Strategic Thinking
for Smaller Businesses and Divisions

For Donna, and for the light of our lives,
our Amanda Noel.

Strategic Thinking
for Smaller Businesses and Divisions

William R. Lasher
Nichols College

First published 1999

2 4 6 8 10 9 7 5 3 2 1

Blackwell Publishers Inc.
350 Main Street
Malden, Massachusetts 02148
USA

Blackwell Publishers Ltd
108 Cowley Road
Oxford OX4 1JF
UK

Library of Congress Cataloging-in-Publication Data

Lasher, William.
    Strategic thinking for smaller businesses and divisions / William R. Lasher.
        p.   cm.
    Includes bibliographical references and index.
    ISBN 0–631–20838–0 (hardcover : alk. paper). — ISBN 0–631–20839–9
(pbk. : alk. paper)
    1. Strategic planning.   2. Small business—Planning.   I. Title.
HD30.28.L374   1999
658.4'012—dc21   98-17509
                                                                         CIP

£38.50

British Library Cataloguing in Publication Data

A CIP catalogue record for this book is available from the British Library.

Typeset in 10 on 11½ pt Sabon
by Ace Filmsetting Ltd, Frome, Somerset
Printed in Great Britain by MPG Books, Bodmin, Cornwall

This book is printed on acid-free paper.

contents

preface

This book is the latest milestone in a 25-year journey in education and commerce that began when I taught business as an adjunct professor. Since then I've helped to run divisions of larger companies, had businesses of my own, written books on business, and become a full-time professor teaching strategy for more years than I like to count. This work is special, however, because it weaves together the threads of those essentially separate experiences, and puts the knowledge I gained there and as an economist in one place.

If you'll join me for a little of the journey, through the pages of this book, I'm sure you won't be disappointed in what you learn. By way of preamble, let's touch briefly on strategic management in general.

Strategic Management

Strategic management is an academic field in the study of business and commerce. It began evolving in the 1950s when people studying management started thinking in long-range terms.

Management scientists soon discovered industrial organization economics (I/O) – a field that studies the issues that make industries more or less competitive. Not surprisingly, they found that the analytic methods of I/O could be applied with great benefit to the management of firms engaged in competitive struggles. That is, understanding the nature of competition makes firms stronger competitors. Hence concepts from management and I/O merged into what eventually became strategy.

Academically, strategy found its home in management rather than economics, and the connection with I/O became increasingly tenuous over time. Indeed, the field's roots there are rarely mentioned today. It's an unusual field in that it generally consists of just one course, the final or capstone offering in business higher education.

Basically, strategy is a disciplined, organized way of thinking about running a business in the long run. It's really nothing more mysterious or exotic than that. The theory just provides us with a framework in which to do that thinking. It gives us a structure that leads from observation to analysis to conclusion in an organized goal-directed way. Further, studying the field drills us on how to do that thinking.

That sounds like we might not need strategic thinking if we consider ourselves logical and well versed in business. But that conclusion is false. It's highly unlikely that anyone could develop the insights and understanding of business situations that come from systematic strategic analysis by themselves.

Strategic Literature

Strategy has spawned a relatively substantial literature; however, most of what has been written is cast in the context of big companies. Indeed, up until now there's been virtually nothing on the shelves of either college or general bookstores on strategic thinking and planning for small business.

That's been a real shame, because an application of the principles of strategy to smaller businesses makes a great deal of sense. The systematic thinking of strategic analysis is capable of bringing some order to the typically chaotic small company. It can take some of the "seat of the pants" flavor out of operations and replace it with careful analysis and well thought out direction.

Virtually all of the ideas behind strategy are applicable to firms of any size. However, the concepts have to be handled carefully when applied in the smaller firm arena. For example, a strategic industry analysis sizes up competition among firms producing similar products. For large firms it's generally national in scope. For small companies, however, the industry must be locally defined for some purposes, but can be considered broadly for others. For example, a restaurant's "industry" for immediate competitive purposes consists of other restaurants within driving distance. For longer-term concerns it includes national chains that might open units in the area. And for the purpose of evaluating performance, it includes similar establishments nationwide.

Because of problems of interpretation like this, a treatment of strategy for smaller businesses will be different from the traditional big company exposition of the subject found in textbooks.

Who Should Read this Book

This book is certainly intended for entrepreneurs who already have or intend to start their own businesses. But beyond that, it should also prove invaluable to anyone whose fortunes are tied to a *relatively* small business operation. By that we mean people involved in managing divisions of larger companies which function essentially like stand-alone businesses themselves.

What this Book will do for You

Strategic Thinking for Smaller Businesses and Divisions explains strategic thinking in clear and direct terms, offers guidance on putting together a workable strategic plan, and goes on to describe the ins and outs of implementing strategies once they're developed. In short, it provides a thorough, step-by-step grounding in the practical aspects of strategic management that will give your business an edge over its rivals and you an advantage over yours. It will also provide invaluable background for students planning careers in organizations of any size.

acknowledgments

I'd like to give a special thanks to Al Bruckner, who has been my editor and friend for it seems like forever, and to Katie Byrne in the Malden office who has helped pull this together in a hundred ways. Thanks also to Tony Grahame for his careful and timely edits, to Simon Eckley for his support, and Rhonda Pearce for her work on the layout and design.

I am also grateful to the following people who reviewed the book at draft stage: Paul Lewis Harmon (University of Utah); William F. Motz, Jr. (Lansing Community College); James K. Swenson (Moorhead State University); Carl E. B. McKenry, Jr. (University of Miami); Paul Dunn (Northeast Louisiana University); Richard E. Baldwin (Cedarville College); and Patricia S. Setlik (William Rainey Harper College).

part I
Strategic Ideas

chapter 1

Introduction to Strategic Thinking

The Concept of Business Strategy

Strategy has to do with deploying resources against an opponent. The word originally comes from the Greek *strategos* meaning a general, or a commander of troops, and tends to have a military flavor, as in arraying an army against an enemy. Today, however, we use the term more generally applying it to any field of endeavor. In business, strategy refers broadly to a marshaling of our economic resources to succeed in the competitive struggle.

But strategy means more than just deploying forces, it also has an implication in terms of scale and time. For example, a small, quick thrust into enemy territory, whether in war or business, isn't a strategic move. We describe something like that as a tactic, a word which also means deploying forces against an opponent. The difference is scale and time in that strategy implies moves that are large, relative to the size of the organization making them, and that generally last for significant periods of time.

This is an important idea. Strategy involves *relatively* big decisions that impact the fundamental nature of companies. For example, opening a ten-person sales office in California isn't a strategic move for a large firm that already operates nationwide. But it probably is a strategic step for a small company based on the East Coast that's never sold its product outside its local area before. The new office is strategic to the smaller company for three reasons. First, the ten-person staff probably represents a large resource commitment relative to the firm's size. Second, the plan probably involves the office being open for a long time if not indefinitely. And third, the move represents a step toward a national rather than a local presence, a major change in the nature of the company. The same move is none of these things to the larger firm, so it's tactical rather than strategic.

Strategy goes hand in hand with the concept of *mission*. A firm's mission is its overall reason for being in business. It's the company's grand goal stated in terms of what it does for its customers, its employees, its stockholders, and everyone else it deals with. A firm's mission can be stated very broadly, but is usually supported by a series of more specific, underlying objectives.

Strategy is essentially *how* the firm interacts with its environment to achieve its mission and associated objectives. Notice that we didn't say how a firm approaches its *market* to achieve its mission. That's because product marketing is only a part of strategy. The concept encompasses marketing as well as everything else the firm does.

Strategy is fundamental. It relates to the way we define the businesses we're in, and the approaches we take to running them. The concept is so broad it's difficult to summarize in a few sentences. It refers to literally everything that shapes our companies including the things they produce, how they develop and acquire products, how they approach markets, and how they interact with employees, suppliers, investors, and the community.

Every company has a strategy, even if its management has never thought about the idea. Then a firm's strategy is simply reflected in the way it operates. In other words, the firm's actions imply an underlying strategy. Put still another way, strategies can be thought out or can "just happen." The latter situation can be a real problem. Strategies that aren't analyzed and planned carefully tend to be created by a haphazard series of decisions most of which are made under pressure. Such an accidental approach to long-run thinking tends to lead to chaotic businesses with exciting but short lives.

Thinking Strategy Through

This last idea, the difference between planned and accidental strategies, leads to what this book is all about. Over the last four decades, scholars and business people have put a great deal of effort into the problems associated with formulating and carrying out business strategy. The result has been the development of a more or less separate field in the study of business known as *Strategic Management*. Essentially, the theory of strategic management is an organized way of *thinking* about business situations, developing solutions to long-term problems, and implementing those solutions. In other words, *strategic thinking* is a systematic approach to analyzing your business's position in its environment, and coming up with ways to make the best of the resources you have, while minimizing your exposure in areas where you're not strong.

A great deal has been written about strategy in the context of large firms, but relatively little has been put down in print about applying its principles to smaller businesses and divisions of larger enterprises. That's unfortunate, because with some important modification strategic thinking is as applicable to smaller firms as it is to bigger ones. In fact, some of the things we'll talk about here have the potential to save entrepreneurs untold grief by explaining how to analyze risky opportunities before investing a lifetime of savings.

We'll also look at some career-saving ideas related to strategic analysis for managers working in divisions of larger companies.

Before going further, however, we'll review how the study of strategy came to where it is today.

The Development of Strategic Thinking

The concept of business strategy began to evolve in the 1950s. It wasn't until then that businesses started making serious long-range plans. Before that time people tended to run companies in a more or less reactive mode. That is, they responded to the needs and conditions immediately surrounding their firms and made only short-term forecasts of the future generally for budgetary purposes.

But then, shortly after the middle of the century, people began to question why some firms were successful in the long run and why others weren't. The idea really strikes home if you look at a list of the fifty largest and most successful companies in the country as of a point in time, and compare it with the same list compiled forty or fifty years earlier. Although many of the companies on the earlier list are also on the later one, a significant number aren't. Realizing that those firms were at a pinnacle of power and influence fifty years ago, you immediately have to wonder how and why they lost their edge. Pondering that question led managers and business scholars to start thinking about how they could avoid the same fate. That is, to avoid falling from prominence into obscurity.

The first reaction was that firms started making long-term plans in which management analyzed the conditions expected in the future and laid out strategies for retaining or improving their competitive positions. Plans basically consisted of two parts, a numerical forecast of financial performance, and written descriptions of what the firms would become as their industries and the economy evolved. The time horizon covered was typically five to ten years.

Long-range planning tended to center around the market for product and the battle with competitors, so plans had a good deal of emphasis on marketing issues and the marketing department. It was also apparent that long-run success depended on a company's people and how they were organized to work together. Hence ideas from the field of organizational behavior were a big part of long-range planning from the beginning. Other functions, like manufacturing, engineering, and finance, tended to be treated on a case-by-case basis.

The Value of the Planning Process

It turned out that the value of long-range planning wasn't primarily in the resulting plan document. That was a good thing to have, but the real benefit was found in the planning process. Planning for the long run forced managements to think carefully about what was going to happen around their companies, and to formulate ideas about how they would respond to those changing conditions. Indeed it led to the idea that companies could themselves take certain actions that would mold the competitive environment to their own advantage.

Business schools picked up the idea and created a course called Business Policy which was designed to be taken at the end of a degree program in business administration. Policy was a case-oriented course that exercised students in applying the management principles they'd learned in other courses to the issue of maintaining long-term performance.

Industrial Organization Economics

As time went on, people engaged in this long-range, forward-looking process noticed the work being done in a branch of economics known as industrial organization (abbreviated I/O). Industrial organization economics studies the competitiveness and structure of industries. It investigates things like the conditions that lead certain industries to consolidate into a few giant firms while others remain fragmented arrays of small companies; and why certain industries are characterized by intense competition while the rivalry in others is mild and "gentlemanly."

The orientation of I/O is governmental. That is, it deals with public (government) policy toward competitive situations, especially in the context of our antitrust laws.[1] However, it turned out that the techniques of analysis used in the field could be applied directly to the problems that long-range planners were wrestling with. In other words, developing an analytic understanding of competition could make firms better competitors. Hence long-range corporate planning began to be augmented with analysis techniques taken from industrial organization.

The Consultants

A parallel development occurred during the 1960s by which time a great many companies had become interested in doing their own long-range planning. A number of consulting firms recognized a market opportunity in that interest, and began to specialize in giving advice on planning. In the course of their work, a few of the leading consultants developed some unique methods of analyzing and presenting competitive information. Those methods were also incorporated into the long-range planning and analysis processes we've been talking about.

---

[1] The antitrust laws make certain activities that limit or reduce competition in American industry illegal.

The Roots of Strategy Today

Hence what we think of as strategy today originated as an amalgamation of three things:

1   General principles of management mainly from the fields of marketing and organizational behavior;
2   The analysis techniques and ideas of industrial organization economics; and
3   Certain unique methods of presentation and analysis developed within the field itself.

In the late 1970s a general agreement was reached that the appropriate name of the field was strategy rather than business policy. Terminology has been changing to that title since then, but you still see an occasional reference to business policy.

The Strategic Process – Analysis, Planning, Implementation, and Control

It's important to realize at the outset of our study that the strategic process has several steps or phases which have to be applied in order. We begin with analysis, which means taking a careful look at the condition of our present environment and where we stand in it. That means studying both the nature of the industry in which a company operates and the firm's own internal condition. A review of how the organization got where it is today is generally an important element of that picture.

The next step is planning, the conceptual center of the entire process. It implies formulating a strategy that creates a fit between the firm's capabilities and the conditions that exist in the surrounding industry. Planning also includes creating a strategic plan document that effectively communicates the results of top management's thinking to whoever else has an interest in the process, such as the rest of management, senior corporate management (in the case of a division) and investors.

Next comes implementation, perhaps the most difficult task of all. This phase involves managing to make the strategy happen through attention to the company's organization, its capabilities and key people, its "culture," and the things that motivate performance. Implementation generally involves creating a series of concrete steps called an action plan that take the strategy from vision into reality. Then it calls for managing to make that series of events happen.

Finally, the control phase entails monitoring the business's progress against plan, and making course corrections to ensure that it's getting where management wants it to go.

Levels of Strategy

There are basically two levels of strategic thinking. The first treats companies in single lines of business. Known as either competitive strategy or line of business strategy, this body of thought deals with how traditional firms approach their environments.[2] Competitive strategy will be our primary focus in this book.

The other idea is corporate strategy. It deals with running a company that consists of two or more divisions operating in different industries. The concept involves managing the divisions in ways that improve their collective performance over what their sum would be if they weren't operating under one corporate umbrella.

Corporate strategy is largely the province of top management at big companies, so we won't dwell on it at length. We'll cover it briefly for two reasons. First, it's important to those who work in divisions of larger companies, because it influences the directives that come from top managements. Those, in turn, affect division-level competitive strategy. The ideas also lead to some important career management observations for divisional employees.

The second reason we'll look into corporate strategy relates to diversification by smaller companies. Firms of moderate size often consider expanding into different lines of business, and the thinking behind corporate strategy can help in those decisions. Hence, we'll have a brief look at the issues involved.

Levels Within Line of Business Strategy

People often talk about strategy below the line of business level. These are put in place by the major functional areas and subordinate departments of the company. For example, it's possible to talk about a company's marketing, manufacturing, or financing strategy within the context of its overall competitive strategy. It's also possible to have departmental or operating strategies below the functional area level. All this can get fairly confusing, so it's a good idea to consider an example at this time (see Example 1-1).

A Hierarchy of Strategies and the Idea of Upward Support

Notice that the actions described in the Baxter example at the functional area and department levels were called strategies. That leads to the idea of a strategic hierarchy as follows:

---

[2] The term competitive has a broader meaning in strategy than in everyday use. Generally competition refers to the rivalry between sellers. In strategy, it includes that and other things such as the competition for inputs.

EXAMPLE 1-1

Baxter Technologies is a manufacturer of sophisticated computer peripheral equipment for industrial customers. Baxter sells the equipment and provides ongoing service at customer sites for a fee. A service contract covers both preventive maintenance and emergency remedial service when machines fail.

The equipment works with the customer's mainframe computer in applications that are typically critical to the user's business. Many of the installations are such that if Baxter's equipment fails, a major portion of the customer's operation comes to an immediate halt. This can happen with respect to the customer's dealings with its own customers or with respect to internal operations. In either event users can lose money rapidly when one of Baxter's products is down.

An element of Baxter's overall strategy is intense service to its customers. The importance of promptly repairing malfunctioning equipment then dictates several strategies or policies in its field service department.

1 Have a service technician (Field Engineer) on site within one hour of receiving an emergency call from a customer.
2 Stock sufficient parts inventory in each technician's truck to repair 95% of failures immediately. Stock enough parts at central service locations to repair all failures within four hours.

Notice that achieving these goals is going to cost Baxter money in both staffing and inventory carrying cost. A speedy dispatch system will also be necessary.

These goals and activities are elements of the Field Engineering Department's strategy which supports a marketing strategy of exceptional service to the customer which supports Baxter's overall strategy in the computer business.

- Corporate Strategy
- Line of Business (Competitive) Strategy
- Functional Area Strategy
- Operating (Department) Strategy

However, some people prefer to reserve the term strategy for the two higher level ideas, calling the functional and operating concepts policies instead. Thus we have corporate and competitive strategy, and functional and operating policies. That usage is more consistent with the traditional use of the word strategy implying only top-level issues. We'll generally use the policy terminology in the remainder of this book, but you should be aware that the language isn't consistent in other literature.

Upward Support

Whether or not we use the word strategy in describing functional and operating policies isn't important once we understand what they are. What is important is that lower-level policies have to support upper-level strategies. In other words, strategic thinking has to be carried down into the organization to ensure an overall, consistent system that works to bring about the company's mission and goals.

This leads to a convenient graphic representation of the idea of competitive strategy and its supporting policies or components. We can think of the line of business strategy as a spoked wheel as shown in figure 1.1. The circumference of the wheel is the overall business's strategy, the spokes are the various functional and departmental policies and the hub is the firm's mission and goals, the load being carried. In order for the wheel to roll smoothly, all the spokes have to support the circumference. If one or more don't do their job, the wheel will bump along for awhile, but isn't likely to last for a long time, or to be able to carry the payload as fast or smoothly as competitors do.

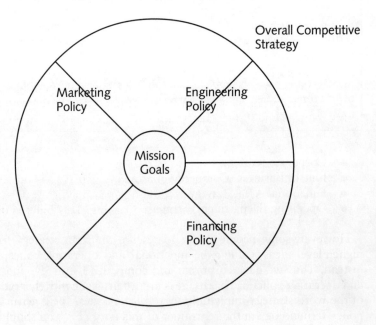

Figure 1.1 The Strategic Wheel

Benefits of Strategic Thinking

Strategic thinking leads to a less chaotic, smoother running organization in which everyone has a sense of where the enterprise is going and their own part in getting it there.

However, the real bottom line in terms of value is that in the long run strategic thinking separates competitive winners from losers. It does that by enhancing a firm's chances of making the right fundamental decisions at the right times. Firms that systematically go through a periodic strategic analysis are in better shape to handle changes in their environments than rivals who operate in a reactive mode. That's because reactive management doesn't allow the time to analyze problems and their long-term implications when they come up suddenly. Strategic thinking gets managers ahead of the game by letting them do most of the analyzing before problems arise. Then it's relatively easy to drop challenging situations into the framework of analysis, and come up with rational, well thought-out solutions quickly.

In other words, strategic thinking provides a background analysis and understanding of business that's available all the time. Managers who think strategically can always lay what's currently going on up against that background and get a better understanding of the long-run implications of current developments and decisions than they otherwise could. Importantly, they can do that better than competitors who don't think strategically.

Strategic Thinking in Large vs. Small Firms

Today, virtually all large companies have bought into the idea of strategic thinking. Most do extensive exercises in strategic planning and analysis annually. That means strategy for them is something they have to do to keep from falling behind rather than something they can choose to do in an effort to get ahead of the competition.

This has a clear implication for managers working in divisions of large companies. To really appreciate what the top brass is thinking, you have to understand the framework of strategic thinking. Further, if you aspire to rise in management, you need to understand how to apply strategic principles to the operation in which you're currently working. This book is designed to help you accomplish both of those objectives.

A Competitive Edge in the Entrepreneurial World

In smaller independent businesses the situation is completely reversed. Only a few small firms plan rationally over long periods. Most are run by the seat of someone's pants and are continually in a state of organized chaos.

That means strategic thinking is a tool you can use to get an edge. If you do it right, strategy is something that will help you to hammer your competition consistently, day after day and year after year. If you've done your strategic homework, you'll be able to react quickly and decisively to almost any problem, because you'll have thought about the issue or something like it before. In the meantime, your competitors will be making quick decisions that aren't thought out and are more likely to be wrong than right.

Avoiding Costly Entrepreneurial Mistakes

In addition, strategic thinking can help you avoid costly mistakes, especially in the early stages of your business and before it's started.

Most entrepreneurs are familiar with the failure rates of new businesses. The statistics are pretty dismal; over 90 percent fail within a few years of getting started. Perhaps more devastating is the fact that a great many of those failures could have been avoided if the entrepreneurs had practiced a little strategic thinking before getting started. In other words, in a great many cases, small businesses that fail can be shown to be strategically ill-advised in the first place.

For example, we've all seen instances in which one restaurant after another fails in the same location. Most of the time successive entrepreneurs buy in because they're getting the food service assets put in place by the first attempt at bargain prices. And they think a different kind of restaurant might succeed or that the earlier attempts didn't work because of the poor skills of the owners. Although such reasoning is occasionally right, more often than not it's something about the location or the surrounding population that dooms every culinary attempt on the site. But that's something that strategic analysis would have revealed in the first place.

In other words, strategic thinking has the potential to keep small business owners from making many of the huge, costly mistakes that are so characteristic of entrepreneurship.

Who Is Responsible for Strategic Thinking and Planning?

It's important to think about where strategic thinking and planning have to be done in an organization and how it should be accomplished. Misunderstanding this concept has brought some large companies a lot of trouble.

The Buck Stops Here

Strategy is ultimately the responsibility of the chief executive officer. He or she is the person that must make long-run decisions with respect to where the firm is going and how it will operate. It's therefore imperative that the

CEO totally understands the analysis phase of strategy and is intimately involved in the creative planning phase. It's also crucially important that the top person be visibly involved in the implementation of the chosen strategy. If they're not, it's less likely that the rest of the organization will buy into the ideas and actions required to make it work.

All this doesn't mean that the top executive has to do all the work him or herself. Subordinate managers can help with a lot of the background thinking and lower-level people can do most of the research necessary for good analysis. Indeed, many large companies have corporate level staffs dedicated to the strategic planning function. Ideally these serve to facilitate the thinking done by top management, but not to do it for them.

This idea deserves special emphasis. The CEO doesn't have to do all of the work behind strategic thinking, but he or she can't delegate the ultimate responsibility for it. In other words, you can use subordinates or even hire a specialist to think about the future and come up with ideas, but ultimately you're responsible for the ideas that get chosen as the firm's strategy.

Some big companies got into trouble with this idea in the 1980s. As strategic planning became more and more popular during the 1960s and 70s, some leading firms created large corporate planning departments staffed with high-powered thinkers. Over time the departments grew very large and even infiltrated down into divisions. In some cases firms had hundreds of people working in planning.

In some cases the planners became so powerful that line managers couldn't make decisions without their approval. That created friction and resentment between the planners and the line organizations they were supposed to be serving. Eventually the house of cards collapsed in what might be described as a revolt of line management.

The problem wasn't in the idea of strategic thinking and planning. It was the fact that strategy had become delegated and bureaucratized so much that it was of negative value to the organization. In the companies that fell into this trap, top management had essentially delegated too much of the strategic thinking function to staff specialists.

We have to keep this lesson in mind. Although strategic issues pervade the entire organization, making strategy is ultimately a top management responsibility which can't be delegated.

Strategic Style

Having considered who is ultimately responsible for strategic thinking and planning, it's logical to ask if there are any general rules about how it should be done. The answer to that question is generally no, but with some reservations. First it's important to realize that no personal style is right for everyone. Some managers lead initiatives themselves taking active, visible roles, while others are better at supervising those to whom they've delegated much of the work. There isn't any one style that works everywhere for everyone, and there isn't any one style that's always ill-advised.

Nevertheless, a few general statements about style and process are possible. First, it's never a good idea to plan strategically in a vacuum. That is, to take the role of the "master strategist" who comes up with the whole analysis and plan by him or herself behind a closed door.

This approach has two problems. First, master strategists aren't likely to think of everything themselves. That is, bouncing ideas around the company's management team just about always produces some thoughts or angles that individuals, no matter how bright they are, don't come up with. Getting some breadth of input is important to the completeness of the planning exercise. The strategy-making CEO doesn't have to take all of the advice offered by the staff, but it's always a good idea to listen to their ideas.

The second point has to do with implementation. As we'll see in Part III, successful implementation requires that the management team "buy into" the concepts behind the firm's strategy. That buy-in is a lot easier to achieve if the team feels they've had a part in developing the overall plan. A team approach is therefore generally a good idea.

chapter 2

Developing Long-Run Thinking

We can think of the business environments in which we work in long- or short-run terms. In general, taking care of everyday operations requires a short-term focus. That's because most of the things we do need to be done now and don't have important long-term implications. We buy from suppliers, pay labor, produce product, sell it, and then collect our money. In the process we create and make deadlines and do a thousand little things in the here and now, and then forget about them immediately.

The Conflict Between the Long and Short Run

However, strategic thinking requires that we maintain a long-run view of our businesses and the environments in which they operate, and keep that view at least in the back of our minds all the time. It's necessary to do this because the long and the short run conflict a great deal. Here's some examples.

EXAMPLE 2-1

Sharon Costello owns a successful Italian restaurant. She prides herself on making breads and pastas fresh on the premises every day. Sharon has good relationships with her suppliers, and has been using most of them for years. The suppliers are very attentive to quality and quick service when Sharon needs something fast.

Recently, a sales representative from a large flour supplier called and offered Sharon an introductory 50 percent discount on a three month supply of flour. The savings is a considerable amount of money.

Problem: What issues should Sharon consider in deciding whether or not to accept the new flour supplier's trial offer?

Analysis: Short-run thinking says Sharon should take the discount and try the new flour to save some money now. If it isn't as good as the flour she's been using, she can always go back to the old supplier.

Long-run thinking says Sharon should consider very carefully what might happen if the flour isn't as good as the kind she's been using. It might imply an inferior product on customer's plates which she'd be stuck with for three months. That much time with substandard bread, pizza crust, and pasta could significantly damage her reputation.

Another important consideration is the impact the purchase would have on her relationship with the current supplier if she needs to go back later. It might take a long time to recover that vendor's good will and willingness to provide extra service when necessary. Another question involves pricing and service after the introductory period. If she expects those to be less attractive than the deal she has now, she probably shouldn't jeopardize her relationship with the current supplier for just the one time cost savings on three months of inventory.

Sharon should probably sample the new vendor's product on a small scale before making a three-month commitment. If its quality is acceptable, and she has reason to believe the service will also be okay, she can negotiate for the introductory offer.

EXAMPLE 2-2

The Aaronson Envelope company employs about 300 people, 50 of which are field sales representatives. Successful sales reps tend to stay with the firm for long periods, so most of the top producers are old hands with the company. Those individuals do, however, leave from time to time. Historically, new reps are hired young with little experience and grow into the sales job. It takes as much as ten years for a rep to develop into a star performer and not all new hires make it. The first two years are especially difficult for both the reps and the company, because beginners don't generally sell enough to cover their own costs. At any time there are ten to fifteen sales people in their first two years.

Aaronson has been having some financial troubles lately. Costs have been sliding upward slowly for several years, and recently several big accounts have been lost to aggressive new competitors. The two forces have come together seemingly suddenly, and profits have taken a serious dive. The once lucrative firm is now barely operating in the black. The controller has suggested cost-cutting as a solution to the problem. Among other actions, he recommends laying off all sales personnel who aren't producing a positive net contribution to profits. This essentially means everyone in sales with less than two years with the company.

Problem: Should Aaronson act on the controller's suggestion and lay off the new sales staff?

Analysis: Short-run thinking says do the layoff because it will cut costs without seriously impacting current sales and improve the profit situation. New sales people can always be hired later on when times are better.

Long-run thinking says that before laying the young sales people off consider the following two issues. First, what will happen in four or five years when normal attrition thins the ranks of the current top producers? Emptying the pipeline of new recruits now will lead to a less than adequate sales force then which is likely to negatively affect the firm's profitability at that time. More importantly, it may have an effect on Aaronson's ability to maintain its market position then. In fact, it makes the firm vulnerable to any future large defection of its senior sales staff, because it removes an entire level of replacements.

The second long-run issue is more subtle, but potentially even more important. Notice that some of Aaronson's accounts were lost to aggressive *new* competitors. Does this mean that the nature of competition in the envelope business has changed? A number of possibilities exist. New entrants could be cut-throat, low-price operators. Or they could be players offering better quality for the same old prices. Or they might be firms with some advantage Aaronson doesn't as yet know about.

Long-run thinking says Aaronson shouldn't do anything until it finds out what's really going on. Perhaps the new situation will dictate that the company should spend more on sales rather than less! Maybe the new firms are succeeding because they've hired some experienced sales people away from existing companies, and Aaronson needs to pay its old hands more to keep them in place. It might then want to hang onto the investment it has in the new people.

Implications

It's important to notice how the long- and short-run objectives conflict in these situations. Business decisions involve this kind of short-run/long-run trade-off all the time. The short-run issues are usually opportunities to gain revenue or reduce spending. That is, they're oriented toward immediate profitability and/or cash flow. The long-term issues are generally more qualitative. They tend to involve things like market position and customer satisfaction. They eventually translate into profit but in a less precise, visible way.

It's also important to realize that solutions don't have to choose one view to the complete exclusion of the other. Some kind of a compromise or trade-off is generally possible. For example, in the second illustration Aaronson might let go of some but not all of its inexperienced sales staff. That would represent a middle-of-the-road option that balances short- and long-run interests.

It's important to understand that what we've just said doesn't mean the short-run solution is never the right answer. This can be especially true for small companies. Suppose in the Aaronson example the profit decline is so bad that the firm is losing money fast. Few small firms can survive very long when day-to-day operations are using cash rather than generating it. In such a situation Aaronson might have to take drastic short-term steps to ensure that there is a long run and simply live with the consequences.

The Right "Mental Attitude"

The point isn't that decisions should favor the long run over the short. It's that *good management demands that we keep the long view in mind all the time.*

Unfortunately, that may be hard to do. If Aaronson waits long enough after its profit problem surfaces to analyze the industrial situation completely, the company could be in big financial trouble before anything's done.

This illustrates the value of periodic strategic thinking. If management goes through an analysis of the envelope business periodically, it won't be surprised by new developments, and will be in a position to respond to problems with quick informed decisions.

Short-Run Biases in American Businesses

A major criticism of American business management is that we're too oriented toward the short run. The criticism certainly seems on target. Let's consider large and small firms separately.

Large Companies

The short-run bias in large companies can be attributed, at least in part, to the focus of senior management on the price performance of the stock of their company. That coupled with the way the stock market operates creates a strong bias toward the immediate.

Boards of directors see maximizing stockholder wealth as the primary objective of management. That goal is most visibly achieved when a stock's price climbs, so boards tend to reward those in charge when stock prices rise with promotions and big compensation packages. Further, top executive compensation is in large part from stock options. These give senior management a direct, immediate interest in raising stock prices.

At the same time, prices on Wall Street are more responsive to earnings and expectations about earnings than to anything else. That means executives are strongly biased toward problem solutions which hold profits up in the short run. In other words there's a general reluctance to sacrifice short-run profitability for long-run position.

Many observers feel that the recent rush into downsizing by major firms is a manifestation of this excessive focus on the short term. In effect, it's feared that businesses are damaging their long-term ability to compete on a global basis by cutting back too far on their human resources today.

The Effect on Divisions

Too much of a short-run focus at the top can create real problems for division managements. Corporate executives force their short-run orientations downward by demanding that division managers keep current profits up in the face of all kinds of difficulties. At the same time, however, they're likely to hold the division executive team responsible when the long-run problems surface later on. This is a perennial problem in survival at the division level. Corporate management is one step removed from the difficulties of running the operation and essentially wants it both ways, i.e., profit now and growth and development in the long run.

The prescription for those working in division management is to be extremely well informed and vocal about the long-term consequences of saving today's profit level. Be sure the top brass know what they're giving up when they opt for the short run. If you don't remind them they'll forget and blame you for the long-run consequences.[1]

Smaller Firms

Smaller businesses tend to be short-run oriented for different reasons.

In a majority of cases, small firm managements haven't given much thought to the long run because:

1 They feel there isn't enough time to think ahead carefully.
2 They don't think it's important to make detailed plans for longer periods.
3 They don't know how to do it.

This says that most small firm managers don't understand long-run thinking. They operate in the short run because that's where they're comfortable.

This isn't to say that entrepreneurs don't have a vision of what they'd like

---

[1] Be careful putting this advice into practice. Too much of an objection can brand you as "negative" or "obstructionist" or "not a team player," and damage your career. It's also not a good idea to say "I told you so" too loudly when you're proven right in the long run.

their firms to become in the distant future. Most have a mind's-eye view of becoming industry leaders and retiring rich and respected. It's rare, however, that they've thought through exactly what has to be done to achieve that goal.

Example 2-2 provides a good illustration of what we mean. It would be rare for a smaller firm faced with Aaronson's problems to think deeply about possible changes in the structure and nature of competition in the industry, and then to be prepared to change anything fundamental about the way it operates in response. However, it's just that kind of thinking that can turn an ordinary company into an industry leader.

Long-Run Thinking in Periods of Growth and Contraction

Continuous planning for the long term can be especially important during periods of rapid growth or contraction. In such times it's especially easy to make mistakes that can hurt later on.

Periods of Rapid Growth

There's usually a great deal of exuberance among management when companies are growing rapidly. This is especially true when the growth is profitable, even if the cash required to support it is a little tight. In such situations managements tend to approve projects and ideas they'd probably reject in more normal times when the outlook isn't quite as rosy. The problem this creates is that assets and programs added during high-growth periods get built into the organization and become difficult to dislodge if things take a turn for the worse. Here's an example based on an actual case history.

EXAMPLE 2-3

Telecom Enterprises Inc. is a small high-tech firm that manufactures a new communications product which it sells to other small companies. There's a strong demand for the product, and sales are growing fast. However, at least half of Telecom's potential customers are chronically short of funds and can't afford to buy it. Conventional bank financing is sometimes available, but the cash-poor customers don't usually qualify because of their weak financial conditions. Telecom could sell almost twice its current volume if financing could be arranged for customers of marginal credit quality.

The Proposal: The company's treasurer thinks that leasing companies[2] might be interested in financing the product if the complex paperwork is prepared and presented correctly. However, customers have no connection with leasing companies nor do they possess the financial sophistication to prepare proposals. The treasurer therefore suggests that Telecom act as liaison between this financing source and the customer. It will locate interested leasing companies, put them together with potential customers, and prepare all the required paperwork.[3] No one at Telecom has experience in leasing, so the treasurer proposes hiring a relatively senior executive from the financial industry for the job. Everyone thinks that the proposal could as much as double sales.

The Action: Already excited about growth, and thrilled by the potential for more, the executive team considers the proposal immediately. Their analysis consists of a comparison between the profit expected on the additional sales and the cost of the new executive including a small staff and the appropriate overheads, expenses, and support. The result is overwhelmingly favorable, and a new Director of Lease Financing is identified, hired and relocated to Telecom's offices.

The Problem Develops: Unfortunately, the leasing program proves to be of marginal value in generating new sales. It seems that leasing companies are concerned with two things: the marginal credit standing of the customers they're being offered and the rapid rate of technological change in Telecom's product. The first concern stems from the fact that financially weak firms have a history of folding up in the middle of leases. The second revolves around the fact that Telecom's product is improving so fast that a unit is likely to be obsolete by the end of the first lease term. This means a second or third term is unlikely which makes it difficult for the leasing company to recover its costs and make a profit.

After several months, it becomes apparent that a few additional sales are being generated through leasing, but not enough to justify the program and its staff. Before long the new director doesn't have enough to do, so she begins to do other things around the company related to finance and marketing. She essentially becomes a resource to handle unusual customer problems which often involve receivables. The resource is nice to have, but its cost really can't be justified. However, because the firm is growing rapidly, and there's plenty of profit rolling in, nobody even thinks about reversing the leasing program decision and letting the new executive go.

Hence the short-run focus on an immediate source of new revenue has resulted in building a continuing, long-term expense into the organization which is essentially a waste of money.

[2] A leasing company buys product from the manufacturer and leases it to the customer. The leasing company's profit depends on the customer's keeping the product through the end of the lease, and the residual value it has at that time.

[3] It isn't unusual for manufacturers to assist their customers in financing product purchases.

The situation described in Example 2-3 is painfully common in fast growing companies. It occurs with respect to people, as described in the example, as well as with respect to facilities. It's especially common to overbuild physical capacity when businesses grow fast. The short-term view is simply that the current rapid growth rate will continue indefinitely, so we had better build an enormous plant. Long-term thinking involves taking a hard look at the economic factors creating the increase in demand and assessing whether or not they'll continue in the long run. When we do that we usually come to the conclusion that smaller increases in capacity are appropriate.

Periods of Contraction

Short-run thinking creates a different kind of problem when companies are shrinking due to a fall in demand.[4] When that happens resources are trimmed starting with people in a traditional lay-off. Eventually, however, the firm reaches a point at which its structure and design need to be changed to accommodate further reduction in size.

For example, suppose a company has a leased computer that's designed to support $20 million in business. If sales shrink to $10 million the machine may have so much more capacity than the firm needs that it wastes money every day in rent and staff to run it.

Moving down to a smaller model, however, usually takes a substantial expenditure. The lease has to be broken, the old equipment moved out and new installed, and a good deal of software and systems may have to be changed.

But in bad times, nobody wants to spend extra money. The short/long-run issue is obvious. It takes long-run thinking to spend today in order to save tomorrow and the next day and for a long time thereafter.

The Importance of Quality

Quality of product or service is a simple idea that has a critical place in long-run thinking. In almost every business there seems to be a tendency for quality to slide downwards over time unless it's watched carefully. This happens in basically two ways.

First, operations tend to become sloppy and inefficient unless they're reviewed regularly. This can lead to cost increases and/or a loss of quality and efficiency in the delivery of the product. The phenomenon is a result of the complacency that comes after an organization does the same thing many times.

---

[4] This isn't the downsizing scenario in which a company chooses to cut its staff even though sales may be strong.

Second, a series of cost-saving decisions can be made, each one of which has a minute, negative effect on quality. Any one is insignificant, but they accumulate into a significant decline.

Two prominent examples in small business are restaurants and dry cleaners. We've all had the experience of finding a great new place to eat only to be disappointed by a mediocre meal when we return a few months later. Dry cleaners seem to be plagued by the same problem. When they first open, our shirts are perfect. Six months later they're returned poorly starched with random wrinkles and bent collars.

The reason, of course, is attention to detail. On opening day the owner/manager is watching everything like a hawk to ensure that nothing gets out the door that isn't perfect. But that's a tough act to keep up. Sooner or later most people slide into a lower level of attentiveness and things deteriorate. Conversely, an obsession with quality is a hallmark of many entrepreneurs who are successful in the long run.

Big companies have the same problem. They've responded by creating quality-control departments to catch downward trends in quality before they get very far. Unfortunately, smaller firms don't generally have that luxury.

We mention quality at this point because it is almost insidiously an element of long-term thinking. In other words, *today's* quality is a long-run issue because if it's lower than yesterday's, a long-term trend may exist that could be fatal if ignored or taken lightly. Put still another way, the long-run thinker watches quality all the time!

Measuring Success

The adjustment in thinking required for the long view is nowhere more important than in how we define success. People generally have a tendency to measure success in terms of profit, expressed either in dollars or as a series of financial ratios like return on sales or equity. In other words, the proverbial "bottom line" is just that, the bottom line of today's profit and loss statement.

But as we've been saying, profits are fleeting things that can be pumped up today at the expense of tomorrow. Long-run thinking, therefore, requires considering something beyond them in taking the measure of how well a firm is doing.

Long-run success implies profitable operations that continue into the distant future, and generally some kind of growth relative to where the firm is today. But so-defined long-run health is related to virtually everything the company does. That includes selling its product, dealing with its employees, doing research and development, and so on. Hence it's difficult to come up with a single measure of long-term success that can be used in a manner comparable to the way we use profitability as a yardstick in the short term.

Thoroughly assessing a firm's present prospects for the long run really requires a full analysis of the type upon which we're about to embark.

Nevertheless it's desirable to have some kind of quick measure that gives an indication of how the firm is doing in a strategic, long-term sense. The best such measure that anyone's been able to come up with is to look at a combination of profitability and the trend in market share.

Although not foolproof, a sustained increase in market share is a good indicator that the company's strategy is well conceived and working. However, a word of caution is appropriate. There are situations in which market share can increase temporarily and give a false indication of success. An obvious case exists when a firm "buys" share by undercutting its rivals' prices, sometimes to the point of selling at a loss. This possibility is why we look at profitability along with share. If share is increasing, but profitability is poor or shrinking, a harder look is appropriate before concluding a company is on the right strategic track.

Another problem with a market share measure for our purposes is that share can be hard to measure with much accuracy. Smaller businesses usually have to define their markets locally or as subsets of larger markets based on the characteristics of what they sell. Under those conditions, it can be hard to get a handle on total market sales. For example, suppose you own a furniture store that specializes in couches and define your market as the population within a 25-mile radius of your store. In such a case, it's probably going to be pretty hard to come up with the total number of couches sold in your market in a year.

chapter 3

An Overview of the Strategic Process for Small Business

Adjusting thinking for the long haul is a first, preliminary step in effective strategic management. The entire strategic process, however, is more involved. We'll cover that process in detail in Parts II and III, but a quick overview is appropriate now to generally indicate what's on the road ahead. It also helps to point out some problem areas now, so we can better appreciate how to handle them later on.

The Strategic Process

The strategic process is charted in figure 3.1. It's important to spend some time studying this overview now.

Notice that there are seven distinct strategic steps listed down the left side of the chart. The nature of each step is more or less evident from its title. We'll talk more about the steps after considering their separation into the three phases shown in the middle and right-hand columns.

Phases of the Strategic Process

First notice that each phase involves a different kind of effort. This means that accomplishing each phase requires different management abilities and resources. These differences turn out to be crucially important, and to lie at the root of many of the problems people have with strategic management. We'll come back to that idea later.

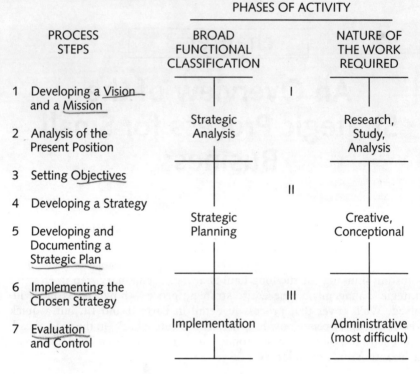

Figure 3.1 The Strategic Process

Phase I – Strategic Analysis

Strategy starts with research and analysis aimed at understanding our business's present situation and what we can reasonably expect it to achieve in the future. Simply stated, we decide where we are and where we want to go.

That sounds easy, almost obvious, but very often it isn't. Establishing where a business is today involves taking a hard, analytical look at what's going on in its industry among customers, suppliers and competitors, and then lining that up against the firm's own strengths and weaknesses. When this is done correctly, it isn't uncommon to find that some of the perceptions we've accumulated by working in the business day-to-day are wrong or at least less than optimal for strategic purposes. Here's an example.

EXAMPLE 3-1

Part of the analysis phase involves defining exactly what business a firm is in. That can sound ridiculously obvious, but it shouldn't. Suppose a firm's predominant business is retailing decorative wall hangings (prints and paintings) in a shopping mall, and that it's reasonably successful. Such a business could define itself as an art gallery or as a specialized furniture store. The distinction may not make a great deal of difference to immediate, day-to-day operations, but it's very significant strategically.

In particular, the definition dictates how the business will attempt to grow. If it's an art gallery, it will cultivate relationships with local painters and sculptors as sources of supply. If it's a furniture store it will buy its goods from distributors. An art gallery will have "openings" and "showings." A furniture store will advertise sales and put discount coupons in the newspaper. An art gallery will target its promotions at an intellectual class of people who buy art for art's sake. A furniture store will target people who are decorating houses and are as interested in size and color as they are in artistic quality. It may also target professional decorators. An art gallery will want employees who know something about painting. A furniture store will hire people who know about decorating.

Notice that the long-term direction of the store changes depending on how its business is defined. Yet the definition doesn't make much difference to what's done every day which is sell paintings and prints from a variety of sources.

We'll have more to say about defining businesses in Part II. For now it's important just to realize that definition is only one of several areas in which an analysis of the present can lead to non-obvious strategic implications.

Phase I Biases

There's a tendency, especially in smaller companies, to assume Phase I analysis is trivial and to skip it. That is, people think they understand their businesses adequately (for strategy) simply because they've been running them for a long time. Further, they assume the vision of success they've had all along is the appropriate one.

Unfortunately, neither of these are usually good assumptions, because people don't tend to think through their environments systematically on a regular basis. Hence, they don't use the knowledge they do have in strategically appropriate ways unless they're guided into it by a formal planning process. That means a Phase I analysis is always appropriate and valuable.

Phase II – Strategic Planning

Once a business determines where it is and where it's going, it's time to think about how it will get from here to there. This is the heart of strategy, figuring out how a firm will do whatever it wants to get done.

Many people have a little trouble grasping exactly what the concept of a firm's strategy means when they're new to the field. Indeed, the Developing a Strategy step within Phase II can be extremely broad, touching in one way or another virtually everything the firm does. To get our thinking straight at the outset, it's a good idea to look at an example now.

EXAMPLE 3-2

Suppose two firms design, manufacture, and sell business and scientific computers. Imagine that the first company provides customers with the fastest, most advanced computing product on the market. Its machines are not only fast, but come equipped with every conceivable, up-to-date feature available. This firm bases its appeal on technological superiority.

The second firm doesn't try to be a technological leader. It provides a service through representatives who custom-design hardware and software solutions to customer problems. The solutions are individually designed, but don't usually utilize the latest (and most expensive) technology.

These approaches to the computer business are two different strategies. One is founded on technology while the other is based on customer service. Several observations are important.

It's possible for both companies to successfully operate in the industry at the same time. They'll generally attract different kinds of customers, but they'll also compete for some of the same buyers.

Their pricing may or may not be substantially different. Advanced technology costs money, but so does service, and it isn't obvious which firm will generally offer lower or higher costs to its customers.

The firm concentrating on technology can't neglect customer service, and the company concentrating on service can't ignore technology. They both have to be at least competent in the other's area of expertise, but they don't have to excel in it.

The strategy difference isn't just a marketing issue. The approach to customers is central to the strategic distinction, but each strategy has implications reaching into virtually every aspect of how the companies are run. For example, staffing and personnel will be very different between the two firms. The technology-based company will have to hire more and better engineers and scientists, while the service-based organization will concentrate on quality sales people and field technicians. The service firm will also need a class of business analyst who can understand customer problems and solve them with computer technology. The same issues are likely to influence how employees are compensated and incentivized. The service-oriented firm will probably lean more towards commissions and bonuses than the technology-oriented company.

In summary, both firms are in the computer business, and both probably have goals that involve growth and becoming an industry leader. However, each defines how it will attempt to achieve those goals differently. These alternative hows illustrate the essence of strategy. In this case the difference in emphasis between technology and customer service defines the basic strategic difference, but it's important to remember that supporting elements, like the human resources policies, are also part of the picture.

Creativity

Notice that Phase II is described as creative and conceptual. It's important to understand how we're using those terms. Phase II isn't just blue sky dreaming; it's more practical. Strategic Planning requires blending a knowledge of a business and its industry with a vision of the future. But that blending is always subject to the constraints and opportunities that surround the business. Here's a simplified analogy.

EXAMPLE 3-3

A pilot planning a trip in a small plane can't just decide where she wants to go and that she'll get there by flying. Pilots are constrained by the plane's capabilities (range, carrying capacity), airport locations, weather, geography and flight regulations. A flight planner has to take all those things and her own flying ability into consideration before taking off. Some destinations just aren't available, like the North Pole, or a spot in the middle of the ocean. Others may be achievable, but not directly, like a spot on the other side of a mountain range that's taller than the plane can climb. The "flight strategy" involves taking all that into consideration in planning a trip from the starting point to a destination.

The same thing is true in business. Suppose in Example 3-2 both companies were based on technology and one was beating the other consistently.

Creative strategy might have involved the losing firm's decision that it couldn't win the game it was playing, defining a new service-based way to compete, and implementing the approach. The process would have required knowledge of the computer business, customer needs, and the strengths and weaknesses of both firms, along with enough creative ability to come up with the idea.

Phase III – Implementation

Once we've formulated and documented a strategy, we can move into Phase III which involves getting the organization to do the things we've decided on. This generally isn't easy. In fact it's usually recognized as the most difficult part of the strategic process.

Implementation is an administrative process that involves developing the right skills within the company, organizing resources effectively to do the job, and motivating people to buy into the strategy and work toward its success. It also deals with blending the strategy with the organization's "culture" and ethics in a way that supports achievement of the business's goals.

Shifting between Phases

It is important to recognize the differences in the nature of the effort required in each of the strategic phases we've been discussing. As the process progresses we move from research and analysis to a sort of constrained creative thinking to a nitty-gritty administrative effort that essentially lasts forever.

Phases I and II can often be accomplished by a few smart people at the top of the organization working more or less by themselves. They generally need some input from others, but usually not very much.

Phase III, on the other hand, touches everyone in the organization. It's described as administrative because it deals with administering behavior and measuring the results.

The strategic management problem, of course, is that people are rarely good at all three of the tasks. Most business executives are good in one, or perhaps two of the areas, but it's rare to find a top executive who's a natural in all three. The most common failure is administration. The people at the top of organizations are generally pretty bright, and come up with great, carefully researched strategies that frequently fail to be effectively implemented.

This means that the practical strategist has to take special care to be effective in all three areas. That sometimes means getting help from others in the organization or from outside experts in the strategic process. At a minimum it means being especially meticulous when addressing areas in which one may be weak or inexperienced.

Strategic Steps

We'll develop the steps carefully in Parts II and III, but a brief preview is in order now.

Developing a Vision and a Mission

A vision of where a company is going involves a mental picture of the businesses the firm will be engaged in five, ten, and fifteen years into the future along with an idea of the company's position within those industries. Part of the picture involves an idea of how the company will be perceived by the groups it influences, such as customers, suppliers, stockholders, and the community in which it operates.

The vision is reflected in a mission statement which summarizes the overall goals and values of the organization as succinctly as possibly. The purpose of the mission statement is to communicate these ideas to interested parties, especially employees.

Developing a mission tends to be somewhat easier in smaller companies than it is in large ones, because big firms generally have diversified operations and more expansion options. Therefore, it's easier to be confused about what they want to do in the long run. That should not, however, lead us to think that the mission concept is unimportant in smaller firms. Formally developing a mission focuses us on the long run and exposes issues we otherwise wouldn't think about. (As in Example 3-1 concerning the art gallery / furniture store.)

Analysis of the Present Position

Analysis of a firm's present position is divided into two parts, external and internal. External analysis means becoming an expert in the firm's industry and developing a thorough understanding of what's currently going on with respect to important issues like competition, technology, demand and regulation. Internal analysis means taking an introspective look at the company's strengths and weaknesses i.e., the things it does and doesn't do well and how important they are.

In a nutshell, effective strategy means developing an approach to the business that produces an advantageous match between the external environment and our internal strengths and weaknesses.

Setting Objectives

We can think of objectives at two levels. Company objectives involve things like market share, customer satisfaction, and profitability. Lower-level objectives are defined at functional department (marketing, manufacturing, etc.) and sub-department levels. They involve things like sales goals, and development schedules. Effective strategic management involves developing top-level objectives that support the firm's mission and lower-level objectives that motivate people's performance while supporting higher-level objectives.

Developing a Strategy

Developing a strategy is such a broad concept that it almost defies description in a few lines. It involves developing a long-run approach to doing business that maximizes the effect of the things the company does well while minimizing the vulnerabilities created by its weaknesses. And all that has to be done within the context of the industrial environment. Look back at the computer companies in Example 3-2. Each has chosen an approach based on using its skills in a way that fills a market need.

Developing and Documenting the Strategic Plan

The Strategic Plan document is a vehicle for recording and communicating the results of the strategic process. It's also a long-term "business plan" that can be used as a management tool and to secure outside financing.

Implementing the Chosen Strategy

Implementation means getting the people in the organization to buy into the strategic ideas management has developed, and to enthusiastically support the concepts in everything they do every day. This is a tough administrative job! When the strategic process fails, it's most likely to happen in implementation.

Evaluation and Control

Evaluation and control means establishing a measurement system and a strategic feedback loop. These allow us to measure progress toward strategic goals and periodically adjust either the strategy, the goals, or the implementation effort to keep the firm on track. The feedback and control process should go on forever.

part II
Creating a Strategic Framework

chapter 4

Developing a Mission and Setting Objectives

DEVELOPING A MISSION

The most fundamental building block of strategy is the concept of mission. Basically, a firm's mission is what it is in business to do. Strategic thinking, however, requires that we expand on that simple definition quite a bit.

Mission: Concept and Statement

A mission can be thought of as an image of the firm that extends through time. It starts in the present describing what the firm is and does today, and progresses into the future creating a picture of what it intends to become.

A good mission is both concrete and visionary. It's concrete in that it defines exactly what business the firm is in (which isn't as obvious as it sounds). And it's visionary in that it includes philosophical ideas and a projection of the competitive position the firm will achieve.

This image is usually presented in a mission statement which serves as an introduction to strategic discussions about the company. The mission statement is also a device for quickly communicating the business's essential nature to interested parties, especially employees.

It's important to understand that the mission is in the mind of the person or group running the company. The mission statement is a written communication of that mental picture. This chapter is about creating meaningful mission statements.

Natural Resistance

People untrained in strategic thinking frequently want to gloss over mission statements, because they think the ideas involved are obvious. It's not uncommon for people to react to the mission statement concept by saying, "How can I have been in this business all these years without knowing what it is and what I want it to become?" Although such a statement sounds logical, it's always worthwhile to go through the exercise of creating a mission statement. The process tends to sharpen our thinking about what we're doing, and often leads to new insights into what's important for the long run.

The Audience for the Mission

The mission statement provides a preamble for any discussion about a company's long-run future. As such it can be a key part of discussions with banks and investors as well as important customers or other business partners.

The statement is most effective, however, in communicating the ideas behind an organization to its employees. A well-prepared mission statement gives them an idea of where the company is going, and an indication of the role they're expected to play in getting it there. This kind of understanding is crucial to successful strategy implementation, because employee support is essential to making any strategic approach happen.

Mission Statement Basics

Essentially, the mission statement tells who we are, what we do, and where we're going.

Good mission statements tend to have three distinct parts. They include (1) a definition of the business the company is in; (2) a statement of the future position the firm hopes to achieve in its industry; and (3) some statement about operating philosophy. The third element is sometimes omitted. An example will clarify the idea.

EXAMPLE 4-1

The Little Chef Restaurant opened in 1997 in Great Neck Long Island, an affluent suburb of New York City. Art Widner, the business's owner, felt that traditional fast-food restaurants like McDonald's and Burger King served mediocre food that often wasn't very fast. He also felt that service and cleanliness at many of the leading fast-food outlets was less than stellar.

In conceiving the Little Chef, he reasoned that a fast-food restaurant offering very high quality food at commensurately high prices could do well in affluent areas where customers were insensitive to the prices of things like hamburgers and french fries. Hence he intends to provide an upscale alternative to the market leaders.

Over the next ten years Art hopes to expand to as many as 15 locations, each in a different, affluent suburb of the city. Art prepared a business plan to secure bank financing for his concept which included the following mission statement:

The Little Chef – Mission

The Little Chef provides a high quality fast-food menu to the residents of the Great Neck area. Our appeal is based on substantially higher quality, faster service and a more upscale decor and cleanliness than offered by the competition.

Our aim is profitable growth by expanding into approximately 15 similar communities in the New York area over the next ten years. Each unit will occupy the same unique, quality differentiated position in its market envisioned for the Great Neck operation.

The Little Chef will continually strive to excel in quality and service offered at a fair price increment above other restaurants. We will operate at all times in an ethical manner putting our customers' interests above all else. At the same time we will be perceived as a credit to the local community and will offer employment opportunities to young people without regard to race or ethnic or social background.

Notice that the first paragraph defines the firm's business – fast food. It doesn't just say restaurant. It also limits the geographical area, which is appropriate for a restaurant.

The next paragraph makes a statement about the future. The firm wants to become a chain, but at the moment it doesn't envision large-scale, nationwide growth. It also makes a statement about market position. The firm will occupy a unique upscale niche that probably only exists in more affluent communities.

Finally, the last paragraph makes some statements about operating policy. Two things will be paramount, the quest for quality and a customer orientation. At the same time, however, there will be a concern for general fairness and being a good business citizen.

Defining the Business

Perhaps the most important thing the process of creating a mission statement does for someone running a small business or a division of a larger company is make them think carefully about the definition of the business. Major strategic errors come from misconceiving that seemingly obvious point.

The classic example of this phenomenon comes from the railroad industry just after World War II. Railroading isn't small business, but the example is worth relating because it illustrates our point so well.

During the nineteenth and early twentieth centuries, railroads were the dominant form of transportation in America. Their immense success tended to make railroad people rather arrogant. They were "railroad men," and weren't interested in being anything else.

But two big changes occurred in the decade after the war that altered the transportation landscape forever. First, the war created an enormous leap forward in aviation technology, which led to an explosive growth in the passenger airline industry. The result was that in a little over ten years, passengers just about stopped taking trains.

The second change was the development of the interstate highway system beginning in the early 1950s. It made transporting lighter freight by truck more efficient than moving it by rail. As a result, that business left the railroads along with the passengers.

Railroads were left with little more than bulk freight, and entered a period in which their fortunes declined dramatically.

In retrospect, we can see the railroads' problem as too narrow a definition of their business, i.e., just "railroading." That narrow, inflexible definition left no option other than suffering the fate of their own iron horses. If railroads companies had defined their business as "transportation," they might have invested in aviation and trucking, and maintained their leadership position in the evolving industry.

Defining the Business – Three Questions to Answer

The best way to approach a business definition is to begin by answering the following fundamental questions:[1]

1   What customer need is the business satisfying?
2   What customer groups are being targeted?
3   What technology is being used to satisfy the need?

Once that's done the business we're really in becomes clear.

Let's analyze the first two questions in a food service context by comparing "Lou's," a family-style, neighborhood restaurant, with "Chez Louis," a high-class establishment specializing in gourmet French cuisine.

The customer need Lou serves is likely to be simply for food to satisfy hunger while incidentally giving Mom a night out of the kitchen. That's a pretty straightforward idea for a restaurant. It implies that quality, quantity and price are the most important service issues as long as Lou's facility is reasonably nice.

---

[1] Derek F. Abele, *Defining the Business: The Starting Point of Strategic Planning* (Englewood Cliffs, NJ: Prentice Hall, 1980), p. 169.

Chez Louis, on the other hand, is providing an entertainment experience. The food is part of a larger package. A romantic atmosphere, detailed service, and a good wine list are likely to be as important as the quality of what Louis puts on his customer's plates. The key point is that the French restaurant isn't really in the business of satisfying hunger, although that happens in the process. It's in the business of providing an evening out, and essentially competes with shows and other entertainment.

The target customer groups are different for the businesses as well. Lou is after whole families whose incomes might be anywhere from high to low. Louis, on the other hand, is probably after a well-heeled clientele who've learned to appreciate the finer things in life and can afford to pay for them. The same family could be in both markets, but probably at different times and for different reasons. Mom and Dad might enjoy a Saturday night out at Chez Louis, but will take the kids and Grandma to Lou's during the week.

The third of our questions deals with how we get our job done. The restaurant example doesn't illustrate this issue well, because both Lou and Louis probably use more or less traditional kitchens and equipment. The transportation industry provides a better example.

Suppose our business is transporting freight. Then it makes a great deal of difference whether we ship in trucks, trains, planes or ships. Clearly trains and ships are appropriate for very heavy freight that doesn't have to get where it's going right away. Planes are in order for lightweight, high-value items, or things that are needed in a big hurry. And trucks fall somewhere in between. The point is that the technology we use to provide the transportation we're selling defines our market and our business. For example, an air transport company wouldn't look for much business shipping automobiles, and we wouldn't expect a great deal of jewelry to travel by train.

A Realistic Mission Statement for Your Business

Sometimes people get carried away when developing mission statements, and produce documents that don't do much good. This usually happens with respect to either breadth of subject matter or physical length.

Overly Broad Statements That Don't Say Anything

To be meaningful mission statements have to be consistent with the size and resources of the organization for which they're written. Entrepreneurs tend to be people of boundless enthusiasm who can sometimes project themselves too far into a successful future. Here's an exaggerated example. Would it make any sense for a neighborhood delicatessen to say that its mission was "feeding America?"

Technically, the statement is reasonable, because anyone from anywhere can walk into the store for a sandwich. The problem, however, is that it doesn't do the business any good. It's so broad that doesn't focus a reader on what the firm is really doing or what it wants to become.

Overly broad mission statements are a problem for big companies too. Saying something like "become a leader in electronics" doesn't do much good without defining what is meant by leader and specifying a field within the enormous electronics industry.

Long Statements That Nobody Reads

At the other extreme, we sometimes run into mission statements that try to say everything conceivable about the business and wind up being so long-winded that the audience loses interest before getting to the end.

Although there aren't any hard and fast rules about length, a good rule of thumb is that mission statements shouldn't be more than a page (500 words) in length. At the same time, it's difficult to imagine getting the job done adequately in less than 150 words.

The Mission and Attention to Change

The mission statement encapsulates a firm's strategy in a few lines. Hence keeping a eye on the mission is a good way for management to monitor whether or not the firm's strategy is appropriate or needs updating as times change.

For example, suppose a firm succeeds by selling at prices below those of its competitors, and that this is reflected in its mission by words like "no frills" and "best value." Then suppose a new rival enters with a lower cost structure and the ability to sell at still lower prices.

The presence of the new entrant means the firm has to lower its costs even more or change its strategy by learning to compete on a basis other than price.

Hence, watching the mission in the context of what's going on in the industry helps management remain on top of the need for changes in operations and/or strategy. In that way it helps firms take timely actions to avoid losing their competitive edges.

Communicating and Buy-In

Keep in mind that the primary audience for a company's mission statement is its employees, and that its purpose is to keep them informed and enthusiastic about the business and where it's going.

That means the mission has to be communicated to the employee group effectively. Doing that right generally means sending the message repeatedly by itself and as part of other communications. In other words, whenever the president makes a speech to an employee group, he or she should find a way to include the essence of the firm's mission. The statement should also be posted conspicuously and printed in the firm's literature wherever possible and appropriate.

One of the most common strategic mistakes managements make is producing a good mission statement, and then keeping it a secret. Without repeated communication and interpretation by top management the best mission statement does little good.

Inconsistent Actions

It should be obvious that a mission statement that conflicts with actual behavior can do more harm than good. This usually happens with respect to statements of ethical or moral values. For example, mission statements that explicitly endorse fair and respectful treatment of workers can have an undermining effect if employees perceive things like promotion and layoffs as being administered arbitrarily and without respect for merit.

A Few More Mission Statement Examples

Let's consider a few examples of mission statements and analyze each one. We'll begin with the Springfield Gallery, a variant on an example we used to illustrate the importance of defining your business in chapter 3.

EXAMPLE 4-2

The Springfield Gallery is a specialty furniture store in Springfield, Massachusetts which carries artistic wall hangings and accessories. It is open to the public, but also wholesales to interior decorators. The owners would like to expand by using some of their floor space as a traditional art gallery carrying original works by local artists.

The Springfield Gallery – Mission Statement

The Springfield Art Gallery retails traditional wall hangings and accessories to middle-class households at moderate prices. Products include original paintings, prints and sculptures ranging in price from $100 to $1,000. The Gallery offers professional advice on decorating themes and color schemes. Discounts are offered to professional decorators on orders over $3,000.

The Gallery operates in a regional shopping mall. The mall's market radius is approximately 40 miles and contains 60,000 households with incomes over $55,000.

Product is procured from commercial wholesalers, manufacturers, and individual artists. In the future, the Gallery will develop relationships with as yet unknown local artists, carrying their work for a reasonable commission.

The Springfield Gallery intends to be the leading source of wall hangings and accessories for households and the decorating trade in the Springfield area.

It's important to realize that the Gallery's mission statement answers the three definitional questions even though some of the answers are implicit. The customer need is for moderately priced decorating items. The target customer population is the 60,000 households in the area with incomes over $55,000. And the technology or delivery technique is traditional retailing. This particular statement also mentions the business's sources of product, which in this case is a critical element of its strategy. The visionary portion spells out the the Gallery's long-term goal, to become the market leader in the area. The long-run idea of adding a traditional gallery for the work of local artists is also included.

Next let's look at Chez Louis, the upscale French restaurant we used as an example earlier in this chapter.

EXAMPLE 4-3: CHEZ LOUIS – MISSION STATEMENT

Chez Louis offers a sophisticated dining experience to more affluent area residents. Elegant French cuisine is coupled with an old-world atmosphere, impeccable service and a superb wine list; these combine to create a memorable evening for discriminating patrons.

A select menu and just two seatings a night ensure that gourmet cuisine is prepared to the most exacting standards by European trained chefs supervised by Louis himself.

Chez Louis will be known as the finest restaurant in the area within three years.

Chez Louis' mission statement seems a little like advertising copy but it's nevertheless effective. It defines the need as an entertainment experience rather than just food. It tells us the customers are more affluent members of the community. And it describes how the task is to be accomplished, through painstaking attention to detail by highly skilled chefs. Finally, it summarizes Louis' vision of the long-run future.

Finally let's look at a personnel consulting business that markets a proprietary software package as well as other services to smaller companies that don't want to staff their own human resources departments.

EXAMPLE 4-5: DENHART HUMAN RESOURCE MANAGEMENT SYSTEMS – MISSION STATEMENT

Denhart Human Resource Management Systems supplies personnel-related services to companies employing up to 3,000 people. We offer smaller businesses a full range of Human Resources services so they can avoid maintaining their own personnel departments. Denharts PC-based software automates most record-keeping and retrieval functions. The software is available alone or combined with comprehensive consulting services.

Denhart strives to be nationally recognized as a source of cutting edge Human Resource Management information and technology for smaller businesses. Denhart maintains an expert staff in each Human Resources specialty as well as in PC-based support systems.

Notice the customers' need is defined implicitly. They need to manage their personnel records and services, but would rather not employ a full-time staff with the appropriate skills. Denhart provides the expert services as needed. The technology of Denhart's approach is a combination of personal consulting and its own computer software. Finally, Denhart is ambitious, it wants to provide its services nationwide.

Setting Objectives

Strategic objectives[2] are part of the process which translates management's visions into reality. Objectives tell the management team what results have

---

[2] We'll use the terms objective and goal interchangeably although some writers make a distinction between the two.

to be accomplished and when they need to happen to make the firm's mission come true. Correctly-developed objectives are the first step in the transition from the concepts reflected in a mission statement to concrete reality.

The Nature of an Objective

An objective is a target set for business performance of some kind. Success is defined as achieving the target while failure is missing it. Of course, there are degrees of success and failure depending on whether the target is made or missed by a little or a lot.

It's important to understand that there are several different kinds of business objectives which must bear definite relationships to one another if they're to be strategically useful.

A few broad strategic objectives are generally implied by a firm's mission statement which are associated with the business as a whole. For example, the Springfield Gallery of Example 4-2 has a goal of becoming a leading source of its product in the area. It's likely that management would amplify that idea by stating some additional goals for the firm in terms of revenue market share or profitability.

In addition to whole company goals, most enterprises establish objectives for departments and sub-departments. For example, Springfield Gallery might establish a separate department for handling the work of local artists, and define goals for the amount of business done in original work.

Finally, it's possible to define short- and long-term objectives which can be developed together or independently of one another.

Strategic thinking requires that the different kinds of objectives work cohesively in support of a firm's mission. This means objectives have to be developed according to several principles which we'll describe in the remainder of this section.

Objectives for Who and What

It's generally accepted today that objectives should be developed for the firm as a whole and for all management units within it. It's only through such a complete set of goals that a firm can be sure everyone is moving in a consistent direction.

Upward Support

Upward support means that the objectives of various sub-units of the organization have to work together to support top-level goals. Sets of objectives that don't do this are quite common, and create major management and strategic problems. Here's an example:

EXAMPLE 4-6

The Bently Company is a medium-sized firm employing about 500 people. It makes and markets electronic communications systems for other medium-sized companies. Bently has developed a new product to replace its standard system which has sold well but is no longer state-of-the-art technology.

The new system isn't completely developed yet, so it has to be sold partly on promised performance and partly on its current capability which is about equal to the old product's. Nevertheless, it's priced higher than the old system because of its expected superior performance.

There's some risk to being an early buyer of the new system, since undiscovered flaws may disrupt operations later on. The old system, on the other hand, has been thoroughly debugged and works perfectly. Both products will be marketed next year which is viewed as a transition period.

One of Bently's strategic objectives is to transition to the new system by the end of next year. Departmental objectives include the following items:

- The product development team has an elaborate series of milestone objectives that will produce a fully operational and tested product by year end.
- The marketing department has an advertising plan and budget designed to introduce the product in a series of trade shows and technical magazines over the next year.
- The training department has already instructed the sales force on the new product and has new customer training as an objective for next year.
- The field service department has an objective of sending every technician to school on the new machine within the next year.
- The sales department has a continuing objective of $4 million per month of product sales which includes both new and old systems.
- The finance department has an objective to implement a procedure to handle billing disputes that may arise over the new system's performance in its first year.

Analysis: First notice what the whole set of objectives does for the company in a broad sense. The overall goal, to get a new product out, is easy to understand, but it's very general and doesn't really tell anybody what to do. The objectives do that. They become more detailed as they reach down into the organization indicating concrete actions that specific departments need to take to make the whole program happen.

Now notice how each department's objectives support the overall goal of getting the new system out within a year. Each specifically addresses something that has to be accomplished in order to make the introduction run smoothly.

However, there is one problem area. One department's objective doesn't support the company goal. Can you pick it out? Spend a minute trying before reading on.

The problem is in sales. In the immediate future, it's likely that the new system will be hard to sell because of its risk and higher price. That means sales people are likely to sell the old product unless they're incentivized to push the new one. The sales department's objective, however, can be achieved by selling any mix of new and old product, including no new product at all! Hence that objective isn't supportive of the company's overall goal of getting the new system accepted and on the market next year.

An upwardly supportive sales objective would include a requirement that a substantial portion of the year's sales, say 60 percent, be in the new product line. Such an objective is likely to be supported by a commission incentive on the new line as well.

Measurability

Objectives have to be measurable to do a firm much good. There are two reasons behind this idea. First, unless a goal is defined on some measurable scale, it's hard to tell whether or not it's being achieved. Second it's generally difficult to know what to do to improve performance on goals that can't be measured.

Easily Measurable Objectives

Objectives that are defined in quantitative terms are usually easy to measure and don't present problems. For example, a company goal might be to achieve $100 million in sales within five years. It's easy to know whether or not that's been achieved. A similar goal at the department level could involve a sales group's booking business of $10 million per month while staying within budgeted spending levels. It's easy to measure both success and remedial action with respect to goals like these, because they're defined on a quantitative scale – sales dollars.

When goals are stated in financial terms, the accounting system tells how well we're doing, and often what kind of corrective action might be called for if we're not doing well. For example, if return on assets (profit/assets) is below plan, management can work on improving profit (by increasing revenue or lowering cost), or on operating with fewer assets.

Measurable objectives aren't always financial. Market share, personnel turnover, and survey scores are usable non-financial measures. Time can also be an objective. For example, a goal of developing a product within a year is a measurable undertaking.

Less Measurable Objectives

Most firms like to state some objectives in more subjective terms. For example, it's common to strive to be a "leader" in some market, or to have a high level of a characteristic like "customer satisfaction," or to strive for recognition with respect to a vaguely defined notion like "excellence."

Objectives like these don't do any harm, but don't do much good either. That's because it's generally not possible to tell to what extent they're being achieved, and because they don't point to any particular action when they aren't being met. For example, how does a firm's management know whether or not the company's performance is "excellent?" And what should be done if the team feels that it isn't?

To be useful subjective objectives like these have to be made measurable. That's generally possible with a little creative thought.

Let's take the goal of excellence as an example. An approach to keeping the goal but making it more useful might involve writing up a questionnaire that asks people to grade the firm on a number of criteria management feels should be included in a definition of excellence. The questionnaire could then be sent to customers, employees, and suppliers.

An initial survey could provide a benchmark grade, and sending it out once a year thereafter would allow the firm to assess whether it was improving on being perceived as an excellent company. Further, an analysis of the responses would identify the areas in which the company was falling down if results dipped. That in turn could be used to define actions for improvement.

Long- vs. Short-Run Objectives

We've already discussed the conflict between the long and short run in chapter 2. The issue resurfaces when we define objectives.

Companies tend to establish long- and short-run goals at different times. Long-run objectives are established implicitly or when we sit down and go through the strategic exercises we're talking about in this book. As we've said, smaller firms frequently don't do this.

Short-term goals, on the other hand, are established when people think about budgets and financial performance, or on the fly, by the seat of the entrepreneur's pants.

If a firm is to be strategically successful, it's important that short-term goals support long-term goals. It's especially important that they don't overtly undermine longer-term efforts. Let's revisit the Bently Company of Example 4-6 to see how this might happen.

EXAMPLE 4-6 – CONTINUED

Bently has been facing increasingly stiff competition from a larger rival over the last two years. The rival makes products over a broader size range than Bently, and has recently been cutting prices in Bently's market segment. As a result, profits have declined to unacceptable levels although the firm isn't actually losing money.

Management fears that the stockholders, descendants of Gerald Bently, the company's founder, are unwilling to accept poor profits and dividends, and are likely to replace the top executives if things get any worse. The executive team is therefore considering selective layoffs to improve short-term financial performance.

One restructuring proposal leaves sales and marketing intact, because they're perceived as the first line of defense against the rival's pricing initiatives. However, it cuts deeply into engineering, field service, and administration, because these functions don't have an immediate impact on sales, and create expenses that reduce current profits.

The proponents of the action argue that the cuts will slow but not stop the new product's introduction. Further, any shortfall in sales of the new system can easily be made up with old system sales.

Analysis: Notice how this proposal jeopardizes Bently's long-term well-being for short-term profitability. The plan will improve profits, but if the engineering and field service departments suffer reductions in their capabilities, the new product's introduction is sure to be compromised. That means the introduction will be slower, and the old product will be around longer.

It's also likely that the new product won't make as favorable an impact on customers as it might have, because it won't be as good and will experience more problems in the field. It will also be less of a state-of-the-art product when it finally does get launched.

The firm can live through all this by stretching the old product out a little longer, but that avoids a key strategic issue. The core of Bently's long-term success is its technical competence versus that of its larger rival and the market's perception of that competence.

Reducing technical capability when it isn't absolutely necessary is probably a big mistake. It's especially problematic if it's done in the middle of a product introduction, because that's when capability is most visible by the market.

The proposed action is likely to put Bently several steps behind in the long-run race to benefit the short term. That's probably a mistake.

However, it's important to understand that if the short-term problem is so severe that the firm could fail, the sacrifice is worthwhile. In the situation described, however, it probably isn't.

Challenging but Achievable Objectives

The purpose of having objectives is to guide and motivate performance. Objectives tell people what to do and define whether or not they're successful. In most companies objectives are also motivational instruments because rewards and bonuses are tied to their achievement. We'll have a great deal more to say about that aspect of managing objectives in Part III. There are, however, a few things about the motivational aspect of goal-setting that we need to notice now.

Objectives should be set to stretch the organization's performance. That is, to guide it into being the most it reasonably can be. In that respect, two obvious mistakes are possible. Objectives can be too hard or too easy.

An objective that's too hard doesn't do anything for the organization, because people just ignore it. They give up before they start, because they don't think there's any chance the goal can be made regardless of their efforts. Hence the impossible objective doesn't influence performance.

An objective that's too easy has the same effect for the opposite reason. People don't perform any differently with the objective in place, because they know it will be made without any extraordinary effort, so they just keep doing what they were doing already.

Objectives that make a difference have to get somewhere in between these extremes. They have to be challenging yet achievable.

Top Down vs. Bottom Up Planning

Objectives tend to be defined during planning and can therefore be affected by planning processes.

A *top down* plan is one imposed on an organization by top management. It can reflect performance the chief executive would *like to see* rather than what's possible given the company's capabilities and the environment. Top down plans tend to create unachievable objectives.

The other extreme is a *bottom up* plan. It's created from the inputs and resource requests of lower-level managers who know it will result in a set of objectives they'll be measured against. The human tendency in that situation is to ask for more than you need, and offer less than you can give. The result is a plan and a set of objectives that are easy to achieve and understate possible performance.

The ideal process begins with simultaneous top down and bottom up exercises which are melded into a challenging yet achievable set of objectives through a negotiating process.

Objectives as Predictions

As we've been saying, objectives should be achievable but stretch an organization. That means good objectives are often unlikely to be entirely achieved.

For example, suppose a business earned $2 million last year, and management would like to see a 20 percent growth to $2.4 million this year. However, suppose that while $2.4 million is possible, it's a tough stretch and not very likely to happen. Suppose $2.2 million is more probable with a good effort by the entire team. It isn't unreasonable for management to set $2.4 million as a stretch objective even though it actually expects the lower figure.

The problem arises if someone uses the $2.4 million as a prediction of what's going to happen rather than a stretch goal. For example, suppose the Treasurer uses it to forecast bank borrowing needs next year. Such a forecast understates the most likely cash need by $0.2 million, because it overstates the most likely profit by that amount. Hence, it's likely to create a banking problem that could have been avoided.

The bottom line here is that it's important to keep track of the assumptions that underlie objectives and be careful how we use them.

Summary

The third step of the strategic process is the creation of a comprehensive set of objectives for the overall company and for every department in it. The objectives have to be thought through so that they build upward through the organization and forward through time in a supportive manner that leads to the achievement of the long-term company mission.

It's a good idea to make up an organization chart showing the firm's departments and the objectives of each systematically and in graphic form. Show the company's overall objectives at the top of the chart. Then step back and review the entire system for consistency, upward and forward support, and usefulness in terms of measurability and meaning.

chapter 5

Analysis of the Present External Position: The Industrial Environment

In a nutshell, strategic thinking means coming up with an approach to business that creates a "fit" between a company's strengths and weaknesses and the conditions existing in the outside environment. For a single line of business company, the outside environment means the industry in which the firm participates. In everyday terms this means we try to do things in ways that take advantage of what we do well while minimizing the exposure caused by things we don't do well or that other companies do better. (It's more or less axiomatic that no one does everything well.)

For example, suppose we're a small computer software firm and happen to be blessed with an exceptional development department. On the other hand, assume we don't have a particularly good marketing force. Under those conditions it makes sense to develop an approach to the software business based on technical superiority rather than on advertising or customer service.

However, that's only the first level of understanding that generally comes out of strategic analysis. More complex results are not only possible but very common. For example, after studying the situation in our illustration, we might come to the conclusion that our marketing department is so weak that we'd fail in spite of our technical superiority and regardless of business approach. In that case we'd need to beef up the sales effort to minimize our vulnerability in that area.

In another possible scenario, we'd find that although we're better at technology than anything else we do, several competitors are better still. Hence we have no basis for a competitive advantage. This situation would be very serious in that it makes long-term survival unlikely. It calls for a complete rethinking of why we're in the business and what actions are necessary if we decide to stay.

Strategic thinking is an organized approach to understanding and solving problems like these. The first step in the process is developing a thorough understanding of the current situation and environment. Such a situation analysis is generally broken into two parts, the external and the internal.

External analysis involves developing a thorough understanding of the industry, while an internal analysis is a study of the firm itself. These two "understandings" are then brought together to build a strategy that fits the company's abilities to its environment. It's important to realize that the fitting process may involve making some changes in the internal set of abilities.

In this chapter we'll present a framework for industry analysis. We'll move on to consider internal analysis in chapter 6. Finally we'll bring the two together when we consider formulating a strategy in chapter 7.

Keep in mind throughout that our focus is on smaller businesses. That orientation is especially important in the industry context because the definition of industry can be very different between large and small companies.

Industry Analysis – Overview

In the rest of this chapter, we'll present industry analysis in several steps. We'll briefly name and summarize the steps, before going into detail about each.

Economic and Operating Profile. The first thing we do is compile a summary of the major distinguishing characteristics of the industry including current size, profitability, growth rate, etc. This provides a background for the more focused analysis that follows.

The Competitive Situation. An analysis of the important competitive forces at work in the industry is our second logical step. In this context competition means not only the rivalry between sellers, but includes concepts like the competition for inputs and the effects of substitute products from other industries. It's important to realise that "competitive" is a broader concept in strategy than we're used to.

The Effects of Change. Next we do an analysis of the factors that are likely to cause significant changes in the way the industry operates. For example, pending government regulation or the likely entry of a major foreign competitor.

Assessment of Industry Structure and Important Rivals. Who are the important competitors, what are their relative sizes, what are their major strengths, and what can they be expected to do in the near future?

Key Success Factors (KSFs). In every business there are a few activities in which any viable competitor must be competent. Further, to be a potential leader, a firm generally has to be exceptionally good with at least one KSF.

Overall Assessment. Is the industry an attractive place for us to be at this time?

Industry Profile

There are a fairly standard list of issues that should be understood about an industry. We'll list each and describe its significance. Putting together an industry profile essentially means writing a brief paragraph summarizing the industry's condition with respect to each of them.

Keep in mind that our goal is to develop an understanding of strategically important issues within our industry. The list of issues we consider in that respect come from industrial organization economics.

Industry Definition

The first profiling task is to define the industry in which the firm being considered operates. The issue can be tricky in the context of smaller businesses. An industry is generally defined as a group of firms producing essentially the same product (or very close substitutes). For large firms this reference group tends to be national in scope. For small companies, however, the industry usually has to be locally defined for some purposes, but can be considered broadly for others.

For example a restaurant's "industry" for immediate competitive purposes consists of other restaurants within driving distance. That's because to a local customer the product produced by a restaurant a thousand miles away isn't a close substitute for a meal in a restaurant nearby. However, if the owner of a local restaurant is thinking about potential new competitors, a national chain is definitely a possibility even though it currently has no units nearby. And if the owner wants to evaluate the business's financial performance, a comparison with similar establishments nationwide is quite appropriate.

Some industries may have to be defined by function as well as geography. Suppose we're a small software company that's developed a computer program for accounting and billing in small hospitals. While such a firm is part of the enormous software industry, the relevant segment for most of our purposes deals only with medical accounting services for smaller facilities. Further, a small software company would probably limit its scope geographically because of the logistical problems associated with servicing customers more than a few hundred miles away. Hence potential customers would be only small hospitals in the local area. Potential rivals, however, could be any size and come from anywhere.

Hence the first task in profiling the relevant industry for a small business is to write down its limits and bounds with respect to customers, rivals, suppliers, and any other groups that might be relevant. The essence of this idea bears repeating. Many (but not all) small businesses compete in geographically limited markets. That fact affects our entire strategic analysis.

Market Size

Once the relevant market has been defined, its size should be estimated in terms of both dollars and physical volume. This is the sales volume that is potentially available to the company. Here again a local or functional character or limitation is usually relevant for smaller businesses.

Growth Rate and Position in Life Cycle

An industry's growth rate is important, because it influences the competitive behavior of the participating firms. In general, competition is less intense in industries that are growing rapidly than in those that are stagnant, expanding slowly or shrinking.

When an industry is growing quickly, the firms in it can expand rapidly without attacking one another, because the overall growth creates plenty of new business for everyone. However, if industry growth slows, the only way individual firms can continue to grow quickly is by taking market share from competitors. Since everyone wants his or her business to grow briskly, low industry growth implies intense competition among the players.

Industry Life Cycle

Most industries go through a predictable growth pattern known as the industry life cycle. They begin in a pioneering stage as the new product is being developed and perfected. If the product is successful, an expansion period of rapid growth follows. Eventually demand and supply stabilize, and sales growth slows or stops as the industry enters a period of maturity.

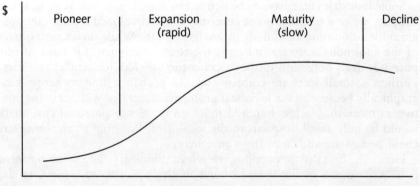

Figure 5.1 Industry Life Cycle

This mature phase can last for a long time, even indefinitely. Eventually, however, most products become obsolete and the industry enters a period of decline. The idea is illustrated in figure 5.1.

The effect of industry growth on competition implies that we can expect a rapid intensification of rivalry as an industry transitions from the expansion phase into the mature phase. Prices generally fall and the number of firms participating shrinks quickly as only the strongest survive.

For these reasons it's important to understand the industry's place in the life cycle and its overall growth situation. Keep in mind that the industry has to be appropriately defined for the small business in question. For example, the restaurant business might be shrinking nationwide while the relevant industry in a particular town is in its expansion phase.

Profitability

The current average level of profitability among firms in the industry is an important issue. Profitability typically varies for two reasons. The first involves temporary ups and downs which result from general economic conditions. These are normal and are not of great strategic importance. A chronically depressed profit level, however, is strategically important and worth understanding. It can be a signal of things like a long-run decline in demand, too many competitors, or technological obsolescence. Unusually high profitability, on the other hand, tends to attract new competitors.

Market Structure – Selling Side

Structure relates to the number of rivals participating in an industry and their relative sizes. A fragmented industry consists of a large number of firms with none dominating the others. At the other extreme, a monopoly is an industry served by only one firm. An oligopoly is an industry dominated by a few large players. Industries containing large powerful firms are said to be concentrated.

Selling side structure is a key determinant of the way participating firms behave. Strategic attacks against a rival several times one's own size, for example, are likely to be ill-advised.

It's important to understand an industry's structure, whether or not it's changing, and why. For example, if an industry is fragmented, it's important to understand what keeps firms from consolidating.

Market Structure – Buying Side

The number and size of buyers is also an important issue in market structure. It makes a big difference whether a firm sells a product to a large number of small buyers or to one or two big customers. In the latter case the customers have a good deal of power over the market relationship.

Vertical Integration

Businesses are vertically integrated when a firm owns either its suppliers or its customers. Owning a supplier is called backward integration while owning a customer is forward integration.

Vertical integration can have an important impact on competition because it can lock competitors out of sources of supply and/or markets. For example, suppose two competing firms buy an input from a particularly cheap supplier. Then suppose one of the two buys the supplier, and either raises its prices to the rival or refuses to sell to it altogether. That puts the rival at a severe disadvantage because it now has to acquire the input somewhere else, probably at a higher price.

Similarly, a competitor who owns a customer will be less concerned about price decreases in the industry than competitors who don't have captive buyers.

Such intricacies indicate that we should understand which competitors are vertically integrated and which aren't.

Barriers to Entry

A profitable industry attracts new entrants. Barriers to entry refer to the things that make it difficult for a new firm to get started. These include things like technical know-how and having enough capital.

Barriers to entry protect existing firms from the competitive potential of others that might enter the industry. High barriers protect insiders' profits, making the industry more attractive for those already in it and less attractive to outsiders. We'll have more to say about barriers to entry later.

The Level of Scale Economies and Capacity Utilization

Scale economies exist when unit cost drops a great deal with increased production. That is, costs are lower as the scale of production increases. This occurs when the production process involves relatively large fixed overhead costs which are spread over more units as volume increases.

The condition is common in automated processes where there's a great deal of machinery associated with production. Automotive manufacturing is the classic example. Processes characterized by manual labor such as those found in the restaurant and garment businesses tend to have fewer scale economies.

Capacity utilization is a related concept. In industries where large fixed facilities exist, unused production capacity means big losses because firms aren't producing enough volume to spread the facility-related overhead adequately, and unit cost can easily become higher than price.

The reason these conditions are important to understanding an industry lies in the reactions they generate among competitors when economic conditions change. When demand drops off, high fixed-cost producers become desperate to keep their own volume up to avoid the sudden losses associated with high overhead. They do that by competing fiercely for whatever business is available using price cuts, advertising, and any other competitive weapons they can find.

All this means that high fixed-cost industries are potentially very volatile, although they can appear calm when times are good.

Product Differentiation

Some industries produce standard, commodity products, while others differentiate their products with attributes and features a great deal. A bushel of wheat, for example, is essentially the same regardless of the farm from which it came. Houses, on the other hand, are quite different depending on their builders even within a size and price range.

Competitive issues are considerably different in industries with differentiated and undifferentiated products. Basically, it's hard to compete based on anything but price if the product or service is a commodity. It's important to understand the degree of product differentiation in an industry because it has a lot to do with the nature of competition and how customers can be influenced.

Technological Change

In recent decades more and more business is conducted in high-tech industries that are subject to rapid technological change. The phenomenon creates strategic issues with respect to both product and production. Up-to-date technology can be a feature of the product offered as in the computer business, or it can be important in production in that it affects cost and/or quality. The introduction of vinyl liners, for example, changed the swimming pool business forever.

It's important to understand exactly how technological change impacts an industry and to what extent competition is based on it.

Analyzing the Competitive Environment

The term competition generally refers to the rivalry between sellers of similar products. In strategy, however, it has a broader meaning. In addition to the traditional rivalry between sellers, strategic competition includes pressures placed on selling companies by their customers and suppliers, by producers of substitute products, and by potential rivals who may not have yet entered the field.

This expanded idea of competition is central to modern strategic thinking, so we'll summarize its five elements for convenient reference before getting into each in some detail. Our perspective is that of a seller of some product or service.

The Elements of Strategic Competition

Traditional Rivalry among Sellers

The Power of Customers to Extract Concessions from Sellers

The Power of Suppliers to Charge Higher Prices for Inputs

The Effect of Substitute Products in Limiting Sellers' Influence
on Buyers

The Restraining Effect on Seller Behavior of Potential Entrants
into the Industry

This expanded view of competition has its roots in industrial organization economics. The latter four effects are traditional areas of inquiry in that field.

The idea of describing all five elements as a unified model of competition was originated by Harvard Professor Michael Porter. Since his publication of the concept in 1980,[1] it's become common in strategic circles to refer to the overall idea as the Five Forces Model, or the Porter Model of competition.

Technique of Competitive Analysis

The five elements are central to strategy in a single line of business setting. The idea behind analysis is to consider an industry in the light of each of the five elements (or forces) one at a time. In each case we describe the issues and players that might affect our company, and make a judgement about whether or not the force is likely to be significant currently or in the future. It usually turns out that only two or three of the five elements represent significant competitive forces.

After analyzing each element we make an overall assessment of the competitive situation in the industry. In general the more intense the competition, the less attractive the business.

Traditional Rivalry among Sellers

Rivalry among sellers, the traditional concept of competition, is generally the most significant of the five elements.

Competition among sellers ranges from mild (sometimes called gentle-

---

[1] Michael E. Porter, *Competitive Strategy: Techniques for Analyzing Industries and Competitors* (New York: Free Press, 1980).

manly) to a level of intensity described as cut-throat. Gentlemanly competition implies that players strive to attract new customers entering the field, but make only mild efforts to attract them away from other competitors. The competition between suppliers of home heating oil is fairly gentlemanly in most areas.

Intense competition means players actively court customers who currently buy from other companies using attractions such as advertising and pricing. The automotive and soft drink industries can be characterized as intensely competitive.

Cut-throat competition implies players may go so far as to use unethical or illegal means to wrest business from rivals.[2]

The Basis of Rivalry among Sellers

Although we generally think of price as the primary basis for competition among sellers, it's only one of a number of weapons with which rivals can attack one another.

Most products are delivered in packages that include attributes such as quality, availability, service, variety, styling, training, and warranties. Competition can be based on offering customers a more desirable set of any combination of attributes than other sellers. This includes but certainly isn't limited to price. For example, better warranties and service are constantly claimed by automobile dealers against their rivals.

The attributes associated with a product are not necessarily real. Imagined attributes generally have to do with an image created by advertising. Beer ads for example, show attractive young adults having intensely good times, ostensibly derived from drinking the featured brand. Yet it's hard to imagine that one beer will lead to a significantly better quality of life than another. Hence advertising itself is a weapon of competitive rivalry.

The first step in a competitive analysis should always be to list the bases on which rivals compete, identifying the issues that may be appropriate for our own business.

Conditions Affecting the Intensity of Rivalry among Sellers

Although every situation needs its own analysis, there are several conditions that contribute to making the competitive climate between sellers more or less intense.[3]

- **Industry Growth.** As we said earlier when discussing profiling an industry, virtually all businesses strive for growth. When an industry

---

[2] Cut-throat competition may include tactics like predatory pricing in which a large firm prices below cost in a restricted area to drive small local companies out of business.

[3] Based on Porter, *Competitive Strategy*, pp. 17–21.

is growing rapidly, each participating firm can grow without attacking others by just getting its share of the new entering business. A problem arises, however, when industry growth slows or stops. Individual firms still want to grow rapidly, but the only way they can get more business is by taking it away from rivals. Hence when industry growth slows or stops, competition heats up quickly. It's also generally true that competition among sellers is more intense in slow-growth industries than in those that are expanding quickly.

- **Economies of Scale and Capacity Utilization.** Competition tends to be more intense when overheads are large and capacity utilization is important. Big overheads imply dramatically large losses when volume falls below the critical break-even level. This gives competitors a big incentive to hold their own sales up as industry volume levels decline.
- **Selling Side Industry Structure.** Competition is generally stronger when all the competitors are about the same size. Each then thinks it can win against the others, so they tend to pick fights with one another. When one firm is much larger, the others tend to follow its lead somewhat meekly.
- **Switching Costs.** Switching costs are the costs a customer incurs in switching from one supplier to another. They can vary from nothing to a lot.

  For example, it doesn't cost anything for a family to switch from one breakfast cereal to another. However, it costs a lot for a company to switch from one computer supplier to another (say from IBM to DEC). That's because the customer's systems are programmed for one maker's product and a substantial reprograming effort is required to switch. Hence the rivalry among cereal makers is intense, while that between suppliers of large computers is relatively mild.
- **Outside Interests and Unexpected Payoffs.** Sometimes strange things can happen when small firms are owned by outside interests. For example suppose one of several competitors in an industry is acquired by a large foreign firm bent on using it to establish a foothold in the US market. The foreign company is likely to compete more intensely than the other rivals are used to because the stakes associated with the battle appear much larger to it than to the others.

The Power of Customers to Extract Concessions from Sellers

This phenomenon is generally referred to as Buyer Power. It exists when the customer controls the interaction between itself and the seller. For example, suppose a small company makes a minor part for General Motors which is its only customer. GM, however, can buy the part from any number of other suppliers. In such a situation, all the power in the relationship is held by the big company. GM can dictate the quality level, delivery terms and just about anything else it wants to including price as long as it leaves just enough profit to stay in business.

Buyer power generally exists when a single customer takes a substantial percentage of a seller's output. Ten percent is a good rule of thumb for its onset.

Large retailers like Sears, K-Mart and Wal-Mart are famous for their effectiveness in using buyer power to negotiate concessions from suppliers.

People often confuse the concept of buyer power with the idea that customers always choose who to buy from and therefore ultimately have the power to determine which firms will survive and which will fail. That concept refers to the collective function of the market over the long term. Buyer power on the other hand refers to specific relationships between individual sellers and their customers.

A strategic analysis always includes an assessment of the degree to which buyer power exists in an industry. In the garment business, for example, many small manufacturing firms sell to a much smaller number of large retailers. That implies the retailers have buyer power even though the ultimate consumer of clothing is the unorganized general population. In the restaurant business, on the other hand, the unorganized population is the direct customer and no buyer power exists. In other words, Sears can wring a price discount from a clothing manufacturer because it has buyer power, but you're not likely to be successful if you walk into a restaurant and try to negotiate a price concession for dinner!

In general, buyer power is stronger when the product is a commodity. That is, the output of one seller isn't very distinguishable from that of another. When that happens the customer can play one seller against another by threatening to take its business elsewhere. When products have some differentiating feature to which the customer becomes accustomed, it's harder to switch to another supplier.

Similarly, low switching costs are associated with buyer power. It's harder for a customer to bargain for concessions if both parties know it has to retool its factory to use someone else's product.

The Power of Suppliers to Charge Higher Prices for Inputs

Supplier Power is essentially the reverse of buyer power. If a supplier provides a crucial input that the seller can't get elsewhere, it's in a position to raise prices until it absorbs much of the seller's profit.

The power of suppliers is generally stronger when they provide most of a particular input, the input is crucial to the seller's process, and there aren't alternative sources. It is weaker when the input is a commodity and there are many suppliers.

It's important to notice that labor is an input to virtually all businesses, and that workers have power over their employers if they can act together to influence the seller's processes. Hence the activity of a labor union is a type of supplier power.

Comparing Buyer and Supplier Power

Buyer power and supplier power are essentially opposite sides of the same coin. Both can also be called market power reflecting the idea that one side or the other has most of the control over the market transaction between a buyer and a seller. However, it's important to notice a particular difference. Suppliers with power can generally exercise it only by raising price. Powerful buyers, on the other hand, have several options. They can demand lower prices, of course, but they're also able to insist on improvements in any of the other attributes associated with the product. For example, they can demand higher quality, better after-sale service, better warranties, free training, and so on.

The Effect of Substitute Products in Limiting Sellers' Power over Buyers

Of course, the seller at the center of our discussion can have market power over its own customers and suppliers. In competitive analysis we're interested in two things that act to limit power over customers. The first is the effect of substitute products.

A substitute is something from another industry that can be used in place of the product being considered. The distinction between a substitute and a differentiated rival is sometimes a little hard to see, so it's worth going through an example or two.

If people drive gas-guzzling cars to work, and gasoline becomes very expensive, they can either buy cars that get better mileage or take public transportation. Taking a bus or train is a substitute for auto transportation via gas guzzlers, while a high mileage car is a rival automotive product differentiated on fuel economy. Notice that we say the substitute comes from a different industry, because the transportation service is the result of a different technology, buses or trains as opposed to cars.

Suppose we're analyzing the market for beer. Wine is a substitute alcoholic beverage that comes from a different industry, produced by a different technology. An imported beer is a rival differentiated on taste and quality even though it may cost as much as wine.

The existence of substitutes limits sellers' market power, because it causes customers to make continuous comparisons of product costs and benefits with those of the substitute. If that comparison becomes unfavorable, customers will switch, and the seller will lose sales. This effectively puts a limit on the price a seller can charge when a substitute exists. That in turn limits the seller's profit potential.

In general a seller's market power is reduced when substitutes exist, are cheap, and don't involve substantial switching costs for the customer.

The Restraining Effect on Seller Behavior of Potential Entrants

The effect of potential entry by new rivals is a major issue in industrial organization and the study of competitive behavior. It's important to note that the issue is the threat of entry, not entry itself. Once entry occurs, the new player is just another rival, and the problems it causes are identical to those we discussed earlier.

It's a basic economic premise that better-than-average profitability in an industry attracts new entrants. Then the presence of the new players increases competition which reduces everyone's profitability. In theory entry goes on until industry profitability is reduced to a normal level, and no longer attracts newcomers.

Obviously, existing firms prefer that new rivals do not enter their industries. Hence they're motivated to behave in ways that discourage newcomers. It is this preemptive behavior that is of interest to us here. Before getting into that, however, we need to expand on a concept we introduced briefly before.

Barriers to Entry

Conditions exist in many industries that make entry difficult for new firms. Suppose, for example, a small company develops a new product on which it's making a great deal of money. If the firm has a patent on the idea, other firms will be precluded from entering the business and eroding its profits. Thus the patent acts as a barrier to entry that protects the firm from potential rivals. When the patent expires, the protection disappears, and entry will probably occur.

A patent is an artificial entry barrier created by law which encourages innovation by protecting the resulting profits for limited periods. Without patents there wouldn't be much incentive to spend money and effort on research, because the economic system would take the rewards away from inventors through the mechanism of entry.

In many industries, natural barriers to entry exist that make it difficult, but usually not impossible, for new firms to enter. Natural economic barriers include things like the following:

- **Capital Requirements.** If it takes a great deal of money to get started, few entrants will be interested unless industry profitability is extremely high.
- **Economies of Scale.** If it takes a large volume to produce a product at a reasonable cost, it may be difficult for a newcomer to sell enough to make a profit.
- **Technical Know-How.** Even though industry processes aren't patent

protected, it can be difficult to operate efficiently if the entrant has limited experience in the field.

- **Access to Distribution.** It can be difficult to get into established distribution channels. In the grocery business, for example, it's very hard for a new producer to get shelf space in supermarkets.
- **Brand Loyalty.** It can be difficult for a new producer to overcome customer preferences for products made by manufacturers they've been using for years.

Entry Deterring Behavior

When barriers to entry are not insurmountable, firms already in a profitable industry are motivated to do things to keep new rivals out. The primary such preemptive action is setting an entry deterring price. This means existing firms independently limit their prices in order to limit their own profitability. This action makes the industry appear less attractive to outsiders who realize they'll have to match the incumbents' pricing.

In effect, existing firms accept lower profits than they could achieve in the short run to guarantee moderately above-average profits in the long run. This is clearly a benefit to customers in the short term, but may be a detriment over the long haul.

Existing firms can accomplish much the same thing by offering non-price benefits to their customers. These include generous warranties, free training, free delivery, an easy returns policy, and so on.

Another entry deterring ploy by existing firms is letting it be known that they will react vigorously to the presence of a newcomer. In other words they'll respond with tactics like price reductions, special promotions, and increased advertising, all things that will make it harder for the newcomer to gain a foothold in the market.

Analysis

The appropriate industry analysis with respect to potential entry is to look at two things. First, ask if industry profitability is now or is expected to be large enough to attract newcomers in any significant number. Next consider the presence or absence of barriers to entry. Put these ideas together and make a judgement about whether the threat of entry is an important issue.

EXAMPLE 5-1

Johnston and Limmerick are lawyers in the small town of Westerly. There are two other firms in town each with two attorneys. The prices for legal work in

Westerly are about one-third lower than those charged in large cities nearby. Each of the six lawyers earns about $100,000 a year. Johnston and Limmerick are thinking about raising their prices. Because of the personal relationship they enjoy with their clients, they don't feel too many would be lost to the other firms in town due to price increases. Should they be concerned about potential entry in addition to business that might be lost to the other firms?

Analysis: The $100,000 average income of the legal community in Westerly, while not huge, would probably be attractive to a number of attorneys who are either looking for work or are working much harder in big city firms. Hence the profit criteria for potential entry is marginally satisfied. Two entry barriers are likely to be relevant. The first is the cost of setting up an office, probably $40,000 or $50,000. A fair amount of money, but by no means an insurmountable obstacle. The second barrier could be more difficult. It involves customer loyalty. Would a newcomer be accepted by the people in Westerly, and are there very many people in town who aren't already clients of one of the existing lawyers? These are judgement calls, but it's reasonable that a newcomer, perhaps charging discount prices, could have a real impact.

On balance, potential entry is probably an issue, and Johnston and Limmerick should be careful. Increasing prices nearer to big city levels might be perceived by potential entrants as an increase in the profitability of the local law industry. That could attract newcomers which in turn could make the lawyer business in Westerly less attractive for those already there.

The Effects of Change

An important element of situation analysis is consideration of things that are likely to cause changes in the industrial landscape. Strategy is essentially planning for the future, so if the environment is expected to change it makes sense to do our best to predict the effects of those changes and incorporate them in our thinking.

Putting this important idea another way, we said earlier that strategy involves approaching business in a way that creates a series of fits between our abilities and the environment. If the environment is expected to change, our current abilities may not fit next year. That means the successful firm will anticipate change and do what it can to adapt its abilities to fit the anticipated scenario as well as the present one.

There are an almost limitless number of things that can be sources of change within an industry. In any given setting it's usually possible to identify a dozen or more items that are causing some alteration in the environment. In most cases, however, only a few changing items are truly significant.

Strategists, therefore, try to identify the three or four most important agents of change that are likely to make long-term differences in the industry.

Once the agents of change are identified, they become part of the environment for which a strategy is crafted.

EXAMPLE 5-2

Wilson Motors makes small engine parts in the industrial Midwest. Labor rates are currently 120 percent of national averages in the heavily unionized area. Wilson is steadily losing business to lower-cost competition. In spite of this, the union at the Wilson shop is currently joining with others in demanding still higher wages and benefits. Management is convinced that labor costs will increase to 140 percent of national averages over the next five years.

Analysis: Increasing labor cost is an agent of change for Wilson. If the trend continues it threatens the company's long-term survival. There are probably four options available to deal with the problem:

1   Close down and go into another business.
2   Try to work with union representatives to make them understand the situation and reduce their demands.
3   Relocate to a non-union area in the South.
4   Try to get cost out of the product somewhere else to compensate for the high labor rate.

Management needs to put the labor issue into its strategic thinking, and move toward selecting and implementing one of the options available to deal with it.

It's helpful to list a few general categories into which many agents of change fall.

- **Changes in Industry Structure.** Industry structure usually changes through entry or consolidation. For example, suppose a town has three supermarkets of about the same size which are only mildly competitive with one another. Then suppose one is offered for sale. Two possibilities exist that have major implications for the remaining stores. An outsider may buy the store and compete more aggressively than the previous owner. Or, one of the other two may buy it creating a market structure in which the third store faces a two-unit chain twice its size.

- **Changes in Demand.** As all entrepreneurs are aware, customer preferences can change overnight as a result of any number of influences including tastes, new products that become available, and changing income levels.

- **Government Regulations.** The government has the ability to impose new regulations on almost anything. These most commonly involve safety and liability.
- **Technological Innovation.** The emergence of a new way to do things can change an industry quickly. The result of a new technology can be a consolidation if the new approach is expensive and only strong firms can afford it. Or it can produce a flood of new entrants if the new way is cheap.

Assessment of Industry Structure and Important Rivals

Our next step is making an assessment of the structure of the industry and identifying the most important competitors. An industry's structure relates to the relative sizes and strengths of the companies in it. A concentrated industry is one that's dominated by a small number of powerful firms. The highest level of concentration is associated with a monopoly where there's only one seller. At the other extreme, an industry made up of many firms, none of which is large enough to dominate the others, is said to be fragmented.

Strategic Group Maps

It's important to segment the market to identify who we're really competing against. For example, suppose we're in the restaurant business in a moderate-sized town, and restaurants in the area fall into three categories. There are fast-food franchises, family-style restaurants, and expensive fine-dining establishments like Chez Louis which we used in an earlier example. It's important to understand that there's little or no competition between the categories. It's virtually all within the segments. We can say that each segment represents a strategic group which acts essentially like an independent industry.

A helpful technique for analyzing the structure of an industry is the strategic group map. Creating a map involves plotting industry players on a two-dimensional set of axes where the scales represent important competitive characteristics. In our restaurant example, we might plot players according to price/quality on one axis and sales volume on the other. The results are likely to look something like figure 5.2.

Notice that the players tend to fall into three clusters, the fast-food segment, the family-style segment, and the fine-dining segment. These are strategic groups. They are essentially independent sub-industries.

This is an important concept, because it contains a lot of very relevant

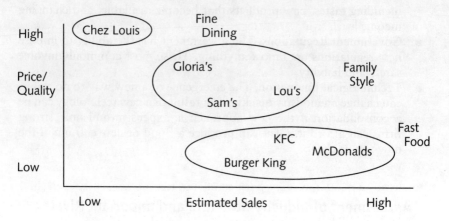

Figure 5.2 Strategic Group Map Local Restaurant Industry

information. For example, the fact that there are a total of seven restaurants in town is nice to know, but says little about the competitive situation for any one of them. The strategic group map, however, indicates that there are several competitors in both the fast-food and family segments, but that Chez Louis has the fine-dining business to itself. This tells us a great deal more about what each unit is facing.

Strategic group maps can be constructed with any two relevant attributes on the axes. If neither of the axes is sales, it's common to include that information on the map by plotting each participant as a circle whose size is proportionate to its revenue or market share.

The Relevant Rivals

It's always important to identify a business's most relevant rivals or closest competitors. There are generally two possibilities. The most important competitor may be the leader in the firm's segment or it may be another firm that's in some sense close by. For example, suppose there are five accounting firms in town, but one is much larger than the others. If the largest firm is the leader in the sense that its pricing and service offerings are imitated by the others, it is the most important competitor to each of those others.

By contrast, suppose there are five similar apparel stores in town, one is larger than the others, but two of the smaller ones are in the same mall. Further assume that the larger store isn't a price or style leader. In such a case it's likely that the most important competitor for each of the mall shops is the other store in that mall, because they compete head-to-head for the same shoppers.

Once a business's relevant rivals have been identified, it's a good idea to develop a knowledge of their strengths, weaknesses, and unusual quirks. For example, suppose a rival restaurant has particularly good food, but also has a reputation for surly service. As long as our food is of acceptable quality we may be able to gain a big competitive edge by making sure our service is especially fast and courteous. That's a lot quicker and easier to do than upgrading the menu.

Experienced strategists recommend actually developing a written competitor profile on more important rivals, and updating it regularly.

Predicting What Relevant Rivals are Likely to do

It's generally a good idea to keep track of what relevant rivals are doing and to try and predict any strategic initiatives they might launch. That way you can have some time to think about an appropriate response.

For example, suppose our clothing store competes with another in basically the same price/quality range. Then the rival announces an expansion and the addition of a higher priced line which it will advertise heavily. This could be a problem if we don't make some kind of response, as the wider appeal of the rival could easily draw business away from our shop. If we anticipate the action we might block it with the addition of a few higher-priced items ourselves, or at least with a counteracting advertising move.

Summarizing Structure and Rivals

The result of the assessment of industry structure and important rivals should be a brief written summary of the issues we've discussed along with a strategic group map and a folder on each important competitor. It's a very good idea to update this file frequently.

Key Success Factors

There are a few things in every line of business that have to be done at least fairly well to survive. For example, a restaurant has to be able to cook at least reasonably good food. If it can't do that, the restaurant is doomed before it starts. It's generally possible to identify three to five things that are critical to success in any business or industry. These skills, capacities, or assets are known as key success factors (KSFs). Here are a few examples:

Industry	KSFs
Groceries	Access to Distribution
Apparel	Design Ability
	Low-cost Manufacturing
Real Estate	Access to Financing

Heavy Manufacturing	Capital
Beverages	Advertising
(beer, soft drinks)	Low-cost Production
	Access to Distribution
Biotech	Research

It's strategically important to identify KSFs for the industry in which we're operating. Once identified, they have to be compared with our firm's internal abilities. We have to be at least competent in all KSFs, but to be successful it's generally necessary to be exceptionally good in at least one. That one exceptional skill or capability then becomes the basis for the firm's strategy.

Recall the example of the two computer companies we used to illustrate the idea of strategy in chapter 3. One was good at technology while the other had a talent for customer service. These were two KSFs for the industry. No firm can ignore either, but it doesn't have to be exceptionally good at both. Recall that in the example each firm based its strategic approach to the business on the thing it did best.

Summarizing the Industry Environment

At this point, we've profiled the industry, considered the elements of strategic competition, looked at the effects of change, diagrammed the industry structure and listed its key success factors. Next it's appropriate to make an overall summary assessing the industry's attractiveness.

In general an industry is attractive if profit prospects are good and competition among rivals is mild, buyers and sellers don't have much power, barriers to entry keep newcomers out, and there are few close substitutes for customers to turn to. The more intense any of the competitive elements are the less attractive the industry becomes. It's also important that change agents aren't driving the industry in an undesirable direction. It would, of course, be unusual to find an industry in which all of these elements are favorable.

The overall attractiveness of an industry is a subjective matter; it all depends on one's perspective. A situation of fairly intense competitive pressure may be attractive to a firm already in the industry, especially if it's in a strong competitive position. The same industry can appear extremely unattractive to a prospective entrant.

chapter 6

Analysis of the Present Position: Internal to the Firm

Once the external analysis is done, we have to lay the result against our firm's capabilities. The essence of strategy is then to create the best fit between the two. The internal analysis, like the external, is broken into several steps which we'll look into in this chapter.

Internal Analysis – Overview

As in chapter 5, we'll quickly list the steps and go on to discuss each in detail. The six steps of internal analysis are as follows:

Recapitulate History. Summarize how the company became what it is today.

Identify the Present Strategy. State the basic elements of the firm's present approach to the business and decide how well it's working.

SWOT Analysis. Summarize the company's Strengths, Weaknesses, Opportunities, and Threats.

Competitive Cost Analysis. Review the firm's cost structure and if possible compare it to that of rivals.

Long Run Problems. Identify the major strategic issues the firm must address in the near future.

Overall Competitive Assessment. Evaluate the firm's Competitive Position against its rivals and judge whether or not it is viable in the long run.

Putting It All Together. Are we in the right place?

Next we'll have a closer look at each step.

Understanding How the Firm Got Where It Is Now

It's generally a good idea to begin a strategic analysis by reviewing how the firm got to where it is today. This should be done by the senior executive group sitting down in a group and retracing the important developments in the firm's history over the last ten or so years or since its inception. While this is going on, someone should document the company's evolution by making a timeline on a blackboard or chart showing the major milestones and decision points.

The entire review should be documented in a brief report which should include the reasoning behind important decisions. It's also helpful to second-guess decisions in the light of later developments to see if they were the right thing to do at the time.

It's very important that this historical review not be used to place the blame for mistakes at anyone's door. Rather it's an exercise to sharpen the team's understanding of the strategies used up until the present, when they've been changed, and how they've worked.

It's also important to realize that this historical recap should not take a great deal of time. Review broad strategic issues, not minute operating details.

Identifying the Present Strategy and Assessing How Well It's Working

As we'll see in subsequent chapters, a firm's strategy is made up of any number of elements that define how it approaches its business environment. A company might strive to be the lowest cost provider of some product or service or to provide a higher-quality item at a higher price. On the other hand it might base its approach on providing a "differentiated" product that's in some ways unique in its field. Or it might seek to serve the needs of a specific segment of the market. In any case the strategy isn't just a single summarizing statement. It's generally a long list of do's and don't's that explain in some detail just how the business is to be run.

As an example, here's a hypothetical strategy for a fast-food chain that might be similar to any of the national franchisors we're all familiar with (see opposite).

Brainstorming the Current Strategy

If the firm's current strategy isn't formally written down, the executive team can develop a strategy statement like the one in Example 6-1 by thinking about the way the company actually does things. If the statement is written, the same brainstorming session should be held to document how things are actually done. That should then be compared with the written statement to see if there are any contradictions or omissions. It's quite common to find that what we say and what we do are two different things.

EXAMPLE 6-1: STRATEGY STATEMENT – SPEEDY BURGER INC.

Offer moderate quality foods at moderate prices in a counter-service setting that enables customers to get in and out quickly.

Limit menu items for efficient operation.

Provide customers with a consistent package among various locations.

Emphasize cleanliness and friendly service at all locations.

Advertise nationally.

Focus advertising primarily on children and families with children.

Expand through franchising and company-owned stores.

Select locations based on a careful study of demographics in target market areas.

Purchase food in quantity under master purchasing agreements for best pricing.

Purchase food only from approved suppliers to ensure quality is high and consistent.

Provide detailed operating instructions for individual stores and enforce compliance strictly.

Hold surprise store inspections to ensure operators are complying with quality and cleanliness guidelines.

Employ entry-level labor to keep costs down and provide part-time jobs for teenagers and seniors.

Notice that the detailed strategy is the sum of a number of specific statements, but that the first statement is fairly broad and gives an overall impression of what's going on. This is fairly common.

How Well is the Current Strategy Working?

The next step is to assess whether or not the current approach is working. That seems straightforward on the surface. In general, a company is successful if it is profitable relative to its competitors and the trends in revenue, profit, and market share are positive.

However, measuring strategic success isn't always easy. That's because we're working in the long run and subtle trends can be very important. For example, suppose a relatively small firm manufactures and sells a unique communications product to other small businesses. Assume the product is customized to each buyer and therefore takes considerable engineering and field-service support. Now suppose that in an effort to improve financial results the company cuts the field-service force. That means it will take longer for customers to get problems that surface after the sale fixed.

This kind of situation leads to a condition of customer dissatisfaction that grows slowly and won't be reflected in sales and financial results for some time. In fact, financial results might appear favorable for quite a while after the cutback due to the expenses saved. Nevertheless the field-service portion of the firm's strategy isn't working, and will probably lead to big problems later on. This is another example of the long-run / short-run tradeoff we discussed earlier.

Unfortunately there isn't any neat formula for assessing the success of a strategy. Certainly the trend in market share and profitability are key measures, but they have to be augmented with a subjective look at a host of other issues that are unique to each business.

Throughout, it's important to keep in mind that strategic success is measured relative to one's rivals. In other words, a 10 percent growth rate may sound great, but isn't if everyone else in the industry is growing at 20 percent. Similarly, a decline in revenue and profit may be the best anyone could do, if the rest of the industry is declining faster.

After the long-term performance issue has been thoroughly discussed and analyzed, the executive team should document its conclusions in a statement about the strategy's effectiveness. That statement should include weak areas and potential fixes.

Hence the present strategy step of our internal analysis should result in two documents. A statement of strategy and a statement of its effectiveness and problems. These serve as a basis for moving forward.

SWOT Analysis – Strengths, Weaknesses, Opportunities, and Threats – The Concept of a Distinctive Competence

The next introspective step in strategic analysis is sizing up what the company can do well and what it can't, and laying that against the external environment. The SWOT analysis does just that. It forces management to make a candid list of internal strengths and weaknesses as well as a compilation of external opportunities and threats. These pave the way for the strategy creation to follow.

Strengths

A strength is something the company either does well relative to others or has that others don't. For example, an ability-related strength might be based on a particularly effective marketing force, or an especially brilliant engineering department.

Strengths can also be things, rights or connections rather than abilities. Owning newer, more efficient planes could be a strength for an airline. Having a patent on a key process is likely to be a strength in a manufacturing company. And having access to the distribution system based on a previous relation with distributors is a strength in the grocery business.

It's important to realize that strengths can be more or less relevant depending on the business we're in and current conditions. For example, suppose we're in some facet of the health-care field and come up with a cure for cancer. Under those conditions, it isn't likely to matter much whether or not we have a strength in marketing! Similarly, suppose we're great personnel managers, so everyone loves working for us. That won't make a big strategic difference if the employment situation is such that firms have ten qualified applicants for every job opening.

Distinctive (Core) Competencies

This last point leads to the concept of a *distinctive competence* which is a strength or competence relative to competitors in something that matters.

Here are some examples. Suppose we're in the garment trade producing ladies' fashions. The ability to design attractive clothing that's also easy to produce is a distinctive competence. If we want to get into the beverage industry, access to distribution and supermarket shelf space is a distinctive competence. If we're in the beer business, designing effective advertising is a distinctive competence.

In a nutshell, a distinctive competence is a strength in something that matters competitively. The term core competence means the same thing.

Distinctive competencies are very important because they provide the basis on which a firm can gain a competitive edge in the marketplace. They can also be viewed as potential *cornerstones of strategy*.

This is a crucial concept. We've been saying all along that strategy is a matter of fitting the company's abilities to the environment. But in order to have something to work with, the company has to be strong in at least one of the things that matter in the industry. It's only on such a match that a strategy can be built.

If strategic analysis reveals that a company doesn't have a distinctive competence, i.e., it isn't strong in some relevant area, it must either build a competence quickly or think about deploying its resources into another field.

Weaknesses

A weakness is something a firm lacks or isn't as good at as its rivals. However, to be a strategic weakness, the deficiency has to create a competitive *vulnerability*. That means it has to be related to an area that matters in the current or prospective business environment. For example, suppose our company offers excellent career opportunities, but isn't good at attracting job applicants and getting people to accept employment. That only creates a vulnerability if there's tough competition for employees. If the local unemployment level is high, and firms have several qualified applications for all their job openings, our weakness in recruiting is more or less irrelevant.

Typical weaknesses include things like obsolete facilities and equipment, sub-par skills in functional areas like marketing or engineering, a poor retail location, a lack of industry or managerial experience, a lack of access to financing, high employee turnover, high labor costs.

If analysis reveals one or more strategic weaknesses (that create important vulnerabilities) it's imperative that strengthening those areas be part of the immediate strategic plan.

Opportunities

Opportunities are situations in which a company has a chance to improve its strategic position by taking a specific, out of the ordinary, action. It's generally an avenue to gaining a competitive edge, or achieving significant growth in some way. Here are a few examples:

- A manufacturing firm has access to a new process with the potential to cut costs dramatically. However, the quality of the process isn't proven, and trying it involves investing substantially in new equipment.
- A company is offered the chance to buy one of several rivals. The purchase will produce immediate growth in sales and profit, but the asking price may not be justified by the benefit.
- A high-tech firm believes it can develop a new product which may be more cost-effective than those of its rivals. Development, however, is costly and may not be successful.
- A regional firm's products have been successful on the east coast. National distribution is possible but expensive.

Notice that opportunities usually involve some investment of effort or financial resources, and generally imply some risk.

Opportunities usually originate outside the company in the form of resources that can be acquired and then used to make operations more effective or chances to gain on rivals in the market place. Less frequently they come from inside like a chance to develop a new product. Hence, although it's common to describe opportunities as external phenomena, that characterization isn't always accurate.

It's also important to appreciate that all opportunities aren't available to everyone. Clearly, internally developed ideas are only available to the company with the vision to develop them. Others, like a new technology or geographic expansion, may appear to be available to any competitor. In fact, however, they're only realistic for those with strong financial resources.

Threats

Threats are generally changes in the external environment that have the potential to seriously disrupt the firm's well-being. The most common threat for small businesses is probably the entry of larger, more powerful rivals into the local arena. Here are a few other examples:

- Technological innovation obsoletes the way firms produce their products, making investments in equipment valueless. This is a common occurrence in electronics manufacturing.
- Union labor demands wages substantially higher than those paid by competitors in other countries or in non-union parts of the country. This is common in the automotive industry.
- Government safety or environmental regulations increase the cost of being in business. The EPA regulates waste disposal, local boards of health enforce sanitation standards on restaurants.
- Customer demand shifts away from the product. Remember movies from the 1940s? Men wore hats!

Summarizing the SWOT Concept

Conducting a SWOT analysis sets us up for the next step, developing a strategy. The exercise begins with brainstorming four lists, our strengths, weaknesses, opportunities and threats.

It isn't uncommon for a item to appear on more than one list. Take the example above in which a firm is offered the opportunity to buy out a competitor. That's certainly an opportunity, but it's also a threat. If the company doesn't take the offer, someone else will. And the purchaser may turn out to be a much more aggressive competitor than the old owner. As another example, employees can be strengths in that they're highly skilled, but they can be weaknesses in that they cost a lot.

Once the lists are made up, it's important to sit back and think about their implications. Remember that the whole idea behind line of business strategy is to match the strengths and weaknesses against the opportunities and threats on a continuing basis. In other words, reviewing the SWOT from time to time keeps us on top of our situation and ready to make strategic shifts when business conditions call for them. If we understand our SWOT we can respond quickly to initiatives from our competitors and keep them off balance with our own.

Competitive Cost Analysis

The one operational factor that underlies all strategic thinking is the importance of being cost-competitive. In nearly any business it's impossible to be successful in the long run if costs are significantly above those of competitors.

Cost is especially important in commodity type businesses where the product or service of one firm is more or less indistinguishable from that of another. In such cases, competition tends to be based on price, so cost relative to the competition makes or breaks the firm.

However, even where differentiated products will support some price differences, a firm's costs can't be far above its competitors if it is to survive and prosper.

It isn't unusual for managements to be surprised by rivals undercutting their pricing. People's first reaction to such a shock is usually that the rival is temporarily selling at or below its own cost to gain market share. However, it often turns out that the rival has some kind of cost advantage, and that others have to scramble to catch up or lose share.

That lesson was brought home to American industry in the 1970s and 1980s when it became apparent that foreign competitors, especially the Japanese and Koreans, could produce similar if not better products than US manufacturers at lower costs. American business suffered some major defeats before streamlining its cost structure and fighting its way back to competitiveness in the 1990s.

The same principle applies in smaller businesses. In the long run you've got to be cost-competitive, and no amount of strategy will save you if you aren't. Strategic thinking provides some ways of looking at cost that help managers stay on top of the issue.

The Concept of Value Chain[1]

The value chain is a structured way of looking at a business's processes and costs that can be strategically insightful. It involves laying functions and processes out along a conceptual line coinciding with the addition of value during the procurement, production, and delivery of the product or service offered. The general model looks is as shown in figure 6.1.[2]

Clearly, the functions within each block are different for different types of businesses, as are the relative importance of the blocks. Nevertheless, all

---

[1] For a detailed treatment see Michael E. Porter, *Competitive Advantage: Creating and Sustaining Superior Performance* (New York: Free Press, 1985).

[2] Based on Porter, *Competitive Advantage*, p. 37.

Figure 6.1 Value Chain Analysis

businesses move whatever they sell from left to right along the line. In any specific application, the blocks can be further broken down into more detailed processes.

The idea behind *value chain analysis* is to identify costs with stages along the line, and compare a firm's performance at each stage with the performance of competitors. Ideally this process shows where the firm is spending too much and where it's effective relative to what others are doing. That knowledge shows management where to concentrate its efforts in becoming or remaining cost-competitive.

It's not always possible to match a competitor's cost in every block, because different firms have advantages in different areas. For example, one firm may have access to a low-cost input that's just not available to others. Labor costs, for instance, tend to be higher in the unionized north than in the non-union south. Northern firms are stuck with that situation in the short run, and can only fix it by incurring the expense of a major move in the longer term.

However, strategic success is dependent on overall cost, not superiority at each stage. Hence a firm that sees itself as behind in one block can make up its shortfall in another, and come out competitively in the end. In other words, expensive production labor can be offset by effective marketing or distribution. The point is that value chain analysis focuses attention on where the problems are and where they might be made up.

Benchmarking

A refinement of the concept is called benchmarking. It involves developing a value chain model in which the costs in each block represent the best anyone can do on that process. Those costs then become an ideal or benchmark against which performance can be measured.

Problems with Value Chain Analysis

The first step in applying value chain analysis is developing an accounting system and an allocation scheme that allows the dividing of a company's own costs among the model blocks. That's always possible, but can be relatively time-consuming and costly, especially if the firm doesn't have a sophisticated accounting system.

The more difficult problem is making a reasonably accurate estimate that breaks out the costs of competitors in the same way. This is often virtually impossible. In most cases, companies are very guarded about cost information, and are especially unwilling to share anything that might help a competitor.

A few large companies have gotten together to share information to their mutual benefit. This, however, can be a legally dangerous thing to do, since such communications could be interpreted as collusion to reduce competition which is illegal under the antitrust laws.

Trade Associations and Benchmarking Groups

Benchmarking frequently provides a more realistic approach to value chain analysis than a direct competitive comparison. Most industries have trade associations or cost-sharing groups that collect cost figures from members and publish averages without disclosing any individual's results. These can be used to estimate an optimal value chain for a business.

Long-Run Problems

The final step in internal analysis is to identify and document strategic problems. These are the big items that management has to address in the coming years. They're usually not surprises, but are things people have known about for a long time. Less frequently management becomes aware of them during the analysis up to this point. Here are a few examples:

- A firm produces machinery in the northern midwest, a heavily unionized area. Its labor costs are 40 percent higher than those of domestic rivals who have relocated to southern states where labor is largely non-union. Foreign competitors pay labor rates 30 percent lower than those in the south. The strategic issue is the cost of labor. Possible strategies include moving south at enormous expense, contracting with offshore manufacturers, and trying to get the union to understand the problem and accept lower compensation.
- Charlie's used to be the only restaurant in a small but rapidly growing town. Business was good and Charlie made an excellent living. The operation is a traditional family-style restaurant. The place is a little old and less than inspiring in terms of style and atmosphere. The food is okay but not great. In the last three years four new restaurants have opened including two fast-food franchises, an Italian place and a very nice family-style franchise with an old-fashioned theme. No one seems to be doing exceptionally well, but Charlie is barely breaking even on a greatly-reduced sales volume. The issue is how Charlie should deal with the new competitive situation.
- New environmental regulations make disposing of waste more costly.

Options include paying to truck the waste away or investing in equipment and changed processes to reduce waste production. The issue is handling waste under the new regulations at a cost that doesn't bankrupt the firm.

- Competitors are beating us with a product that isn't as good as ours by using innovative advertising and packaging. We depend on pure sales(wo)manship which frequently doesn't work. The issue is managing our marketing effort.
- Our factory and equipment are old and inefficient. Should we build a new one or upgrade the old one? If we build, where should we go? The issue is our old facility and the opportunity to move to a better place.

Long-Run Problems and the Plan

It's absolutely essential that all long-term problems be identified and addressed when formulating strategy. A strategy that doesn't offer a solution to all of a firm's major issues is simply incomplete, and is probably just putting off a major problem that's likely to become worse before it's finally addressed.

Such problems often have both a strategic and an operational dimension. While a long-run approach to the problem has to be worked out, in smaller businesses it's often necessary to do something quickly to stay in business long enough to implement the long-run fix.

Take Charlie's restaurant, for example. He probably has to renovate his establishment to remain competitive with his new rivals. But he may also have to do something like reduce prices or launch a promotion to stay in business until that's done.

Hence a strategic plan should include a strategy to deal with issues, as well as immediate action-steps to get something started quickly. We'll have a great deal more to say about the action-steps later on.

Overall Competitive Assessment

Our next step is to make an overall assessment of the firm's competitive position. A quantitative approach to this task involves rating (scoring) the company's position relative to its rivals on a number of separate issues, and then putting the several scores together to come up with one aggregate measure.[3] The appropriate issues are generally the industry's key success factors plus a fairly standard group of other things like quality, customer satisfaction, financial condition, and market position. The aggregating proc-

---

[3] See Arthur A. Thompson and A. J. Strickland, *Strategic Management, Concepts and Cases*, 10th edn (Irwin–McGraw-Hill, 1998).

ess is generally some kind of a weighted averaging that gives consideration to the relative importance of the separate measures.

There's some danger in producing an aggregate measure like this. A single overall score on anything as complex as competitive position is bound to oversimplify the real situation. It's especially dangerous if one of the important measures is rated as critically low.

For example, suppose a firm is doing well on every strategic issue, but owes so much money it can't meet its debt service obligations. It would receive a poor grade on financial condition, but might have a good overall grade if its scores were high on everything else. This would give the impression of a strong competitive position even though the business was actually on the verge of failure. It would be like saying a person with advanced heart disease was in good overall health if his other systems were working well.

Despite this reservation, it's a good idea to develop an overall measure of competitive position for the firm we're interested in and its chief rivals. It's then possible to rank our company relative to its competition.

The Rating and Computational Procedure

The rating procedure is as follows:

1 Choose the strategically important issues on which the competitors are to be scored and assign a weight to each.
2 Assign each competitor a grade from 1 (lowest) to 10 (highest) on each issue.
3 Calculate a weighted average grade for each competitor.
4 Rank the competitors on the basis of the weighted average grade and evaluate the results.

EXAMPLE 6-1

The Dexter Company is a small manufacturer of sheet-metal parts which it sells to companies that assemble a variety of finished products. Dexter's products include diverse items such as lawn mower housings and cabinets for computer peripherals. There are a large number of sheet-metal shops nationwide, but shipping expense keeps competition relatively local. Dexter has two important rivals, Forbes Sheetmetal Inc. and Dobbs Stamping Co.

Assemblers tend to work repeatedly with only two or three sheet-metal fabricators as long as cost and quality remain competitive. This means Dexter's Key Success Factors are the low-cost production and established connections with assemblers.

Other important measures of competitive viability are reputation, quality, engineering and financial condition. Management feels that cost and engineering are twice as important as the other measures which are all about equally important. These relative judgements of importance provide a raw weighting of the issues.

Dexter's management has graded itself and its rivals on the important issues as follows:

	Dexter	Forbes	Dobbs
Low Cost	8	6	9
Connections	10	9	9
Reputation	8	7	9
Quality	7	9	8
Engineering	7	5	6
Finances	5	2	7

Develop an overall competitive score and ranking for Dexter and its rivals.

Solution: Write out the measures and the raw weights then calculate weights for computation by dividing each raw weight by the sum of raw weights. This is just stating the factors as percents in decimal form. Note that they add to 1.0:

Measure	Raw Weight	Weight
Low Cost	2	.250
Connections	1	.125
Reputation	1	.125
Quality	1	.125
Engineering	2	.250
Finances	1	.125
	8	1.000

Next multiply each company's grade on each measure by the measure's weight and sum for each firm to get the three weighted average grades.

Measure	Wt	Dexter Grd	GrdxWt	Forbes Grd	GrdxWt	Dobbs Grd	GrdxWt
Low Cost	.250	8	2.000	6	1.500	9	2.250
Connections	.125	10	1.250	8	1.000	8	1.000
Reputation	.125	8	2.000	7	.875	8	1.000
Quality	.125	7	.875	10	1.250	8	1.000
Engineering	.250	7	1.750	10	2.500	6	1.500
Finances	.125	5	.625	2	.250	7	.875
Overall Grade			8.500		7.375		7.625

First notice that using this procedure Dexter rates itself first by a fairly wide margin. Also notice that Forbes appears to be in the same ballpark as the other two firms in spite of its very low grade in financial position. This is an illustration of the danger we described earlier. Notice that Dexter's finances are in pretty bad shape too, but it comes out on top overall anyway.

Of course, it's also possible to take a qualitative approach to rating and ranking the various competitors in an industry. That means we step back and subjectively consider all the things we've put together about the industry and the companies in it. We stroke our chins thoughtfully, and then place all the players in a ranked order based on our judgment. People who don't like math tend to favor this method while technical folks prefer the numerical approach. It isn't a bad idea to do both and reconcile any differences that come up.

Putting It All Together – A Self-Assessment

At this point it's a good idea to step back and take a long look at everything we've done so far with an open mind. That is, before we become embroiled in developing a strategy, we need to at least consider the possibility that we're not in the right business.

It's important to keep in mind that small businesses fail all the time. There's a tendency to ride a failing operation out to the last gasp, closing the doors only when the owner is absolutely bankrupt. This generally isn't the most graceful way to exit a field, and almost always costs a great deal more than a more controlled exit made earlier.

Look at the example we gave of Charlie's restaurant. It's quite possible that while Charlie did okay in a small town where he was the only player, he just isn't equipped to compete with sophisticated, well-financed operations like the franchises that have moved in recently. Maybe the best thing for him to do is to close down now and go into something else.

The end of the situation analysis phase is a good time to look at this decision. Although strategic thinking is a great tool, it isn't magic, and it can't make an impossible situation viable.

Put another way, a business's best strategy may be to close. If that's done while the business is still making money, the owner may be able to sell to someone who has the resources to make it survive and prosper.

On the other hand, if the self-assessment looks reasonably good, it's time to tackle crafting a strategy.

chapter 7

Developing a Strategy

An effective strategy takes advantage of a fit between a firm's internal abilities and its external environment. If that fit is correctly conceived and effectively managed it gives the company an edge in the struggle with its rivals and a better chance at winning the long-run competitive game. In this chapter we'll look at the process of coming up with fits and examine some specific situations in which certain generic approaches work well.

The Nature of the Strategy Making Task

Building a strategy deals with defining what a firm has to do to fit into its environment. In other words, strategy deals with figuring out just how we go about fitting our firm's abilities to the industry's needs.

Let's reconsider Example 3-2 in which two firms used different strategic approaches to the computer business. Recall that both made and marketed computers. One was an engineering leader but had a weak marketing force, so it based its appeal on a technically advanced product. The other had an exceptional talent for customer relations, but was weak in engineering, so it based its approach on understanding and solving customer problems.

It's important to understand that both companies can do well only if there are at least two kinds of customer, one that requires advanced computing power and one that doesn't. If both segments exist, then both companies can base their strategy on their strengths, which match the needs of the respective segments. Further, appealing to the right segment's need minimizes each firm's vulnerability to its weakness.

Putting together a strategy involves the process either firm goes through as it recognizes its abilities, the needs of its market segment, and the match between the two; and then defines actions which capitalize on that match.

It's important to notice that so far we've described both firms' strategies in only the broadest terms. Each complete strategy would actually have many elements that support the concepts of being technology-based or service-based. For example, the technical firm might do some of the following things that the service-oriented firm probably wouldn't:

Identify customers in scientific fields in business, government, and academia which are likely to need extra computing power.

Develop marketing programs designed to appeal to scientists and engineers rather than to business managers. These would include seminars and symposiums on science and computing.

Actively recruit the best computer scientists for its own research staff.

Devote proportionately more funding to research than to advertising or promotion.

Building the technical firm's strategy would involve developing this list of activities along with others that would round out the entire business approach.

Creating Strategies in General

Most of the problems we learn to deal with in books are structured, and we can apply more or less the same solution technique every time we run into a variation on the situation. For example, in physics we'd use the same formula to figure out how hard a dropped weight will hit the ground in every problem even though we might make adjustments for variables like height or air resistance between problems.

Building a strategy isn't like that. It's a more free-form exercise than most of the other things we're used to. The task is accomplished by taking the knowledge from internal and external analyses and putting it together with principles we'll learn in this chapter. But there isn't any rigid or standard way of doing that. It's a matter of creatively synthesizing information and coming up with a unique package that fits the situation we're up against.

In general, two well-trained people looking at the same strategic problem come up with similar but not identical solutions. People without strategic training, however, often come up with solutions that have big problems and aren't likely to work.

The Concept of Competitive Advantage[1]

The concept of competitive advantage is a useful way to think about the ideas we've been talking about up until now and linking them with strategy.

---

[1] For a detailed treatment see Michael E. Porter, *Competitive Advantage* (New York: Free Press, 1985).

A competitive advantage is some kind of an edge a company uses to win over its rivals again and again in the business arena. It's generally based on some skill, talent, or asset the firm has that its rivals don't. We've described those things as strengths or distinctive competences.

Good strategy produces a sustainable competitive advantage based on at least one distinctive competence that's used effectively. In other words, there's a hierarchy of ideas involved as shown in the following.

STRENGTH

↓

DISTINCTIVE COMPETENCE

↓

BASIS OF STRATEGY

↓

COMPETITIVE ADVANTAGE

In words, the cause-and-effect relationship can be stated as follows: A strength in something that matters is a distinctive competence, which can be used as a basis of strategy, which if implemented effectively can produce a competitive advantage, which can be sustained over a long period.

Notice that this statement is conditional. It uses the words can and if, not will. This implies that just having a strength in the right thing doesn't guarantee success without a lot of work to make it happen.

For example, suppose a high-tech firm has a strength in engineering, that might seem to lead directly to success in the market, but it doesn't. Suppose for example, the engineering department produces a stream of "nifty" gadgets that the engineers like but which are only mildly interesting to customers. That's not likely to produce a big win against rivals in the marketplace.

In order to be strategically successful, the engineering department has to be managed into coming up with a series of innovations that rivals can't match, and that win big with customers on important issues again and again.

This is an important idea. It takes more than having the right stuff to be a strategic success. The right stuff also has to be used in the right way.

Generic Strategies[2]

There are three situations in which the basic elements of the right strategy are indicated fairly clearly. The strategic approaches that fit these cases are known as generic strategies.

The three generics are:

Low-Cost Leadership,

Differentiation, and

Focus (Niche).

We'll talk about each at some length.

Overall Cost Leadership

The cost leadership strategy is just what the name implies: A firm employing the approach strives to be the lowest-cost producer of whatever product or service it offers. Having that lowest cost then gives the firm a competitive edge over its rivals.

The Advantages of a Low-Cost Strategy

A low-cost strategy, even if the firm doesn't actually achieve the lowest cost in the industry, yields several advantages.

Price Competition

The primary issue is that having a relatively low cost gives a firm extra maneuvering room in pricing battles with rival sellers. The lower our own costs, the more easily we can match others' pricing initiatives and attack them with our own.

Pricing against Potential Entrants

Having a low cost blunts the threat posed by potential entrants. They know they'll have to match the prices of strong firms already in the industry, and that they'll have a hard time getting their costs as low as those of the

---

[2]   Based on Porter, *Competitive Strategy*, 1980, ch. 2.

seasoned firms. They'll be reluctant to try if it's known that one or more incumbents has very low costs and can drop prices further in response to an entry move.

Low-Cost and Substitute Products

Buyers only use substitutes when their pricing makes them attractive relative to the industry's product. Having a low cost makes it possible to keep prices down if substitutes start to become a problem.

Bargaining with Buyers

Low-cost leadership can give some protection against buyer power in that a powerful customer can't bargain prices down below the lowest price the next lowest-cost producer is willing to offer. And at that price, the low-cost leader can still make a profit.

Several Close Rivals

In industries where the low-cost approach is appropriate, it's likely that more than one firm will pursue the strategy at the same time. If several firms achieve costs that are close to one another's, the industry can continue indefinitely with all of them jockeying for a lead position.

Cost and Prices

A company that successfully achieves the industry's lowest cost doesn't necessarily offer lower prices than its rivals although it obviously might. Profits from a low-cost approach can be made by selling at the same price as others and earning a bigger margin per unit or by undercutting rivals' pricing for a lower margin on a larger volume.

Cost Means Total Cost

The low-cost approach doesn't just mean striving for the lowest production cost. Low-cost producers generally have a theme of austerity and budget-consciousness that runs through the entire company. Human resources tend to be stretched thin in all areas, facilities are spartan, and when people travel they go economy class.

In a firm that successfully implements a low-cost strategy, the whole organization thinks about saving money all the time. Doing things inexpensively becomes more than a theme; it borders on being an obsession. Cost reduction becomes part of the corporate culture, and people develop value systems that respect and esteem saving money. If the idea is implemented well employees are willing to sacrifice their own time and comfort in the cause of austerity.

How a Low-Cost Leadership Position is Achieved

Several observations are important in understanding how low-cost leaders stay ahead.

Attention to Detail

The first and generally most important requirement for low-cost leadership is a scrupulous attention to detail starting with top management and continuing all the way down to the supervisor level. This is especially true in small businesses. Keeping costs down takes constant vigilance on physical operations and meticulous reviews of spending.

In the restaurant business, for example, it's important to watch for waste in ordering and preparing foods, to monitor portion sizes, and to keep a constant eye on excess labor. In retailing, inventory losses and control over price discounting are crucial as are getting the most out of promotional spending. In manufacturing, the biggest problems are usually in controlling inventory to minimize breakage, theft, and obsolesence and in managing overhead spending.

Automated Processes and Scale Economies

In many fields achieving low cost means replacing people with machines which in turn requires keeping volume up to achieve scale economies. That is, the overhead associated with machinery has to be spread over a large unit output to keep cost down.

Reinventing Processes

Occasionally a cost advantage can be achieved by eliminating process steps or coming up with an altogether better way of doing something.

When a Low-Cost Strategy is Appropriate

Although cost is important in virtually every business, the low-cost leadership strategy is far from universally appropriate. Several characteristics of industries and products tend to make a low-cost approach more valuable.

Strong Price Competition

When price competition is vigorous, even if other competitive weapons are in use, a low-cost strategy can give a producer an extra edge.

Commodity Products

A low-cost strategy makes the most sense when the product is a commodity, i.e., there isn't much difference between one producer's output and another's, and there isn't much opportunity for producers to differentiate themselves even if they want to. In such a situation, the dominant weapon of competitive rivalry is virtually always price. Hence having the lowest cost gives a competitor an edge over rivals, because it has more pricing flexibility than they do. However, it's important to understand that in commodity businesses all rivals usually have something of a low cost approach, and everyone's costs and prices are generally pretty close together. That's because any firm whose costs (and therefore prices) are more than a few percent out of line with the others won't survive.

Low Switching Costs

Switching costs are the costs buyers incur in moving from one supplier to another. When these are low or non-extant, buyers are more responsive to price differentials than when it's expensive to change vendors. Hence low switching costs tend to breed price-competitive markets in which it's a big advantage to have a cost leadership position.

Risks Associated with a Low-Cost Strategy

There are two main sources of risk associated with striving for cost leadership. One is external while the other is internal.

Somebody Else Does it Better

Many low-cost processes require quite a substantial investment in machinery, facilities and procedures to achieve their cost advantages. The danger always exists that someone will come up with a breakthrough (usually technological), creating a process that does the job more cheaply. If that happens the investments in process and equipment can be lost along with the cost advantage.

Low-Cost Myopia

Companies sometimes get so fixated on low cost that they lose sight of other things going on in the market. For example, customer preferences often shift over time toward products with more features or higher quality or better support. That leaves the low-cost producer with a problem because its product is usually low in features or quality.

The Low-Cost/Quality Issue

It's important to think about the implication of a low-cost strategy when the product isn't a commodity that's produced in only one version by everyone.

Where the product or service has a quality range and/or a variable number of included features, a low-cost strategy generally constrains a producer to operate at the bottom of the range with a minimum of features.

We'll come back to this point shortly.

EXAMPLE 7-1

The RoughWear Company manufactures blue jeans and work clothing for private label sale by large retailers like Sears and Penney's (private label items are marketed under the retailer's brand name although they're produced by other firms). The retailers place orders containing exact product specifications and generally give contracts to the lowest price bidder that's qualified to do the work.

Retailers try to spread their business among several suppliers to keep them actively competing with one another and to guarantee their source should one supplier fail to deliver. Timely delivery and consistent quality are also important to the retailers, but virtually all suppliers perform well on those factors.

A low-cost producer strategy is appropriate for RoughWear since there is little opportunity to compete on anything but price.

However, the strategy creates an ethical problem. Securing the lowest cost in the garment business generally means contracting labor out to job shops in less developed countries. These firms keep costs down by operating sweatshops that pay subsistence wages to workers that are often children. In many cases, workers are virtually slaves.

If you suddenly found yourself in charge of RoughWear, how would you alter the firm's strategy to address this problem? Is there a problem? Is there a way out?

Differentiation

A differentiation strategy implies incorporating features or attributes into a product or service that make it more desirable to some buyers. Two points are crucial to the concept:

1   The differentiated product generally costs more than the undifferenti-
    ated version, and
2   the differentiated version still maintains a broad appeal among buyers.

In other words, the differentiating feature is generally a betterment of
some kind that most customers find desirable, but may or may not be willing
to pay extra for.

For example, suppose an automobile manufacturer offers a car with an
engine that's both more powerful and more fuel-efficient than others. The
car would be *differentiated* by a higher quality engine. Virtually anyone
would want the better engine if it didn't cost more. This means the differentiating feature has *broad appeal*.

Alternatively imagine that the manufacturer differentiated the car by putting
on a very durable exterior coating which came in only one color, purple.
Although people would like the extra protection, many wouldn't want it
because of the color. In that case the differentiating feature would not have a
broad appeal.

A differentiating feature can be an optional addition that's available
for an added cost. The car engine, for example, could be an optional upgrade
from a basic model. On the other hand, a feature can be made part of the basic
product. The better engine, for example, could be a standard feature differentiating the car from rivals but not from other models in its own line.

Bases for Differentiation

Probably the most common differentiating feature is wrapped up in the idea
of quality. Almost everything we buy, from food to clothes to cars to houses,
can be had in higher quality versions that perform better but cost more.

Beyond that, however, a great deal of differentiation is based on some
specific attribute of a product or the package that comes along with it.
Products can be differentiated on availability, quick delivery, variety of
options in style or color, warranty protection, training offered, convenient
distribution and so on.

It's also possible to differentiate on price or overall cost to a user. Notice
that differentiating on price isn't the same as a low-cost leadership strategy.
In the low-cost situation, price is usually the dominant if not the only basis
for competition. Here low price is one of many possible bases for differentiation, and may be offered along with other features.

Differentiation Based on Perception

It's important to realize that differentiating features can be concrete, demon-
strable things, or they can exist as perceptions in the customer's mind. In
that case they may or not reflect reality.

Real features are easy to understand. One dry cleaner consistently returns clothes cleaner and better pressed than another, one restaurant has better food than another, one builder offers a larger house for the same money than another. These things are verifiable by the user.

Other differences, however, can't easily be demonstrated and may or may not be real. For example, what makes one wristwatch better than another, or one home furnace, or one brand of beer? Although such products are all marketed based on differentiation strategies, much of the differentiation is artificial and put in the buyer's mind by advertising.

In such cases, image can be as important as anything real. Beer commercials are a good example. Budweiser, Coors and Miller are priced similarly, and seem to be of about the same quality. So their makers spend a great deal promoting an image of youth, attractiveness, and fun associated with using the product. The brand people buy has a lot to do with which ad they find most appealing.

Making Differentiation Work

Differentiation, whether real or perceived, generally costs the seller money. Real features have real costs while perceptions cost money to create through advertising. At the same time differentiated products generally sell at higher prices than their plain vanilla counterparts.

Clearly, the key to successful differentiation is adding features that cost less to produce than buyers are willing to pay.

In our automotive example, suppose the better engine cost the manufacturer an additional $500 to produce and install. Some buyers would have to be willing to pay that plus a reasonable markup to make the idea worthwhile. If they weren't, the whole differentiation initiative would be a waste of time and money.

The Competitive Advantages of Differentiation

The big competitive benefit of a differentiated product is that it creates customer loyalty. It does that by giving buyers something that fits their needs better than the undifferentiated product or the offerings of competitors.

Differentiated products save money, are especially effective, are easy to use, or are just aesthetically pleasing. Features that do these things create products to which customers become attached, making them reluctant to switch to other brands or substitutes.

At the same time, loyalty blunts the threat of entry, because potential entrants know they'll have a harder time prying loyal buyers away from incumbent firms. It also helps to deal with buyer power. In order to exercise their power, buyers have to be willing to move to other suppliers, but that's hard when they're attached to a differentiated product.

Risks in a Differentiation Strategy

The risks associated with differentiation can be divided into two categories. The first consists of things that happen after the strategy has been established, while the second includes problems that occur while trying to find and implement a basis for differentiation.

Risks after the Fact

The biggest risk is probably from copiers. A differentiation that's successful but easy to copy can quickly be imitated by rivals mitigating its benefits. Then the cost of developing and implementing the feature may be lost.

The second risk comes from fickle customers. It isn't uncommon for users to migrate away from features they seemed staunchly attached to only a short time earlier. This too can have the effect of wasting the effort put into differentiating.

Risks of Getting There

It's possible to spend a lot of money developing a differentiating feature that doesn't appeal to enough customers to be worthwhile. This happens quite a bit in small business, because entrepreneurs confuse what appeals to them with what appeals to customers. For example, suppose a furniture retailer loves expensive fine art. A few of his customers share his passion, so he decides to differentiate his showroom by incorporating an art gallery, and devotes 20 percent of his space to expensive, collectible paintings. However, it turns out that the bulk of his clientele are in an economic bracket that makes buying better art difficult if not impossible. Hence the differentiating feature doesn't attract many people and he loses sales on what he would have normally displayed in the space devoted to art.

Sometimes an organization doesn't effectively signal the value of a differentiating feature. For example, a small college may have an excellent program in accounting that rivals anything larger, more expensive schools have to offer. Its advertising, however, features only its business programs and doesn't say anything specific about accounting. The value of the differentiating feature is lost, because it's kept secret.

Overpricing a differentiated product generally defeats its purpose. Better restaurants do this all the time. Fine-dining is frequently offered in suburban locations, but the establishments don't usually last long. They tend to charge twice (or more) what good but not great local establishments do. People like the idea, but not at the price.

EXAMPLE 7-2

Harry Gardner operates a store that sells good quality furniture and a wide range of appliances including TV and stereo equipment in Lancaster, New Hampshire, a rural town with a population of about 20,000. The nearest city is Manchester, 75 miles away. Harry has been in business in Lancaster for over 20 years making a good but not spectacular living.

Suppose a large discount chain has been trying to open a store in Lancaster for several years but has been blocked by the town council due to vigorous opposition from merchants like Harry and a few people concerned about maintaining the town's New England character. The merchants fear the fate of countless rural retailers who were forced out of business shortly after big discount stores opened in their towns. Others residents, however, see the presence of a retailing giant as a step toward a higher level of economic prosperity in Lancaster, and want to see its proposal approved. The issue has been hotly contested for some time.

Unfortunately for Harry, the council has just approved zoning for the discounter, and construction is scheduled to start in a few months. Harry is petrified. He's 45 years-old and doesn't know anything but the business he's in. Is there any way he can survive near a retailing giant that sells the same things he does?

Solution: Harry is in for a tough battle, but it isn't a foregone conclusion that the discounter will put him out of business if he makes the right strategic choices.

The chain's strategy is probably one of low-cost leadership in which they pass their cost advantage on to customers in the form of low pricing. They may also strive to differentiate themselves based on customer service. They define that as a helpful, friendly attitude in the store. Discounters don't, however, provide much after-sale service, and their sales people are not particularly knowledgeable about the technical specifications of products.

Harry clearly can't match the big store on price, but he may survive if he chooses a strategy that differentiates his store on something it doesn't try to do. After-sale service seems like a good place to start. Harry might consider hiring a technician and opening his own appliance service department. Then he can claim to take care of the customer throughout the life of the purchase, something big discounters don't do. He can also provide knowledge and advice on the technical quality of products, especially TVs and stereos. A stereo installation service might be a good idea.

If Harry differentiates his store on advice and service, some customers may be willing to pay somewhat more for appliances, TVs, and stereos purchased from him.

The fact that Harry sells better furniture may also offer a possibility for strategic differentiation. Discounters generally carry only small amounts of low-end furniture, so Harry may be able to differentiate himself by creating an image of a high-quality, full-line home furnishing and equipment center.

The risk in all this is that people will find out all they need to know about products at Harry's, and then buy from the discount store for less.

The Role of Cost in Differentiation Strategies

It's important not to get the idea that cost is only important to firms that use the low-cost leadership strategy. In that situation, it's the paramount issue that eclipses just about everything else.

Differentiators have to control cost too, because it's a central element in business performance. In fact, most businesses list cost-control as an element of strategy regardless of their overriding strategic theme.

A Hybrid Strategy – Best Cost Provider[3]

Recall that earlier we said a low-cost leadership strategy generally constrained a seller to operate at the low end of the quality/feature spectrum when the product or service being sold was not a commodity. Operating with higher quality and/or features generally involves some kind of a differentiation strategy.

It's possible to combine a cost leadership strategy with a differentiation approach by selecting a quality/feature range above the bottom, and striving to be the lowest-cost producer in that range. The idea is represented graphically in figure 7.1.

For example, a seller might choose to provide a medium-quality product at a slightly below-average price or a fairly high-quality item at a mid-range price.

The idea is easy to visualize in the context of a restaurant. Suppose an independent restaurateur competes with mid-range family-style restaurants like units of the Denny's or Howard Johnson's chains. A viable strategy would be to match their food quality, beat their service, and provide the package at a noticeably lower price.

The best cost-provider strategy fits a vast number of situations, because buyers often shy away from minimum-quality products. Hence a best cost strategy in the medium range has tremendous flexibility.

---

[3] Thompson and Strickland, *Strategic Management*, pp. 152–4.

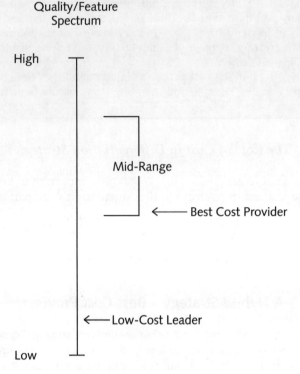

Quality/Feature
Spectrum

Figure 7.1   Best Cost Provider

Focus (Niche) Strategies

A focus or niche strategy identifies a market segment whose needs are not well served by the industry's broad-based sellers, and constructs a product/ service approach which caters specifically to that segment.[4]

In general, customers in a targetable niche market can get along with standard products, but need to make some adaptation, incur an extra cost, or suffer an inconvenience to do so.

The focus strategist tailors its product or service specifically to the needs of the niche customers. Ideally the result is a relatively small market segment in which the niche player is the only seller. In other words, its product fits the limited group's needs so well they virtually eliminate other sellers from consideration as long as the focuser's pricing is within reason.

---

[4] We *focus* our attention on a *niche* in the market. We'll use the terms interchangeably.

The difference between a focus strategy and an extreme case of differentiation is that a differentiated product retains a broad appeal across the entire market. A niche product is generally of little interest to buyers outside the niche.

EXAMPLE 7-3

Sam Haverty has wide feet, at least a EEEE width, and has always had trouble finding shoes that fit. Sam's biggest complaint is a lack of selection. He has to buy whatever he can squeeze into rather than being able to select a style and color he likes. He's met several other people with the same problem who are equally frustrated by the trouble they have finding shoes.

Sam has an idea for a business venture using a focus strategy. He'll start a company that produces shoes in extremely wide sizes offering a reasonably broad selection of styles and colors. The firm will market the shoes in small stores dedicated to wide styles. Part of the strategy involves putting just one store in each metropolitan area. Sam reasons that once people with wide feet find out about the stores, they won't mind traveling a distance to get their shoes, and he won't have to put a store in every shopping mall the way large shoe companies do.

Notice that Sam is addressing a true niche market in that his targeted buyers are poorly served by traditional shoe manufacturers and others have no interest in wide shoes.

Sam's strategy will create a problem at the production stage of the value chain, because only a relatively small number of shoes of each size and style will be produced. That means unit production costs will be high.

However, the deficiency will be made up in the distribution stage. Only one store in each metropolitan area will be needed, and marketing and distribution costs will be lower than those of traditional shoe-sellers.

Overall, Sam's plan represents what looks like a viable niche strategy. The target market is indeed poorly served, and his business will make a big difference to its customers. Major shoe companies don't make many wide sizes, because they don't want to incur the production and inventory expense of carrying low-volume items in all their stores. Sam's strategy compensates for that effect by having fewer stores which avoids expenses related to both inventory and store operations.

Sam's big risk is that he's depending on buyers traveling to him, but that seems like a reasonable gamble.

The focus strategy is very common in small business, because a variety of focus criteria lend themselves to small individual enterprises. For example, suppose a town is 75 miles from the nearest complete shopping area. The town has several kinds of retail store including food, hardware and most necessities, but there's no place to buy clothing. That means residents have to make a 150-mile round trip to buy something to wear. That makes the town a geographically defined niche for a clothing store. Notice that such a business opportunity isn't likely to grow, but is likely to control a captive market for some time.

The Strengths of a Niche Strategy

A true niche can be very attractive because it represents an insulated position that can last indefinitely.

The niche supplier becomes extremely good at serving the needs of its customers. This creates a situation in which there are no rivals, and it's difficult for new competitors to enter. Newcomers are unlikely because they have to overcome the incumbent's expertise and fight for every one of the limited number of customers available. Further, if the niche is small, there isn't much incentive to enter, because there isn't much money to be made. Hence others stay away of their own accord.

Niche buyers don't have much power either, because there's no source other than the niche supplier for the customized product they need.

The Risks and Disadvantages of a Niche Strategy

A niche strategy is an odd business situation in that it can be bad for a seller to be too successful in terms of either profitability or growth. That's because noticeable success is likely to attract new entrants, which spells the end of the niche situation.

The result of entry may not be too bad if entrants are other small firms against which the original player can fight effectively. It's a disaster, however, if the niche attracts the attention of one or more of the industry's major players. They can bring resources into the segment the smaller firm can't hope to match.

Hence a niche opportunity has to walk a fine line. It has to be big enough and offer enough growth to be worth an entrepreneur's time and investment. But it shouldn't be large enough or have sufficient potential to interest a major player.

An exception to this rule exists if a successful niche firm can sell out to an entering large rival. This can provide a lucrative exit for the entrepreneur that avoids a one-sided fight he or she isn't likely to win.

EXAMPLE 7-3 – CONTINUED

Suppose Sam's chain of stores selling wide shoes is very successful. Imagine that major shoe companies notice Sam and realize that the wide-foot segment is bigger than they thought it was. They therefore begin to produce wide shoes of their own in a variety of styles.

This is likely to be a big problem for Sam, because the large shoe companies will make the new sizes available in their many stores. That in turn will make it unnecessary for customers to travel to Sam's unique locations. This is likely to spell the end of Sam's niche market opportunity.

Unfortunately, no big company is likely to be interested in buying him out, because they have all the production and retailing capacity they need already.

On the other hand, if Sam is moderately successful, and the big companies continue to see wide sizes as an unimportant segment, he can coexist with them indefinitely.

Focus Segments Defined by Price, Quality, and Features

The definition of a niche can get a little fuzzy around the edges. For example, it's possible to define a niche with quality and price that are so high they create a unique image and are affordable to only a few buyers. Rolls Royce automobiles and Rolex watches cater to such market segments.

It's debatable, however, whether these are really niches, because the products would probably be broadly attractive if they weren't so expensive. Hence they're better defined as cases of extreme differentiation.

The idea can work the other way too. A segment at the low end of a market can be thought of as a niche if only a few buyers are interested in a bare-bones product or service at a rock-bottom price.

Offensive and Defensive Strategies

Some strategies can be characterized as offensive or defensive in terms of their desired effect on the competition. There's a difference between offensive and defensive moves in business just as there is in a military or sport context. However, in business it's harder to tell one from another.

In war or football, an offensive move generally attempts to take territory away from an enemy, while defensive moves either counter enemy offenses or strengthen against potential attacks. In these physical endeavors, offense generally means taking possession of territory by moving forward, while defense means resisting the enemy's forward movement. Hence, it's easy to tell which side is on the offensive and which is on the defensive.

In business, market share is roughly analogous to territory. Hence moves to gain share are offensive while those to prevent a competitor from gaining it are defensive. The problem is that the same move can be either offensive or defensive, so it can be hard to tell what's going on.

For example, a price cut can be part of an aggressive attempt to increase sales in a particular line at the expense of the competition. Or it can be a response to price cutting, increased advertising, or improved quality on the part of a rival. In the first case the cut is an offensive move, in the latter case it's defensive.

The difference lies in the intent of the overall strategy which is usually reflected in a number of moves undertaken at the same time. For example, a major offensive move is likely to involve a price cut and increased advertising and a new product variation along with a promotion of some kind. A cut by itself is more likely to be a defensive response.

It's important to realize that a significant, favorable change in market share just about always comes from some kind of offensive move. Further, successful offensives are usually linked to competences that create competitive advantages.

Suppose a restaurant launches an advertising and discounting program to increase its share of the local market. If it doesn't have a competence in the quality of its food relative to rivals, share will slip back to the original point immediately after the promotion is over. If, on the other hand, the promotion is coupled with superior food (or service, or atmosphere) some of those who tried based on the promotion will remain customers and share will be increased.

Timing Competitive Actions[5]

There are often strategic benefits to doing something first or avoiding being the first to do it. For example, suppose several firms are developing a new product. The first to get the product to market may capture customers who attach a loyalty to the first seller that's hard for others to break later.

In other situations a first mover can lock up sources of supply and access to distribution or hire hard-to-find people with critical skills.

Conversely, situations exist in which moving first has a cost. Sometimes the first firm to use a new product or process makes a lot of costly errors that are avoided by those who use the idea later after learning from the pioneer's mistakes.

---

[5] Based on Porter, *Competitive Strategy*, pp. 232–3.

Careful study can often discern whether the rewards associated with doing something first are likely to be worth the risks.

In industries in which smaller firms compete with larger companies, a late-mover strategy is generally appropriate for the smaller players. They let the big firm take the risks of trying new ideas and copy only those that are successful.

This is an especially good approach to hardware-based ideas that require substantial investments. It's generally better to let the industry leaders pioneer new technology and then jump in later when the big guys have the bugs ironed out.

On the other hand, small innovations that don't cost much can be low-risk ventures that are appropriate ways for little players to get ahead.

Strategic Issues in Emerging Industries[6]

Industries are emerging when a new concept or technology appears to have the potential to create a business but no one is quite sure whether the whole idea will work or how much of a market it will create. There's generally quite a bit of activity, but there may not be many sales dollars flowing in. Personal computers were an emerging industry in the early 1980s, and biotech has been in an emerging status for some time.

Emerging industries are often populated by small firms, so the strategic issues they encounter are important to us here. The following characteristics are common in emerging situations:

There's little certainty about how or whether the industry's future will develop. Hence being in the field is a gamble.

Technical know-how is critical in determining the winners. Each player guards what it knows jealously.

Firms have problems obtaining resources. Access to adequate financing is critical.

Barriers to entry are low, so new and more powerful players are possible at any time.

Customers are difficult to secure because the product is unproven.

Several years of losses precede profitable operations.

Successful strategies in emerging industries often include one or more of the following elements:

Concentrate on perfecting technology even if it means neglecting something else.
If a particular way of doing things is shown to be superior, adopt it quickly.

---

[6] Based on Porter, *Competitive Strategy*, ch. 10.

Try to capture the advantages of acting first with customers and suppliers.

Favor bold, high-risk strategies to win customers rather than conservative wait-and-see approaches. The first player with a practical product generally has an edge for some time.

Tie up enough financing to fund operations for substantially longer than appears to be necessary.

Fragmented Industries[7]

An industry is fragmented when it is populated by a large number of smaller firms, and no one company has the size or power to dominate the market. Most industries emerge in a fragmented state and slowly consolidate into more concentrated structures. The automobile industry provides a familiar example. There were a number of American car-makers in the 1920s and 1930s that are just memories today. Names like Studebaker, Auburn, and Packard are gone, and only GM, Ford and Chrysler remain.

Economists consider consolidation a more or less natural phenomenon in industries where there are benefits to being bigger. Such benefits are called economies of scale. Automobiles, for example, can be made more cheaply when they're mass-produced (Henry Ford invented the assembly line) than when they're made a few at a time.

The implication of scale economies is that if one firm in a fragmented industry gets a little bigger than the others, it picks up a competitive advantage that puts it even further ahead. Clearly the phenomenon drives the industry toward control by a few large firms, often forcing all smaller players out of business.

However, conditions sometimes exist that short-circuit the consolidation process, and keep the industry fragmented indefinitely. The most common such condition is a local character attached to the product or service being offered. Dry cleaners, auto mechanics, and restaurants provide good examples. The market for each is limited to the population within a reasonable traveling distance of the point of sale, so the industries continue to be populated by large numbers of relatively small firms.[8]

Other conditions that keep industries fragmented include an absence of scale economies in production such as in advertising, the garment industry and business forms printing; and the high transportation cost of certain products like concrete.

---

[7] For a thorough discussion, see Porter, *Competitive Strategy*, 1980, ch. 9.

[8] In some industries, while individual businesses remain small, scale advantages are available to chains. In fast food for example, firms like MacDonald's benefit from centralized activities (training, advertising etc.) and have come to dominate the industry. Hence it's arguable whether the fast-food segment of the restaurant industry is fragmented or concentrated.

Strategic Options for Fragmented Industries

It's important for smaller businesses to understand the fragmentation concept and what forces keep the industry they're in fragmented. The value of the idea is especially relevant in defining the industry the firm is in for immediate competitive purposes. A restaurant, for example, competes only with other restaurants within a relatively short driving distance. A garment manufacturer or a parts fabricator faces no such geographic limitation even though they're in similarly fragmented fields.

The fact that the industry is fragmented, however, places no restrictions on the nature of strategy. In other words, the strategic elements of differentiation, low cost, or focus can apply as well to fragmented operations as to other businesses.

Developing a Strategy – Summary

Developing a strategy involves sitting down with the results of the situation analysis and the ideas we've presented in this chapter, and developing the important elements of a strategic approach to your business. You'll notice that we haven't told you exactly how to do that. That's because there isn't any right way to do it. Here are a few guidelines to get started:

- The first step is to decide whether the company's situation is close to one of the generics, or can better be thought of as a combination of elements from more than one. It's very common in smaller businesses to differentiate on some aspect of the product or service and overlay that with a concentration on keeping costs as low as possible.
- First make an overall summarizing statement of the strategic approach and then start writing down things that have to be done to support the broader idea. Work from the general to the detailed.

part III

Strategic Planning and Implementation

chapter 8

Implementation and Control

IMPLEMENTING THE CHOSEN STRATEGY

Implementation is generally considered to be the most difficult part of the strategic process. As we said at the outset of our study of strategy, implementation requires a different set of skills from strategic analysis or developing strategy. Those activities tend to be intellectual, requiring creativity and vision. Implementation, on the other hand, is basically an administrative task. It involves working with people, procedures, information, and the structure of the organization to make the visionary ideas developed earlier come true.

The Nature of the Implementation Problem

Implementation is hard because it generates conflict and it's time-consuming. The conflict comes from the fact that strategic change usually isn't welcomed by everyone. There are always some people who see change as either inappropriate or threatening and resist it. That makes moving the organization in a new direction difficult.

Implementation is time-consuming, because it has to be done throughout the entire organization and essentially forever. A senior manager can't just write a memo explaining a new strategy and forget it. He or she has to work with subordinate managers at all levels making sure they understand what the strategy means to their operations and that they install systems and controls to make it happen. That overseeing, monitoring task is more or less endless.

Implementation tends to be more difficult in larger companies than in smaller ones. That's because the larger the company the more distance there is between the chief executive and front-line managers, and the more people there are whose attitudes and methods may have to change. Indeed, the implementation phase is where strategy fails most often in big companies. There's generally no shortage of bright, talented people at the top, so excellent strategies are developed. But the companies contain so much inertia that the effort to make changes falters and collapses before it pervades the organization.

In smaller companies it's easier for top people to carry the implementation right down to the working level, so there's less reason to fail once a strategic vision is established. That doesn't imply, however, that implementation is easy or will happen by itself. It still takes a lot of work!

Implementation Start-up or Change

It's important to notice that strategy implementation occurs at a business's start and when a change is called for later on. The issues are the same, but change is by far the more difficult process.

An Overview of the Implementation Process

Strategic thinking offers a framework for the implementation task. It consists of breaking the job into several pieces that can be considered independently and then melded together. Unlike the steps in the earlier strategic phases however, these don't have to be accomplished sequentially, but go on at essentially the same time.

The elements of implementation are:

Designing the Organizational Structure.
Managing Competences.
Selecting Key People.
Budgeting To Support Strategy.
Strategic Support Systems.
Incentive Systems.
Managing the "Corporate Culture."

We'll consider each in some detail.

Designing the Organizational Structure

A company's organizational structure refers to the basis for the pattern of reporting relationships reflected on its organization chart. The organizational structure defines the way in which work activities are grouped together for management purposes. For example, in a functional organization everyone in marketing reports to one person regardless of what product they work on. In a product organization everyone who works on Product A reports to the same person regardless of what function they perform.

There are four common bases for business organization: functional, geographic, product, and matrix. We'll talk about each shortly, but first we need to develop the idea of a strategically essential function.

Strategically Essential Functions

Strategically essential functions are those that are especially important to a business's well-being. They're the things that have to be done, not only right but exceptionally well, to ensure survival and success given the firm's strategic approach.

Recall once again Example 3-2 about the two computer companies. One firm based its appeal on having the most technically advanced computers on the market. Its most essential function is probably research and development. The other firm's strategy was tied to customer service. Its strategically essential function is likely to be marketing. Both firms have to do their essential functions very well to succeed in their approach to the computer business.

Essential functions can also be areas in which a firm is vulnerable. For example, suppose a restaurant has great food but poor service, because for some reason it's hard to hire mature, committed employees. Service isn't the firm's strategic strength, but it's critical, because if it gets worse instead of better the business may fail.

The strategically essential concept is like asking what functions (sales, manufacturing, accounting, etc.) are most important to a company. In one sense it's possible to argue that all functions are important because the business will fail without any one of them. In another sense, however, the important functions are the ones that need attention, the ones that aren't routine. These generally include the strengths the company's strategy is based on and weak or dangerous areas.

Organizing Around Strategically Essential Functions

It's a fundamental of strategic thinking that strategically essential functions be located visibly and report to senior executives high in the organization. Put another way, this means the activities and their results need to be in front of top management and regularly command their attention.

This makes good sense. If a critical function is buried in the bowels of a department, it can be poorly managed for a long time and create major problems before attracting top management's attention.

Most of the time companies organize around such activities more or less naturally, because they're performed by major organizational units. Then no special attention has to be paid to organizing in support of the activities. For example, many strategies are keyed to marketing. If the marketing department is a key organizational unit reporting to the CEO, it's automatically in the right place. We'll discuss some exceptions later on.

The crux of this idea is visibility and attention to the details of decisions about the function by top management. It's well illustrated by the elevation of the Information Function to a vice presidential level in many companies with the increasing importance of computers.

The Functional Organization

The functional organization is the most common in single line of business companies. In it people are grouped according to the nature of their jobs, and report to an executive in charge of all similar activities. For example, anyone who does anything related to marketing or sales reports to the Vice President of Marketing, everyone in the factory reports to the manufacturing VP, and everyone in finance or accounting reports to the CFO. The organization chart is represented in figure 8.1.

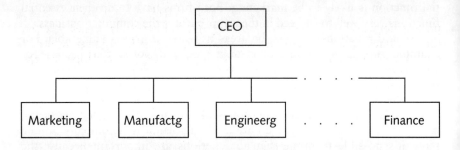

Figure 8.1 A Functional Organization

The functional organization is the most common because strategically essential functions are typically defined along functional lines. These include things like engineering excellence, low-cost manufacturing, creative talent in marketing and so forth.

Geographic Organization

Functional organizations work well for most single line of business companies. However, there are some notable exceptions. Imagine a firm that services equipment installed at customer sites nationwide using technicians that are permanently located near concentrations of equipment. The strategically important activity is efficient service which is performed in geographically dispersed locations. Further, it's difficult to manage service from a distance. Hence, it makes sense to organize geographically and put senior managers near the organizations for which they're responsible.

The geographic organization chart is represented in figure 8.2.

Product-Line Organization

Sometimes a firm's strategic thrust naturally divides along product lines. For example, suppose an architectural firm designs both residences and shop-

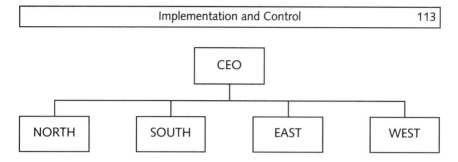

Figure 8.2   A Geographic Organization

ping centers, and finds enormous market and technical differences between the two lines. In such a case, it makes strategic sense to organize into two separate departments, one for the commercial business and one for the residential.

The organization chart would be as represented in figure 8.3.

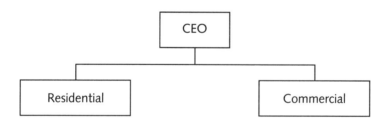

Figure 8.3   A Product Line Organization

The Practical Hybrid

In most real situations, product-line and geographic organizations are partial hybrids with the functional approach, because certain administrative functions serve all the strategically essential departments. In our architectural firm for example, there's no need for the residential and commercial operations to have their own finance and personnel functions. Central departments can generally do such jobs more efficiently. A realistic organization chart would look like that in figure 8.4.

Keep in mind that the residential and commercial divisions would have their own marketing and production departments.

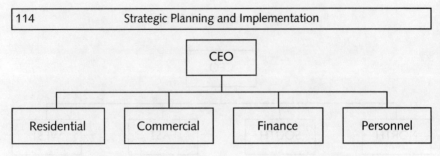

Figure 8.4 The Practical Hybrid of a Product Line Organization

Matrix Organization

Sometimes two strategically important ways to divide a firm's activities exist at the same time, and it's difficult to organize in a way that's supportive to both. In such cases, the matrix organization can make up for the deficiencies that arise with either of the traditional structures.

To illustrate, imagine a technical firm that has two products. One is a expensive, new state-of-the-art machine, which is also risky, because no one is entirely sure the design will work out. The other is less exciting, but well tested and has great customer acceptance. The firm is organized along functional lines, but there's a competition between the product lines for resources within functional departments. The engineering department likes to work on the new product, because it's state-of-the-art technology, while the marketing department tends to emphasize the old product, because it's easier to sell. How can the company be organized in a way that maintains the importance of the traditional business functions (marketing, engineering, etc.) but ensures that appropriate attention is given to both lines?

The answer is sometimes a matrix organization which overlays one structure across the other. The organization chart looks something like that represented in figure 8.5:

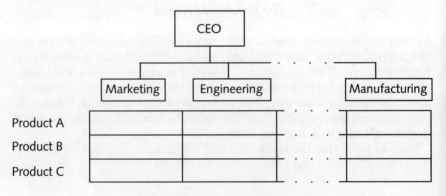

Figure 8.5 A Matrix Organization

In this case the product structure is overlayed on the functional structure which remains the company's basic organization. People report to the heads of the various functional departments at the top of the matrix, but each product is represented by a manager who has "dotted line" authority over activity pertaining to his product in each function.

The idea is that the product managers have to approve the allocation of resources to the products within each department. They are graded on the success and profitability of their products, so they're incentivized to fight for resources, but only to the extent the benefits exceed the cost. In theory this produces a near optimal allocation of resources among the products.

The system works, but has its costs. These include the product manager organization itself, which isn't cheap, and a decrease in the company's flexibility. The latter comes from the fact that two approvals are required for virtually everything, and a lot of additional communication is necessary to keep product managers informed. It also requires an elaborate financial system to develop product-line costs.

It's important to notice two things. First, the boxes in the matrix generally contain activities rather than permanent personnel. And second, nobody has two bosses, because the product manager's authority is "dotted line," implying a veto power rather than direct control.

Problems in Organizing Around Strategically Essential Functions

Sometimes strategy critical activities don't neatly match organizational building blocks and some creative thinking is called for.

Critical Functions That Seem Routine

Occasionally a function that's usually routine takes on strategic importance calling for special attention. For example, in most companies that aren't in high technology, the computer handles the company's financial books and does some record keeping in a few other areas like inventory or customer records. In such cases, the management information systems (MIS) department (which programs and operates the computer) doesn't represent a critical function, and generally reports somewhere in the finance organization, usually to the controller. In such cases finance generally isn't a strategy critical function either, so the computing function doesn't get a lot of top-level attention.

But sometimes a record-keeping function can become strategically very important. An airline reservation system is a good example. While it's conceptually just a record of everyone's flights, it's also a leading edge of the marketing effort. That means it doesn't make sense to have the group that keeps the books deep within the finance department handle the reservations system just because they're both computer applications. The reservations system should report higher in the organization, probably to the head of marketing.

Similar things happen in small businesses all the time. Field service can go from routine to critical if the firm's strategic emphasis changes to product reliability from something else. That might call for making the service organization a separate department reporting to the president. Likewise, purchasing and inventory control can become critical if the firm's thrust moves to filling orders immediately.

Activities Strung Between Departments

Sometimes a strategy critical activity involves a process that's shared by several departments. Handling an order from receipt through final acceptance by a customer is a classic example.

Imagine a specialized technical product that has to be configured for individual customer needs. A sales person takes an order from a customer and forwards it to an administrative order entry group at headquarters. A copy of the order is sent to finance for a customer credit check. If credit is approved, the order is routed through a technical department that makes the configuration, and goes on to inventory where parts are pulled or orders placed on production if the parts aren't available. When it's ready to go, the order is configured and tested by production before packing and shipping. When it finally arrives at the customer's site, field technicians unpack and install it.

Now, suppose rapid and accurate order filling and delivery are part of a customer-service strategy at this company. Notice how many departments are part of the critical order process.

Situations like this are organizationally difficult, because it's generally not practical to organize around the function. For example, we wouldn't want to create an order/shipping department reporting to the president. The solution can involve specially created task forces to monitor and report on critical functions that cross departmental lines.

Rules About Organization Structures

There's really only one rule about organizing to support strategy, and that is that there are no hard and fast rules. No way of putting the pieces together is always right and no reasonably logical approach is always wrong.

However, there are some things that it's generally a good idea to avoid. The worst of these is probably what might be called a good old boy organization. Here's an example. Harry is one of the company's founders. He was originally in charge of marketing but now he runs manufacturing. Harry always liked advertising so he kept that when he moved over to manufacturing.

This organization makes no sense at all because the current head of marketing doesn't have the control she needs to run strategic initiatives which would generally include advertising.

Situations like this come up from time to time due to human relations or historical accident. They're especially common in smaller companies. Strategic thinking says we should avoid them whenever possible.

Managing Competences

Strategic success depends on having abilities in areas that matter in a company's competitive arena. We've called these abilities competences. They're things like an engineering expertise for a company in the technical field, or a flair for marketing in a business where customers can be influenced by things outside of the product itself.

It's a good idea to identify and list all the competences that a player in an industry might bring to bear. This includes the things your own company is good at as well as things others are or might be good at. These abilities will be related to the list of KSFs developed in the situation analysis phase of the firm's strategic analysis, but may also include a few other things.

There are two important points to be made about items on the competence/KSF list. First, a successful firm generally has to be especially good in at least one competence area. This special competence usually forms the basis of the company's strategy. Second, no company can be a viable competitor if it's completely devoid of ability in one or more of the areas on the list.

This means implementing competences implies sharpening and maintaining a leading-edge talent, and being sure at least a minimum ability is maintained in other areas. Most firms have to pay attention to both ideas.

Our Own Area of Strength

Maintaining the firm's own central competence means staying on top of the state of the art in the field, continually observing what others are doing to make sure they're not getting ahead, and keeping resources up to date. Forging ahead in your own area means actively looking for innovative ways to get an edge on the competition and taking the initiative to put ideas that develop into practice.

For example, suppose several exclusive restaurants compete for the fine-dining trade in a city all basing their appeal primarily on the quality of their food and drink. One competitor might try to forge ahead by hiring a well-known French chef and advertising his or her reputation. If they're on the ball, the other restaurants will counter with their own food and drink-based initiative like a special menu or an expanded wine cellar to avoid losing position in the core area to the first restaurant.

Philosophy and Ethics

People have different philosophical and ethical ideas, and it's a good idea to expose the issues and hire people who think the same way. For example, suppose the head of an advertising agency thinks she may acquire a cigarette account sometime in the future although she doesn't have any tobacco business now. It wouldn't be a good idea to hire employees who are so adamantly opposed to smoking that they'll refuse to work on the contract if it's landed.

Compensation Issues

Money is often a problem for smaller businesses when they compete for key people, because they can't match the compensation packages, including fringe benefits, offered by bigger, more stable companies.

That means the small firm has to offer something else. The freedom and excitement of working in an entrepreneurial environment can help, but it's generally not enough. Nearly everyone with employment options has to be attracted at least in part with money or the promise of it. That's usually accomplished by offering key people bonuses or equity stakes in the firm if it's very successful. Stock options are an effective way to accomplish the equity alternative. We'll talk about bonus plans at some length later in this chapter.

Budgeting to Support Strategy

A budget is a plan for spending money. Each department has one that describes how it will spend its allocation of funds on people, assets, and expenses. (Spending on assets is called the capital budget.) The consolidated sum of all department budgets is the company's budget. Hence, a firm's budget contains information on how money is allocated among its various departments and among different kinds of resources.

Strategy has to be Supported with Money

It should be axiomatic that a strategically successful organization has to be supported by a budget that provides implementers with the resources they need to get their job done. That means critical activities involving distinctive competences have to be supplied with enough money, people, and assets to keep the ability current, and exercise it in the marketplace.

This is a straightforward concept, but it doesn't happen in a surprising number of cases, because of the short-run/long-run conflict we've talked about before. Funds that support strategic initiatives usually don't bring bottom-line improvements right away. In fact they tend to depress short-term profits. That makes people reluctant to fund the resource buildups necessary to put strategic actions in place.

Large and small firms suffer from this difficulty, but large companies seem to have learned to allocate resources to the long run better than smaller firms. As we've been saying, however, long-term success in any size firm depends on getting past this obstacle and allocating adequate funding to strategic issues.

Strategic Changes and the Budget

Relatively sudden changes in strategy can occur in a context that makes the problem worse. They're often conceived and implemented in times of financial stress. That is, firms tend to change their strategic approach to business in response to conditions that cause their competitive positions to deteriorate, generally along with profitability. That means a strategic change is likely to be implemented at the same time as a cost-cutting program designed to improve profitability.

As a result, it isn't unusual for a department to be asked to do something entirely new and different while spending less than it did before the change. For example, a marketing department might be asked to launch a new product while maintaining its sales in older products with a 10 percent budget reduction.

Clearly, that situation presents a potential for strategic failure. Unless the department was spending very inefficiently before the change, it's unlikely it will be able to do everything it previously did plus a significant new function on the same money.

The rationale usually goes something like this: cut 15 percent out of the department's budget for normal activities by operating more efficiently and working harder, and then give back 5 percent to launch the new product. It sounds reasonable, but is usually very difficult.

Strategic Support Systems

A support system is something associated with a way of doing business that makes a particular strategy possible or enhances its effectiveness. Here's an example:

Suppose a company services computer equipment installed at customer sites. Routine preventive maintenance can be scheduled in advance, but service to get failed equipment back on line needs to be done in a hurry. That means if the firm wants to offer emergency service, a dispatch system needs to locate technicians in the field and route them to customers who have equipment down. Hence, dispatch is a support system that enables the company to provide emergency service.

If the firm's competitive strategy is based on providing quick response to emergency calls, it's easy to see that the quality of the supporting dispatch system is critical to the success of the strategy.

In businesses of any complexity most strategies need support systems to work at all. How well the strategies turn out is often determined, among other things, by the quality of the support system. In our service example, if the dispatch system can't get technicians on site within a few hours of a customer's call, the company's emergency service strategy is likely to be a failure.

Common support systems include dispatch, inventory control, order entry, cost accounting, customer information databases, maintenance, and equipment diagnostics. Notice that not all support systems are completely informational like dispatch in the example. Maintenance systems support any business that relies on equipment, but they're especially critical in firms like airlines where equipment failures carry big penalties. In that case, support includes both scheduling and actually doing the maintenance work.

Supporting Strategic Information

Managing a business strategically requires knowing how well it's doing against its strategic objectives. For example, if a firm's long-term objective is to be the industry's leader in customer satisfaction, it has to be able to define and measure customer satisfaction. If it can't, management won't know if the goal is being achieved or if the things it's doing are moving the business in the right direction. We talked about these ideas in chapter 4 when we discussed setting objectives.

This concept implies that a firm has to be able to collect strategically relevant information to manage strategy well. In many cases that doesn't create a special problem, because the relevant information is collected whether the company is being strategically managed or not. For example, suppose a long-term goal involves achieving a 20 percent return on equity (ROE). The accounting system automatically captures data and produces reports that tell whether that's happening, so nothing special has to be done for strategic management purposes.

However, some strategic information isn't likely to be collected as a matter of routine. Customer satisfaction is a good example. Management generally has to define what it means by customer satisfaction, take surveys, and track the results to create a system in which the firm's performance on the issue can be measured. Stated another way, a customer satisfaction information system has to be developed and maintained in order to strategically manage the business.

A system that captures this kind of information can be thought of as another kind of strategic support system.

Implementation and Support Systems

It should be clear that an important part of strategy implementation is making sure the necessary support systems are in place, adequate, and functioning properly. Exactly how that's done depends on the situation.

It's generally a good idea to list the elements of the firm's strategies, and then think about the support systems each explicitly or implicitly requires. Then you can work on whether or not they're available. For example, if shipping customer orders within two days of receipt is part of a strategy, it's necessary to ask if the company's inventory, procurement, and production systems are up to that task.

Incentive Systems

Successful strategy implementation requires that employees buy into the company's strategic plans and objectives. Buy-in can be thought of as having two dimensions. The first is a philosophical agreement with the firm's mission and methods. The second is a commitment to doing one's part to get the company's strategy to work. It's nice to have employees committed in both ways, but the second idea is the one that really counts in terms of results. In other words, it's extremely important that employees be committed to doing their own parts of strategic tasks, which for this discussion we'll assume are relatively well-defined.

As a result of the importance of individual buy in, a body of thought associated with motivating people to behave in ways that achieve strategic results has developed. Specifically, it's desirable to motivate performance that efficiently supports strategy. Undirected enthusiasm, while better than a negative or neutral attitude, isn't very effective. Hence motivation has two dimensions, developing energetic enthusiasm and making sure it's applied to the right activities.

Motivating Employees

Companies take a wide variety of approaches to motivating employees. Some firms hold inspirational meetings on a regular basis to pump up morale and get people enthusiastic about common goals. Japanese firms are famous for having daily assemblies at which people sing songs and do exercises together to foster a team spirit.

Other motivational techniques are more focused on individuals. Most systems overtly reward good performance, and punish undesirable behavior by withholding rewards and relegating poor performers to undesirable tasks.

There are three basic approaches to rewarding good performance. These involve granting the performer recognition, promotion, and incentive compensation (money). Clearly the approaches are interrelated. Promotion, for example, usually involves a pay increase and an element of recognition.

Recognition

Recognition includes giving plaques, awards, and holding ceremonies as well as less formally praising people who do good jobs. It has a positive effect in that it fosters a convivial atmosphere and supports morale, but it has a limited impact on driving employees to work extra long and hard to get things done. People seem most motivated to do that when more tangible personal rewards are at stake.

Promotion

Rewarding with promotion has the desired effect on performance, but its use as a motivator is limited by the number of opportunities available. Promotions can also have a negative effect on those who aren't promoted, a group that generally outnumbers those who are advanced. This creates a problem when there are a number of good performers but only a few promotions available. Second-place finishers can feel like losers even though their performance was quite good.

Compensation

This leaves compensation as management's most effective motivational tool. It comes in two forms, periodic salary increases and incentive bonuses.

Salary increases work as motivators, but they tend to have less of an immediate psychological impact than bonuses. For example, suppose a person making $50,000 does very well against her objectives and deserves to be rewarded. Her salary increase might be 6 percent rather than a routine 3 percent. The difference is an extra $1,500 to be received over the next twelve months. Nice, but not too exciting

Contrast that with a person who's paid a $40,000 base salary along with a performance bonus that can vary from zero to $20,000 and averages about $10,000 over all employees in the job category. (Total compensation is the same $50,000.) To that person, outstanding performance means as much as a $20,000 lump sum at year end. This is a much more significant psychological motivator for most people than the salary increase alone.

The bottom line of all this is that incentive bonus systems are our most effective and flexible approach to motivating performance. However, some important issues have to be considered if such a system is to fully achieve its potential. In fact, a poorly administered bonus system can be a waste of money or even have a negative motivational impact.

Incentive (Bonus) Compensation Systems

Incentive compensation systems work best if they're designed keeping a few simple rules in mind. Let's spend a little time on each after seeing how such systems work.

How Incentive Systems Work

Bonuses are paid on the degree to which some measure of performance, the basis, is achieved. The simplest system just pays an amount proportional to the achievement of a target defined in terms of the basis.

For example, suppose Harry's bonus is based on company profit paying him $10,000 if the firm achieves its plan of $500,000. A simple bonus system just pays proportionately larger or smaller amounts based on performance over or under the $500,000 target. A profit of $600,000, for example, is 120 percent of plan, so Harry would get 120 percent of his target bonus or $12,000.

Simple systems can run into definitional problems. For example, if the firm loses money does Harry get a negative bonus and owe his employer money? Generally not, of course. Or what if the target profit is break even, $0. What does Harry get if the company earns $1,000?

Most of the time bonus systems are defined with a zero minimum, a target amount paid at planned performance, and include a limit if plan is exceeded by a great deal.

Choosing the Basis for Incentive Compensation

There are three issues involved in choosing bases for bonuses. They must be measurable, strategy supportive, and under the control of the person being paid.

Measurability Clearly, results deserving a bonus have to be precisely measurable and not open to interpretation or dispute. Revenue and profit are good bases in the sense that they're readily measurable. Other bases are softer and more difficult to pin down. Customer satisfaction, for example, is desirable and a logical concept on which to pay a bonus, but it's much harder to measure.

It's a mistake to try to pay bonuses on soft concepts like customer satisfaction or quality unless they're defined and measured in ways that don't lead to arguments. If they aren't, it's likely employees will perceive better results than management and feel cheated out of a portion of their bonus money. The negative morale implications of such disputes can easily wipe out the positive effects of the whole incentive plan.

Strategy Supportive Incentive bases need to be things that lead to making long-run strategy happen. Examples include opening a new sales territory, achieving a certain level of revenue growth, and developing a new product on schedule.

Sometimes companies make mistakes in this regard. It's common to see short-term profit included as a major, if not the only, basis for a bonus system. This can lead to the kind of short-term/long-term problem we've discussed before. That is, achieving short-term profits precludes devoting resources to long-term programs necessary for strategic success.

It's crucially important to select incentive bases carefully, because targets in those measures will probably be achieved whether they're really good for the company in the long run or not.

Control   Bonuses should be based on things that the person being paid can control. If they're not, most of the benefit of the system is lost. For example, an inventory manager might be paid on having low obsolescence and shrinkage, an accounting manager on how long it takes to close the books, an engineering manager on developing a product quickly, a manufacturing manager on making shipment dates, and so on.

The problem this concept creates is that the bonus system is necessarily quite complicated. Just about every person in management has to have individually designed bases and goals. That means administering the system takes a lot of work. It's easier, but less effective, to bonus everyone on the same scale.

A related mistake that's fairly common is basing bonuses on things tied to the performance of the company as a whole, like revenue or profit. The rationale is that those bases foster team spirit and a sense of striving for the common good. The problem is that such a system loses its ability to make people put out extra effort to do specific, strategy supportive things.

For example, suppose a department has to work all night to make a certain deadline. If making it just contributes to the common good, which in a roundabout way enhances profit that creates bonuses, people aren't likely to be excited about staying past nine o'clock. If, on the other hand, their bonuses are tied to deadlines, and they can see dollars slipping out of their hands if they go home, they're much more likely to stick it out until the job is done.

Mixed Bases   Compromises are generally advisable. That is, the best of several worlds can be achieved by splitting a bonus into more than one part, each with a different basis. Splitting too finely, however, can reduce the impact of any one thing to insignificance.

Incentive Pay as a Percentage of Total Compensation

The best results are generally achieved when incentive pay is a significant part of total compensation. People aren't as committed to achieving program goals if the incentive is a small extra on top of their normal income as when it's a bigger part of what they live on. The idea is that people should come to depend on receiving at least the target bonus level.

For example, consider a management employee who earns $40,000 plus a bonus that can range from $0 to $20,000 and averages $10,000. That person will come to depend on the incentive, and move heaven and earth to be sure it's paid. That generally leads to better performance and receiving a little more than the $10,000.

Contrast that with a person whose salary is $50,000 who receives a $2,000 bonus if things go exceptionally well. Here the bonus is an extra, something to play with. The employee's lifestyle doesn't change if he doesn't get it. Therefore he doesn't have nearly as big an incentive to make things happen as the first employee.

Aligning Job Definitions with the Compensation System

When incentive pay is a significant portion of compensation, it's beneficial to define jobs in ways that are consistent with the system. This is accomplished relatively easily by defining jobs in terms of results rather than work activities.

For example, don't hire an engineer to do product development work. Hire her to develop a product with a given set of specifications in less than one year. Don't hire someone to do the firm's accounting. Hire him to keep the financial records with less than 1 percent error, close the books in three days at the end of every month, and collect 98 percent of all receivables. Don't hire someone to sell. Hire her to sell at least $2 million a year. And so on.

When jobs are defined in terms of the results people are expected to accomplish, it's relatively easy to create bonus systems based on those results.

Administration and the Problem of Uncontrollable Factors

An incentive compensation system is a delicate thing. It can be one of management's most effective tools for motivating performance, but relatively simple errors in its design or administration can make it useless or turn it into a morale negative.

In general it's critically important that the incentive system be administered fairly and impartially. Unfortunately, that's often easier said than done.

Defining the conditions under which people receive bonuses is a particularly sensitive area. The decision isn't as simple as it seems because of the existence of uncontrollable external factors that affect performance on bonus measures. The issue is whether a person whose performance has been as good as can be expected should receive a bonus if an outside force beyond his control causes a shortfall in the bonus measure.

For example, suppose a purchasing manager's plan depends on his negotiating prices below some standard on a key input. Then suppose a strike or natural disaster causes a shortage in the supply of the item which leads to a big price increase that causes him to completely miss the goal. However, assume everyone agrees that under those conditions no one could have achieved the goal, and the purchasing manager did as well as anyone could. Should he get all or part or none of his bonus?

A rigid enforcement of the incentive system argues that he should not get anything. A more liberal interpretation stressing the intent of incentives would award him at least part of the money. Either approach has problems.

Denying a bonus in the face of unforseen and impossible conditions will obviously demotivate employees. Giving the bonus, however, calls for a judgement on how bad outside influences have to get before the system is overriden. Once management starts to make exceptions the incentive system can be perceived as an instrument of favoritism, and claims of outside influence can become the norm rather than the exception. That weakens the entire plan, and creates morale problems for those who feel less than favored.

There isn't a universally right answer to this kind of question. It's always a judgement call, but the appearance of fairness and impartiality is always crucial.

Corporate Culture

Corporate culture is a broad term that refers to the overall way organizations operate. It's like a company's personality. It encompasses rules and procedures, moral and ethical values, and the way people perceive themselves and the company relative to the rest of the world. It includes the firm's history, its heroes, its legends and "war stories," and everything that makes it what it is. A key element of culture is the level of loyalty and dedication employees have to the firm, and how they perceive the firm feels about them.

Some companies have extravagant cultures. People travel first class, take customers and themselves to fancy restaurants, go on retreats, and have lavish offices. Others are penny-pinching and austere. Some firms operate ethically and morally because it's the right thing to do. Others do whatever makes the most money regardless of the ethical implications. Along those lines, some businesses knowingly break the law calculating that the penalty will be less than the probable profit to be made from the illegal behavior, and will only be imposed if they're caught.

Corporate Culture and Strategy

Corporate culture can be extremely important to making strategy work. Remember that a large part of implementation is getting the employee group behind management's chosen strategy. That can be relatively easy if the ideas and methods behind the strategy are consistent with the customs, values, and expectations of the employees. However, if that consistency isn't there, getting employee buy-in can be difficult to the point of impossibility.

Simply stated, developing a culture that supports a firm's strategy pays really big dividends. A strategy supportive culture is almost like getting something for nothing from the employee team. Conversely, a cultural mismatch means management is fighting an uphill battle every day.

A Culture that Rewards Performing for the Company

Perhaps the most valuable and illustrative attribute a culture can have is a spirit of high performance for the sake of the organization. We want to form a culture that rewards strategy supportive effort with peer approval. For example, suppose an employee stays at work all night to meet a deadline. Management should recognize such performance, but it's even better if the employee receives sincere admiration from his peers for putting out the effort. That is, the most desirable corporate culture includes an attitude that applauds self-sacrifice for the good of the company.

Contrast that with an attitude in which other employees ridicule the hard-working employee for letting management take advantage of him by doing more than the job for which he's paid.

Culture as a Competence and a Competitive Advantage

In some businesses the culture is directly tied to a distinctive competence and the firm's competitive advantage in the market place. Sales-oriented companies are often good examples. If the firm's competitive advantage is a high-powered sales force, a flashy, sales-oriented culture may be a must. Maintenance of that culture is, in fact, the central competence on which the firm's strategy is based.

Culture and Strategic Change

Most of the time cultures are fairly consistent with strategy, because they tend to grow up together as organizations develop, i.e., it's unlikely that a company will last long if there isn't a reasonable match between its culture and its mission and strategy.

Culture-related problems usually arise when a change in strategy is necessary. If the change is radical, corporate culture can be a major problem, and even derail the initiative.

Over time, organizations tend to attract and retain people who are comfortable with the cultures in place. As those people stay longer, they become more and more invested in the existing way of doing things, and that makes it hard to change culture to support a new strategy while those people are around. In other words, the longer an organization has been operating along a cultural path, the more inertia it has, and the more difficult it is to change. Larger organizations have more trouble changing than smaller ones, because there are more entrenched individuals with interests in the old way of doing things.

EXAMPLE 8-1

Imagine, for example, a conservative bank that runs by rules, regulations, committee decisions, and audits. Think about the kind of people who are happy in that environment. We'd generally expect conservative, systematic people who like order and predictability in their lives and who don't take very many chances.

Contrast that with the people we'd generally expect to find in a sales-oriented organization that runs on marketing enthusiasm and excitement generated with flashy advertising, prizes, awards, parties, and trips to exotic places. A well-known firm like Mary Kay Cosmetics might be a good example. It's hard to imagine the bankers lasting very long at Mary Kay or the cosmetics salespeople doing well at the bank.

Now imagine that the bank isn't doing well. Small business customers are complaining that it's difficult to deal with the bank, because it's hard to get a decision out of the bureaucratic maze of committees and auditors. Further, the bankers don't seem to understand their customer's needs and are slow to grant reasonable loans. As a result the best customers (stable small and medium-sized businesses) are leaving for other banks.

In response to this the bank's board of directors appoints a new president, charging that he make the organization more "marketing-oriented" and "responsive" to customers. No one thinks the bank should address its market like a cosmetics company, but everyone feels a movement in that direction is in order.

Think about the kinds of problems the new president would face. The bank's management team is a conservative, rule-oriented group of people. They probably don't agree that being very marketing-oriented toward loan customers is appropriate for a bank. They may see that as conflicting with its moral responsibility to provide safety for depositors. In fact, they're probably proud of the structure of checks and balances that makes their loans safe. Further, even if they wanted to become more marketing-oriented, they're unlikely to have any idea of how to do it.

The managers in place work for the bank because their personalities are consistent with its conservative style. Over the years they've been encouraged and rewarded with raises and promotions for behaving that way. Now the new president wants them to do an almost total about-face and behave differently. The firm's reward structure will change so that the behavior that's been successful for most of their careers may now be viewed negatively and lose them their jobs. Many will simply be unable to make the change.

Culture and the Implementor of Strategic Change

This phenomenon can be an enormous problem. Yet situations arise all the time in which strategies have to change. Two extreme negative results are possible with an infinite variety of outcomes in between.

At one extreme, it isn't at all unusual for the implementation to simply fail. Nothing really changes and the organization continues as before. At the other extreme, the change causes a mass exodus of people in key positions which seriously damages the firm.

The implementor's task is to navigate between these opposite poles getting the strategy successfully implemented with a minimum loss of human talent and expertise. The implementor should operate in two steps. First, identify areas in which the strategy and the culture are inconsistent. Second, develop a program to change one or both so that they are reasonably consistent.

There isn't any rule about how to make strategic/culture changes like these. A general approach should involve the following:

1 Explain why the changes are necessary, and how each individual's behavior is expected to alter to match the new regime. Be sure people know what is wanted. It's very common for employees not to understand the new way and to be afraid to ask for clarification.
2 Define measurement criteria for success in meeting the new challenge.
3 Give people a reasonable chance to accept the new way and alter their behavior.

Above all work slowly. Implementing a major change to a long-standing culture immediately is likely to result in failure.

CONTROL – EVALUATION AND ADJUSTMENT

Implementation and control can be thought of separately or as parts of a single process. Both refer to the administrative things that have to be done to make a strategy work. It's important to realize that those administrative processes go on forever. No company can ever be put on a strategic autopilot and allowed to fly itself. A more or less continuous adjusting is always necessary.

Nevertheless, it's convenient to think of implementation as happening early in the life of a strategic thrust when a firm is getting a major new approach started. Control then, is associated with periods between major changes when minor adjustments are made to a relatively stable set of ideas.

Control Processes and the Feedback Loop

Control refers to the process by which a system's progress toward a goal is monitored, evaluated, and adjusted to ensure the goal is reached in a reasonable time. Steering a car is a good example. If we just point a car along a road and hold the gas pedal down, we aren't likely to get very far without the control process called steering. It involves continuously checking that the vehicle is on the right course, noting the extent to which it isn't, and adjusting direction with a steering wheel. Most of us make the comparisons and adjustments associated with steering with little conscious thought.

Control involves the idea of a feedback loop as shown in figure 8.6.

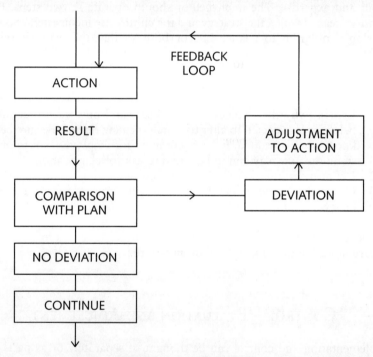

Figure 8.6 Feedback Loop

Strategic Control

Strategic control involves exactly this idea. The process begins with an action to implement some strategy. After a while, the organization's progress toward its strategic goals is compared with the plan. If progress is as expected, no action needs to be taken until the next comparison. A deviation, however, calls for either an adjustment to the implementation effort to move the organization back toward its original track, or an alteration in the goal to reflect changed conditions or thinking.

Although the idea is straightforward, a few important points about the process in a strategic context should be brought out.

Goals and Measurements

Meaningful control requires that strategic goals be stated in measurable terms. If they aren't, there isn't any way to make the comparison with the plan shown in figure 8.6. We've talked about this idea before, but it's worth emphasizing again here. Suppose a firm's goal is stated as achieving "total customer satisfaction" with no further amplification of the idea. A year after implementation it's hard to know whether that goal is being achieved totally, substantially, a little, or not at all. It's much easier to tell how well the firm is doing on its way to a revenue or profit target, because progress toward those goals is easily measurable.

The customer satisfaction idea can be used as a workable goal if it's broken down into components and surveyed periodically to develop a numerical score that permits measurement and self-assessment.

But even that isn't quite enough. A time frame is generally necessary to make a statement of progress meaningful. That implies the plan has to project how long achieving the firm's strategic goals is expected to take, and how rapidly progress will be made along the way. In other words, a good strategic plan will define milestones for major goals against which progress can be measured.

The Comparison with Planned Performance

Comparing progress with the plan in a strategic context includes at least three separate elements. As time passes, evaluations have to be made of the effects of (1) the implementation effort; (2) changes in the environment; and (3) changes in management's understanding and analysis of the environment.

This is in marked contrast with the automotive steering example. There, the road's direction represents the entire environment. The environment doesn't change as the car progresses, and the driver's view isn't subject to much misinterpretation.

Validating The Analysis and Assumptions

Recall that the strategic process began with a situation analysis that involved studying and developing an understanding of the firm's industry (external analysis) as well as its own capabilities and weaknesses (internal analysis). That analysis process often calls for making judgments about things from imperfect and incomplete information, and for making assumptions about the future and what others are likely to do.

As time passes, new and better information becomes available that can change management's understanding of the environment and the assumptions made about the future. It's important to understand that the control process involves adapting to that better information as it becomes available.

Changing the Implementation, The Goal, or the Strategy in Response to New Information

Adapting to new strategic information can mean changing the implementation effort, strategic goals, or the strategy itself. Changing just the implementation effort is analogous to making a steering adjustment when driving a car. It's usually appropriate when the new information doesn't reflect a major revelation about the environment.

In the strategic context, however, it's also possible to discover new information that's important enough to modify a long-term goal or make a change to the strategy itself. These latter situations have no analogy in the steering wheel example.

EXAMPLE 8-2

Bill Sinclair opened a family-style restaurant in Wilmington last year. Before getting started he did a little research, and found that based on industry norms, the population within a two-mile radius could be expected to support an additional restaurant.

A major element of Bill's strategy involved a pirate theme and game area designed to appeal to young children. He also dressed the staff in pirate costumes, and trained them to make a big fuss over kids. The expectation was that children's enthusiasm would influence their parents to come in. Bill had great expectations for the pirate idea and planned to open two more stores within three years.

The initial plan involved little paid advertising, but depended on word of mouth among children to spread information about the place. However Bill did experiment with some direct mailings and discount coupons.

Case 1: Suppose business hasn't been as good as expected, and Bill is trying to find out why. A number of customers told him they stumbled across his establishment, and that most of the community didn't know he was there. This new information might indicate that Bill needs to advertise more and that direct mail probably doesn't work well for his business. Adjusting his advertising would represent a change in the implementation process as a result of new information.

Case 2: Again suppose business has been slower than expected, and Bill finds that while kids love his place, parents get sick of the pirate theme and come back only infrequently.

This information is likely to affect Bill's long-term goal of opening more restaurants, since the concept's appeal is mediocre and the first unit is unlikely to be able to provide cash for expansion.

Case 3: Finally, suppose Bill, in response to weak business, takes a look at some new census information and discovers the local population consists mostly of people over fifty who don't have young children. This new information is serious with respect to Bill's strategy of appealing to youngsters in his present location. It probably calls for a reformating of the restaurant's theme into something that's likely to appeal to retirees. That's a major strategic change.

Changes in the Environment

Similar comments apply to changes in the business environment. For example in our illustration, it's possible that new competition could have entered the Wilmington area since Bill opened his doors. Strategic control requires that changes be made to a firm's strategy or its implementation style in response to such new conditions.

Evaluating the Implementation Effort

Finally, the effectiveness of the implementation effort has to be assessed and adjusted in the control process. For example, Bill might find his pirate strategy well founded except for an error in staffing. Suppose he hired a few servers who needed work but resent dressing up in pirate costumes. They've therefore been less than courteous to customers, and find it especially difficult to be jolly and entertaining with children. This is strictly an implementation problem that has to be fixed by reassigning them or terminating the problem employees' employment.

Summary – Strategic Control

In summary we can say that strategic control is conceptually the same as any control or steering process, but has more variables than most. In most processes we steer a along a constant course toward a stable target. Like driving down a road, we move the system back toward the correct path when it drifts off.

In strategy we have to steer along a course that can change within a changing environment, while heading toward a movable goal. And in addition, we occasionally have to change vehicles.

chapter 9

Strategy and Business Planning

Planning is a big part of modern business life, especially in larger companies. Well-run firms project the future constantly within formal planning systems. They address everything from cash flow and short-term profits to long-run strategy on a regular basis. The product of this activity is a series of documents called business plans which serve as frameworks for forward thinking. In this book we're interested in strategic planning for the long run, but it's important to understand the entire planning system and see how short- and long-run plans fit together. It's also important to understand how planning differs between large and small companies.

Business Planning

The easiest way to describe business planning is in terms of its result. The process produces a document called a *business plan* which is a conceptual model of what a business unit will be in times to come. Typically, business plans look something like magazines (containing charts and graphs instead of pictures), and contain both words and numbers which together describe their businesses.

The numbers in plans are mainly projections of the firms' financial statements. The words describe the business generally and also amplify the numbers. It's important to keep in mind that everything in a business plan is based on assumptions about the business environment made by the planners, so the picture portrayed represents what will happen only if the assumptions come true.

Overall, a good plan conveys a fairly complete image of a company including information on products and markets, technology, employees, equipment, facilities, and capital as well as expected financial performance.

The Outline of a Typical Business Plan

There's a great deal of difference in the substance of plans for different companies, but most use a relatively standard outline similar to the following list of chapter or section headings.

Contents	Operations
Executive Summary	Management and Personnel
Mission and Strategy	Financial Projections
Market Analysis	Contingencies

The table of contents is an outline of the entire document while the executive summary is a one-page condensation of its important points.[1]

The mission and strategy section summarizes the firm's long-term direction. The market analysis explains how and why the business will succeed in its competitive environment despite the fact that others may have failed. Operations explains how the firm actually does whatever it's in business to do. The section on management and personnel usually describes the qualifications of key people and details expected personnel needs.

The financial section is a forecast of future financial results and is the company's "financial plan." Contingencies explains the actions management will take if results turn out less favorably than expected.

The Purpose of Business Planning

Business plans are intended for two major groups, the firm's management and outside investors.

The Value of Planning in Management

Planning yields several management-related benefits. The first has to do with the planning process while the others deal with using the result.

Process

The process of creating a plan can pull a disparate group of executives into a cohesive unit with common goals. Going through it together helps everyone

---

[1] The purpose of the executive summary in a business plan is rather unique. Summaries are usually prepared so busy people can avoid reading entire documents. In a business plan the intention is exactly the opposite. Plans are usually used to solicit funding from banks or venture capital companies who receive and reject a great many based on only a quick look. The intention of a business plan's executive summary is to catch readers' interest so they read it all.

understand the organization's objectives, why they're important and how they'll be achieved. The process makes the team think about what has to be done in the planning period, what it will take, and helps to ensure that everyone understands his or her task.

A Road Map

After it's written, a properly used business plan becomes a road map for running a business. The process of management review calls for comparing operating performance with plan, and investigating deviations. Making such comparisons is generally the best way to understand a company's problems and get at solutions. We discussed this idea under strategic control in the last chapter.

The Plan as a Set of Goals

A business plan generally forecasts a future that management would like to see happen, given where things are today. Hence it can be thought of as a set of goals, for both the company and for individual departments.

Plans generally contain revenue and expense targets as well as a variety of product and process development goals. Since different people are responsible for different goals, many can be assigned to individuals or groups and tied to an incentive compensation system.

Predicting Financing Needs

Financial planning is crucial when firms forecast outside financing needs. Financial planning techniques let businesses predict when they'll have to raise money from outside sources.

Investors

A business plan is the primary vehicle for communicating management's vision of the business's future to investors. It estimates future cash flow and predicts the character of the enterprise in years to come. The financial information tells stockholders the returns they can expect, and shows lenders where the money to repay loans is expected to come from.

Business Planning in Divisions of Large Companies

Big companies tend to be made up of smaller divisions which function as more or less independent firms within their own markets. In most large companies the planning process is going on almost continually as divisions produce plans which are consolidated to create overall corporate forecasts.

The process is a major avenue of communication between division and corporate management. Top management's acceptance of a plan is its stamp of approval on the way division management is handling its responsibility. Then, after the fact, virtually everything divisions do is compared with the plan. Success and failure are defined as whether or not the plan is achieved or surpassed.

Four Kinds of Business Plan

There are four distinct kinds of business plan. Large companies generally do all four, each of which results in a separate document or series of documents. Small companies tend to plan only once, producing a single document that has some of the attributes of the four separate exercises.

The four variations are:

1   Strategic Planning,
2   Operational Planning,
3   Budgeting, and
4   Forecasting.[2,3]

The types of planning differ in three ways. They cover periods of different length (sometimes referred to as the planning horizon), they address different kinds of issues, and they contain different levels of financial detail.

Strategic Planning

The strategic plan is a vehicle to document the things we've been talking about in this book. Strategy deals with broad concepts like a business's fundamental nature and what kinds of customers it serves. It's an exercise in long-term thinking intended to predict what the business will become over a long period, usually five years. We won't dwell on the ideas behind strategy now because we've already discussed them at length.

Strategic plans generally explain ideas and concepts and contain far more words than numbers. Like all plans they contain financial projections, but they're approximate and aren't backed up with great detail. The

---

[2]   Terminology isn't consistent. There are Annual Operating Budgets and Long-Term Forecasts. The terms Outlook and View are also used from time to time. The most important issue separating the types of planning is the length of the period covered.

Multi-year (usually 5) – Long-term, strategic.

One to two years – Intermediate-term, operating.

3 to 6 months – Short-term, budgetary.

2 weeks to 3 months – Very short-term, forecast.

[3]   Budgets and Forecasts are usually abbreviated plans that are primarily financial.

plan's final (usually the fifth) year generally shows virtually ideal financial performance.

Strategic Plans are frequently called Long-Range Plans or Five Year Plans.

Operational Planning

Operational Planning has to do with running the business on a day-to-day basis. Most companies prepare an Annual Operating Plan that defines the way the firm will be run in the coming twelve months. It generally tries to forecast in some detail how much will be sold, which customers will buy, and what prices will be charged. It also details the sources and costs of inputs and equipment and what the firm expects to earn.

On a conceptual, philosophical level, the annual plan deals with how long-term strategies are implemented in the shorter run. This includes statements of method and approach as well as the establishment of shorter-term goals for things like revenue and profit. Sales quotas and product development milestones are also usually in an annual plan along with compensation and bonus plans.

It's important to realize that financial projections are a lot more precise and detailed in operational than in strategic planning. Typically Annual Operating Plans are about even mixes of words and numbers.

Budgeting

When conditions in an industry change rapidly, an annual plan can be out-of-date long before the end of the year it covers. That means the last months of the plan become progressively less useful as a guide in running the business. Budgets are short-term updates of annual plans that generally cover three-month quarters. They're essentially substituted for the quarters of the annual plan as an immediate operating guide. In some firms they also contain more supporting detail than that included in the annual plan. In other words, in terms of everyday operations, a budget does much the same thing as an annual plan but for a shorter period.

However, the budgetary time frame is too short to make important changes in the nature of the businesses. Therefore, policy and longer-term direction aren't generally discussed in budgets as they are in annual plans. In other words, budgets do very little direction-setting, they just lay out and explain detailed performance. As a result, budgets have relatively fewer words and more financial detail than annual plans. It's clearly possible to describe a budget as an operating plan, because like the annual plan it deals with routine operations.

Forecasting

Forecasts are quick estimates of financial results usually in the very short run. Essentially they're projections of where a business's financial momentum will carry it over the short term. They're generally almost all numbers containing few if any words.

Forecasts are commonly put together to estimate cash flows in and out of the company and when management becomes concerned about how the company will close out a profit period.

Forecasting is especially important with respect to cash. A company has to have an accurate picture of the cash ins and outs coming up if it's to be sure it can pay its bills and employees. When temporary shortages are expected, bank borrowing has to be arranged to keep the firm solvent until collections catch up with disbursements.

A *cash forecast* is a financial projection made to predict short-term cash needs. Big companies do them monthly.

Comparing the Kinds of Business Planning

It's a good idea to visualize the different kinds of plan arrayed along a horizontal line as illustrated in figure 9.1. The broad, conceptual thinking of strategic planning is on one end, while the numerical detail of forecasting is on the other.

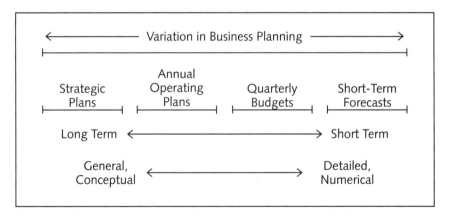

Figure 9.1   Variation in Business Planning

Moving from left to right, the planning period (horizon) gets shorter, and the documents become less qualitative and more quantitative. That is, they change from being mostly words to mostly numbers.

Ideally, companies practice the whole range of planning activity. That's what most big companies do, producing all the different documents as part of a coordinated planning system. In such a system strategic and annual plans are each produced yearly about six months apart.[4] Four quarterly budgets and a number of forecasts are also usually done.[5]

The Financial Plan

The set of projected financial statements included in any of the business plans we've been talking about can be described as the company's financial plan. The process of creating such projections is called financial planning.

It's important to appreciate the different roles played by these financial projections in the four planning documents. Every business plan must include financial projections, but they're of secondary importance in strategic planning which deals more with concepts and ideas than with numbers.

In annual planning financial projections are the most important part of the exercise. They're surrounded by supporting discussion, but in essence, a company's financial projections are its business plan.

Budgets and forecasts, on the other hand, are almost entirely financial-planning exercises. The numbers are central, and aren't surrounded by much of anything.

Relating Planning Activity in Small and Large Firms

In small business planning activity tends to be compressed into one document known simply as "The Business Plan." It's usually produced when the firm needs money. That's generally when it's getting started and sometimes later on for expansion or other needs.

The relation of the small company business plan to the full range of planning activity found in larger firms is illustrated in figure 9.2.

The content of the (small company) business plan overlaps three of the big firm exercises. It encompasses all of operational (annual) planning and parts of strategic planning and budgeting.

The entrepreneur's plan has to do everything for his or her business that the large firm's annual plan does for it. That is, supply a convincing rationale for the actions planned in the next year supported with dollar, headcount, and production projections.

Things are a little different in the strategy area where the small business

---

[4] Notice that the Strategic Plan is revised annually even though it covers five or more years.

[5] Firms in stable industries may omit budgets and much of the forecasting we've described. For example, the revenues of public utilities are based on population which doesn't change rapidly. It's therefore not usually necessary for utilities to rebudget quarterly to keep up with changing conditions. High-tech businesses are just the opposite. Technology changes rapidly, and the best firms replan constantly.

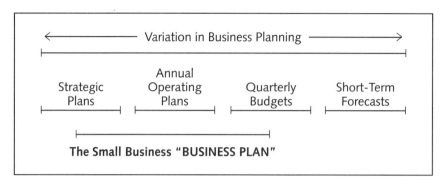

Variation in Business Planning →

| Strategic Plans | Annual Operating Plans | Quarterly Budgets | Short-Term Forecasts |

The Small Business "BUSINESS PLAN"

Figure 9.2   Business Planning in Large and Small Companies

plan isn't expected to be quite as complete as a full-blown strategic plan. For example, the small business plan doesn't have to deal with the broadest strategic issues such as the choice of this business over another. That decision is already in the past.

It is strategically important, however, that a small business plan establish that the planned market exists and can be served by the business in question. The plan must also make some insightful projections as to what the enterprise will become in three to five years.

Finally, a small business plan must get beneath a big company annual plan in terms of precision by projecting the first year in budget-like detail. Hence the small company business plan is a mix of strategy and operations with a touch of very short term forecasting thrown in. This isn't generally a problem as we will discuss in the next section.

Strategic Planning Documents

In large firms the strategic planning exercise is separated from shorter-term planning, and results in a separate document whose format is dictated by corporate management. Most formats parallel the general business plan outline given earlier in this chapter with appropriate emphasis on long-term issues and strategic analysis. Divisions produce individual plans in accordance with the format which are consolidated into an overall company plan. This procedure gives division management a convenient vehicle to record the strategic ideas and analyses we've talked about in our first eight chapters.

In small businesses documenting strategy is a little more subtle, because most companies don't execute a separate long-term plan. Therefore, strategy has to be included in the company's "all-purpose" business plan. That works fairly well because small business plans generally cover the appropriate period of time (three to five years). It's important to realize, however, that the level of detail varies with the year in such a document. The first year is presented in great detail, while subsequent years are projected with less precision, consistent with a strategic exercise.

It's also important to understand that the verbal treatment of concepts in a small business plan has to include both the short term and the long term. In other words, it has to include broad strategic arguments like why a market exists and how the firm's strategy will reach it as well as tactical issues such as how many salespeople will operate in New England and what their quotas will be.

There isn't any fixed or universal format for combining long- and short-term presentations in a business plan. Clearly the mission and strategy sections come right out of long-term thinking. But the sections on the market, operations, and finance each have to address both time frames internally. It's generally best to begin with a broad strategic analysis, and then progressively narrow the focus into shorter-term tactical issues within each section.

The Strategic Audit

A strategic audit is a review of a company's situation by a person trained in business planning and strategic thinking. The auditor reviews all available information about the industry and the firm and conducts a series of interviews with management and key individuals inside and outside the company. He or she then makes a judgement about whether the firm is strategically on the right track or needs to make some adjustments.

A *strategic audit program* is a series of questions about how the company does its strategic analysis, planning, and implementation. The program divides the audit into several sections that roughly parallel our first eight chapters, and gives it a structure and format.

An outside strategic auditor can be a good idea for two reasons. First, the person has expertise in strategic thinking and analysis that generally can't be matched by anyone in the company. Second, an outsider brings objectivity to the process. There's always a tendency for people in organizations to say the things they think the boss wants to hear. Hence if the company's owner wants to be sure of an unbiased opinion, it's a good idea to hire an outsider. On the negative side, an outsider may not have as much industry knowledge as people working in the company.

The Strategic Planning Process

Strategic planning is a top management responsibility. The firm's strategy and its written plan are ultimately the responsibility of the owner, CEO, or division president, but that person generally draws heavily on the knowledge and experience of the next level of management down.

A Series of Senior Management Meetings

Strategic planning is commonly accomplished in a series of meetings of the executive team. It's a good idea to hold these meetings off-site to ensure getting people's undivided attention.

The first meeting should recap the company's strategic history within its industry and establish where it is today. This sets the stage for a thorough analysis of the present environment which can be the subject of the second meeting. It's common practice to give people research assignments before each meeting and have them report the results to the group to get things started.

Subsequent meetings work through finding or refining an appropriate mission, establishing the right goals and objectives, identifying competences, crafting the best possible strategy, and establishing an approach to the implementation and control effort.

There's no rule for exactly how many meetings and how much time all this should take. However, it isn't a good idea to try to get it all done in one long session, even over several days. There needs to be a period during which people can digest and reflect on the material in each stage if the results are to be well thought-out.

The process we're describing should result in the production of a strategic business plan like the ones we've described in this chapter and a separate action plan for its implementation.

The Action Plan

The biggest strategic failure of American companies is that they create great strategic plans and then fail to implement them effectively. Plans are written and put on the shelf until the next year when they're taken down, dusted off, and revised; only to be returned to the shelf again.

What's usually missing is an action plan to take the strategy from thinking into reality. An action plan details what has to be done differently after the strategy meetings are over. A successful action plan has to be developed and supported by top management and be filled with measurable milestones against which progress can be checked. Strategy implementors have to be concrete and precise about what they want to get done and what they're willing to pay to achieve their goals.

Here's an example. Suppose an engineering-oriented high-tech firm makes a strategic decision to become more focused on marketing. How should this change be made to happen? Too often the CEO exhorts the executive staff to "think marketing" and leaves them largely to their own devices.

What the CEO should really do might be something like this:

- Meet with department managers to explain the goal and assure their buy-in.
- Establish an exact definition of "market focused."
- Establish measurements of market focus and define the goal in measurable terms.
- Assign responsibility for the implementation at key operating levels.
- Establish a timetable including milestones and dates for achieving the goal.
- Determine the resources necessary (staffing, training, equipment, advertising) to become market focused.
- Establish a budget for the transition.
- Lay out hiring and training plans to achieve the appropriate staffing.
- Kick-off the implementation.
- Continuously monitor progress against milestones and make changes as necessary.

These ideas along with dates, names, dollar amounts and specific goals are an action plan. Strategies and strategy changes that aren't supported by such a plan aren't likely to happen!

The Role and Importance of a Facilitator

A facilitator is an outsider who conducts the executive staff's series of strategic meetings. He or she is a person trained in strategic analysis and thinking like a strategic auditor.

Strategy meetings conducted without a facilitator tend to drift off on tangents and become lost in interesting but irrelevant minutiae. The meeting topic is the future which is subject to opinion and an infinite series of conjectures and variations. That can provide fodder for arguments and discussions that go on forever.

In a common pattern of events, the meeting starts smoothly, and then drifts off-course for most of the allotted time. At the eleventh hour people realize they haven't accomplished what they set out to do, and rush to finish on time. The result is that although the team met on strategy for a whole day, only a single rushed hour was actually spent on strategically relevant work.

A facilitator versed in strategic thinking recognizes when a meeting is drifting or has dwelt on an issue too long, and gently nudges conversation back to important issues. He or she also knows when a group is ready to move on to another phase or step, and thereby ensures that steady progress is made.

part IV

Strategic Issues for Small Businesses

chapter 10

Marketing and Sales: The Strategic Center of Small Business

Marketing is generally at the heart of strategy in a single line of business company. That should be fairly obvious, because no business can exist without a market for its product and a credible way to connect itself with that market. It's only after those are established that the other elements of strategy become important.

This central position of marketing is especially true for small businesses. As a general rule the primary issue faced by smaller companies is generating sales. Typically, entrepreneurs spend more than three-quarters of their time selling or managing the sales effort. For that reason it's important that we spend some time studying a few strategically important points related to the marketing (and sales) function in a small business.

Terminology

The term *marketing strategy* has a somewhat different meaning within the marketing function than the one we attach to it in the study of strategic management.

In the language of strategic management, a firm's marketing strategy is the set of policies (strategies) adopted by its marketing function in support of its overall strategy. Broadly-speaking, that means the approach the company takes to making and maintaining its connection with the market in which it participates.

Terminology within the marketing discipline is somewhat more focused although the underlying meaning is essentially the same. There, *marketing strategy* generally refers to the way a firm defines its *target market* and chooses a *marketing mix*. The expression *marketing mix* traditionally includes policies and decisions related to product characteristics, promotional activities, physical distribution, and pricing. We'll talk about each of these ideas before moving on to a few other important issues.

The Target Market

The target market is the group of customers the firm intends to reach. The term market segment generally means the same thing. A target can be defined geographically, economically, in terms of product attributes, or in any other logical way. Typical geographic definitions might be all the people in a particular town, or everyone on the East Coast. An economic definition might be all families with incomes between $40,000 and $60,000 a year, or anyone who's able to spend $80,000 on a sports car.[1] Attribute-based definitions might include people who are interested in contemporary as opposed to traditional furniture, those who like a particular ethnic food, or businesses that need an especially powerful computer.

It's very common to define a market with a combination of criteria, especially in smaller businesses. For example, a furniture store's target market might be people interested in the type of furniture the store carries, who live within a reasonable driving distance.

The target market concept is closely related to the idea of differentiation we discussed in chapter 7. Recall that in competitive strategy differentiation implies adding features to a product that make it especially appealing to some customers. Features usually have a cost, so while most are generally appealing, not all customers will be interested. Hence differentiation can be a way to segment a market. For example a firm might offer very high-quality merchandise at a high price which effectively limits its market to people with upper-level incomes.

However, differentiation doesn't always create a meaningful market segmentation. For example, an Italian restaurant is differentiated on the fact that it's Italian but still competes for the same customers as the neighboring Chinese and traditional restaurants.

It's important to realize that product differentiation is only one way to define a segment. Other ways tend to be more associated with the customers themselves like geography or income.

The word *niche* is sometimes used to describe a segment or target market in the sense we've been discussing. That can create confusion with respect to competitive strategy where it implies a group of customers with needs so special they're poorly served by existing firms. A niche player then tailors a product specifically to their needs. A niche is clearly a target market, but all target markets aren't niches.

---

[1] This definition includes wealthy people as well as people who love cars enough to spend a large portion of their resources on one. The distinction makes a big difference in how the firm attempts to reach its customers.

Marketing Mix

The marketing mix consists of four elements the firm combines to reach its target market. These are the company's product, pricing policies, use of advertising, and its channel of distribution. We'll discuss each separately.

Product or Service

A company's product or service is, of course, whatever it sells (we'll just say product for convenience, meaning product or service). Recall that strategically companies are in business to fill customer needs. A product's basic requirement is that it satisfy the need the firm is out to fill. Beyond that the product contains attributes relating to style, image, efficiency, convenience, cost, and a host of other things.

It's especially important to realize that most products are packages rather than just the items being sold. The typical package includes things like delivery, service, warranty, training and any other support that comes along with the purchase. A brand name is also generally an element of the package. Some brands have better attributes than others in terms of quality and reliability. In some cases the distinction is real while in others it's image created by advertising.

In most cases the definition of the firm's product isn't entirely a given with respect to the marketing effort. In other words, modifications and additions are generally possible to make products more salable, especially with respect to peripheral attributes like warranty and support.

For example, in an earlier chapter we used an illustration in which a small merchant was concerned about a large discount store opening in his town. We made the point that he might survive against the larger store by providing a level of service and product expertise not offered by large discounters. In this situation the entrepreneur would be adding attributes to his product package to differentiate it from the large chain's offering. Thus he might create a viable segment for his business.

Advertising and Promotion

A firm's approach to advertising involves how much it spends, the media used, and the nature and content of the message. Advertising has two basic functions: informational and persuasive. The informational element informs the market about the company and its product and educates consumers on what the product does. The persuasive element attempts to convince people to buy the firm's product, usually instead of competing brands. The extent to which advertising is aimed at educating rather than persuading depends on how long the product has been around, whether it's been changed recently, and how well it's known.

Advertising along with pricing creates an image of the firm and its products in the minds of potential customers. This concept of image is an important element of strategy. At its simplest, image focuses on either quality or economy. High-quality goods are generally expected to carry high prices while economical merchandise is of lower quality.

It's strategically important that a firm's abilities, its target market, and the image presented by its advertising and pricing be consistent. For example, it's possible to say anything in advertising, but it would obviously be foolish for a store carrying discount-grade merchandise to advertise it as being of an exclusive quality. People would respond to the ad, but would be disappointed or dissatisfied. In any event the inconsistency would cause more problems than good in the long run.

Promotional activities are similar to advertising. The term is sometimes used to include advertising, but is technically a little different. Promotions are events staged from time to time to inform users about products or to stimulate immediate purchases. They include trade shows, samples and coupons, and point of purchase displays.

The same strategic principles that apply to advertising are relevant for promotions. Basically the image conveyed has to be consistent with the firm's abilities and its market segment.

Distribution Channel

The distribution channel is the route through which a firm sends its products to customers. The idea is a non-issue for the majority of small businesses that deal directly with their end customers. For example, retailers, restaurants, plumbers, and lawyers simply sell to those who need their products and services. The choice of distribution channel mainly comes up in manufacturing.

Most manufacturers don't sell directly to the end users of their products, but go through a chain of "middlemen" that can include distributors, wholesalers, and retailers. Industrial products are often sold through agents or brokers who operate on commissions. The choice and availability of a channel is an element in the firm's approach to its market.

In some cases a firm's success depends more on acceptance by a link in the distribution chain than by the end customer. This is particularly true in the grocery business where getting a product on supermarket shelves is crucial.

However, in most smaller businesses the distribution channel generally isn't a strategically important variable. In other words it's usually either obvious or something the firm can't do much about.

Pricing

Pricing is a deceptively complex issue. A firm's prices have to be high enough to cover cost, overhead, and allow for a reasonable profit, while being low enough to attract business and keep the firm competitive. Price is also related to image in that it has to be consistent with the quality perceived in a firm's products.

Pricing can create problems in small business because people don't realize when they're not covering all their costs or are not competitive.

For example, suppose a retailer marks up cost by one third to arrive at selling price. That implies an item which sells for $10 costs $7.50 and leaves $2.50 as a contribution toward overhead and profit. But whether or not the $2.50 covers overhead and leaves enough for a reasonable profit depends on volume. And that depends on the competitiveness of the $10 price, the store's location, advertising, how well the store is meeting its target market's needs, and what other stores are doing at the time.

Sales and discounts make things even more complicated. If the typical item lists for $10, it isn't likely that the retailer is getting that much on his or her average sale. The effective price recognizes the fact that a percentage of the store's merchandise is sold at a discount. The average effective price might be $9 which would reduce the contribution to profit and overhead substantially.

It isn't at all unusual to find small businesses whose pricing structures don't lead to profitable operation even under favorable assumptions about volume. Then if volume falters, the result is quick failure.

Pricing is conceptually anchored in three places. First, price has to be competitively viable. That means if it's higher than the competition's there has to be a reason, usually based on a value-enhancing differentiation. Second, price leads to profitability after cost and overhead, and that has to be good enough to keep the business going. Third, price affects volume which also leads to profitability. The idea is illustrated in figure 10.1.

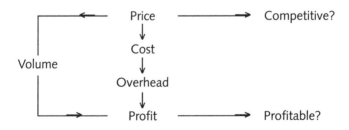

Figure 10.1   Pricing in Business Operations

It's important that small businesses understand their own cost structures, pricing, and the effect of volume on the viability of their businesses. There are several financial techniques for doing that. We'll look into one, the break-even analysis, in a later chapter.

Advertising in Small Business – A Strategic Problem

Small business owners give advertising very mixed reviews. Conventional wisdom says that businesses perish without advertising, but in interviews many entrepreneurs maintain that the increased sales from paid advertising often don't cover its cost. They maintain that success comes from word-of-mouth information passed from satisfied customers to the community. That's generally a long, slow process. To appreciate why these mixed opinions on advertising exist, it's necessary to understand a few basics.

The Target Market and the Trading Area

We've already discussed the idea of a target market. It's the group of buyers to whom the firm's product or service appeals. The group can be defined in any number of ways including taste, income, and geography.

The trading area is the geographical area from which the firm can reasonably expect to draw customers. Notice that the trading area idea overlaps the target market concept when the latter is defined geographically.

The trading area is an important concept for most small firms, because they can't expect to sell to customers too far away. Restaurants are a good example. People will rarely drive more than a few minutes to eat unless the meal represents a very special experience.

Notice that the trading area for large firms is usually a large region if not the entire country, because they have outlets all over and are therefore near virtually everyone.

Advertising Media

Advertising media are the forms of communication that carry advertising messages. They include newspapers, magazines, radio, TV, handbills, direct mailings, and signs. Each medium presents an advertiser's message and sells space or time in its own way. They also reach audiences in differently defined areas.

Advertising Strategy

It obviously makes strategic sense to match a firm's advertising to its target market and trading area. An advertisement is wasted to the extent it reaches people outside of the trading area or not in the target market, because those people are very unlikely to buy from the advertiser.

Let's make that point more precisely. Suppose a bicycle shop's advertisement is read in another city. It's unlikely to generate any business, because people won't travel between towns to buy bikes they can get locally. Further, the ad is also lost on anyone, anywhere who isn't interested in bicycling.

This implies that the perfectly distributed ad would reach only bicycle enthusiasts near the advertiser. That's generally not possible, but serves as a definition of efficiency. The closer an advertiser can get to that standard, the more effective his or her advertising dollar is likely to be.

Advertising Media and Cost

The cost of advertising in a medium is proportional to the number of consumers it reaches. Hence time on nationwide TV is very expensive, while it's relatively cheap on local cable channels. Newspapers, which tend to be the advertising workhorses for smaller businesses, operate in the same way. An ad in a large metropolitan paper is many times the cost of the same thing in a suburban weekly.

The cost of advertising is also related to the amount the advertiser does. This idea has two dimensions, size and frequency. In a newspaper, for example, a large ad costs less per column inch than a small one, and an ad run many times costs less per "insertion" than something run just once.

It's important to understand that the scale of discounting in advertising is enormous. Large advertisers pay a fraction of the cost per unit of exposure (column inches, airtime, etc.) paid by small advertisers. Of course, the cost of designing and setting up the ad is also much higher per exposure if it's used only a few times.

Why Advertising is so Problematic for Small Businesses

The problem faced by most small businesses with respect to advertising is the difficulty of matching media coverage with their target markets and/or trading areas.

Smaller firms often have very limited trading areas. This is especially true in retailing where the distance people will travel to reach a particular store is limited.

In general, however, advertising media tend to cover relatively large areas. Major newspapers, for example, cover entire cities.

That means most of the paper's coverage is outside of the trading areas of small businesses that target parts of the city or surrounding suburbs. That means an ad run in a metropolitan newspaper by a small business is usually largely wasted, because it's distributed substantially outside of the business's trading area.

Large newspapers address this problem by including local sections distributed only within sectors of the city and charging commensurately lower rates for ads in those sectors. This helps, but generally not enough. Local and community newspapers, usually weeklies, also help, but seem to be a good deal less effective as advertising vehicles than larger papers. People tend to read both the local and the metropolitan paper, but do most of their shopping from the larger of the two.

All this implies that the distribution structure and pricing of traditional media advertising makes it inefficient for many small businesses. Clearly signs, handbills and direct mail advertising aren't affected by this phenomenon. However, their effectiveness is limited relative to newspapers and the electronic media.

No one has come up with a general solution to this problem. Efficient advertising continues to be a major problem for the majority of small businesses, and probably will remain so in the forseeable future.

The Content of Advertising

Small businesses frequently don't do good jobs when designing their ads. They often concentrate more on their own qualities than on what the customer needs. For example, an ad that leads with the fact that a firm has been in business locally for 15 years doesn't do much to attract business. That fact is nice to gain credibility after an initial interest is aroused and the customer is close to choosing a vendor, but it doesn't attract buyers in the first place.

Similarly, ads with pictures of the firm's owners or staff generally aren't a good idea. Real pictures (as opposed to posed shots using professional models) are more likely to turn off people than attract them. The advertiser is probably too old, too young, too fat, too thin, or looks like somebody's in-laws who they never liked anyway.

What Advertisements Should Do

A good ad should immediately answer three questions for potential customers. It should tell them (1) why they should buy the product; (2) why they should buy it from the advertiser; and (3) why they should buy it now. Further, the answers should be couched in terms of benefits available to the buyer.

For the first question this means stressing the attributes or price of the product. For example:

> Summer fun in a swimming pool
> A 12× zoom on a camcorder
> A car with superior comfort and performance
> A well-built house in a beautiful neighborhood

For the second question it generally means stressing the benefits the seller has that others may not. These may include:

> Lowest price
> Biggest selection
> Best or most skilled and reliable service
> Convenient location

Keep in mind the emphasis here is on benefits to the buyer. The fact that an advertiser is "nicer" than the competition or has been here for a long time isn't relevant unless the buyer gets something from it.

The third issue should impart some urgency to the purchase decision. People tend to procrastinate on most decisions, and the longer they put off buying the less likely it is they'll remember an ad and buy from the advertiser. This logic is behind the fact that retailers, big and small, always seem to be having some kind of sale that "ends tomorrow."

Market Research

The value of market research has been recognized since the 1940s. Large companies do a great deal of research, but small businesses rarely make use of this valuable tool. Typically entrepreneurs are either unaware of the value of the information available or are put off by the cost of professional research companies.

It's true that large-scale studies made by professional researchers are too expensive for the majority of small companies. However, a great deal of information can be gathered using seat-of-the-pants techniques that don't cost a lot.

For our purposes market research can be divided into two broad areas. The first is aimed at discovering things about the market and its potential without reference to the business doing the research. For example, it's valuable to know who has what share, whether people would be interested in a particular new product, the income distribution of buying units, family sizes, and so on. A good deal of this kind of information is available without cost from public sources. Local governments have census information that's available for the asking, and the federal government publishes a great deal of economic information broken down by industry.

The second research area deals with finding out how a particular business is doing. This research answers questions like whether the community generally knows about the firm's existence, how satisfied its customers are, and what they specifically like and don't like about it. In particular, it's a good idea to know if customers are upset to the point of going elsewhere, and why former customers left.

This last idea is particularly important for small companies. Customers that are very upset with a business usually tell management about their problem, perhaps while asking for a refund. Customers who are mildly dissatisfied usually don't say anything. They just don't come back. We've all had an experience with a dry cleaner or restaurant that goes slowly downhill. After a few disappointments we just start going someplace else.

Typically entrepreneurs don't know there's a problem until sales fall off and their reputations are seriously damaged. Even then the cause often remains a mystery. Is the problem product quality, poor service, the staff's attitude or a combination of things?

Entrepreneurs faced with declining sales typically operate on intuition with respect to the reason behind the decline. That leads to hit-and-miss solutions that usually don't work. That's a tragedy because most of the time a little focused market research would have revealed the problem.

Designing a Research Program[2]

In general, market research is as simple as observing people's behavior or asking questions about important issues. However, to get meaningful results care has to be taken with respect to how the observations are made, how the questions are written and presented, and who's asked to answer. There are five steps in the market research process:

1 Defining the problem.
2 Determining the required information.
3 Planning how the information will be gathered.
4 Conducting the research.
5 Analyzing the data.

Defining the Problem

Research should always have some informational goal. Whether there's a specific problem that needs fixing (usually poor sales) or just a need for general information, it's necessary to exactly define the research goal before starting.

Determining the Required Information

Next the researcher has to decide what information will shed light on the problem, and design a series of observations or questions that will elicit that information. Every effort should be made to define the information in concise, quantifiable units. Even the simplest research project has to be carefully thought-out in advance in this respect. If it isn't the results tend to be anecdotal and don't lead to clear conclusions.

For example, suppose a restaurant is having problems and exiting customers are asked their general opinions about the establishment. Everyone will answer in conversational terms which will be filtered through the researcher's interpretation as the responses are recorded. The result is likely to be an imprecise collection of descriptions from which it's hard to draw conclusions.

---

[2] Hal B. Pickle and Royce L. Abrahamson, *Small Business Management* (New York: John Wiley and Sons, 1986), pp. 327–8.

It's much better to ask a series of short, objective questions that can be answered on a scale. The results can then be summarized and tend to show problems clearly. For example, ask people to rate each of the following on a scale of 1–10. The salad, the entree, the drinks, the service, prices, atmosphere, etc. When 30 or 40 people have been polled, compile averages for each question and analyze the results. They're likely to pinpoint what customers perceive as the establishment's problems.

Planning how the Information will be Gathered

Planning the survey means deciding who will be observed or asked questions. It's generally impossible to survey all customers or the entire population of an area, so a representative sample has to be selected.

It's very important that the sample questioned or observed represent a fair cross-section of the target population. Care must be taken in this phase, because it's easy to make a mistake that will result in a biased result. Biases come from asking the wrong questions or failing to observe a representative group of people. Here's an example:

Suppose a supermarket wants to find out about the preferences of customers, so management designs a short questionnaire and hires someone to stand at the door and ask exiting customers the questions. But suppose the person hired is a high-school student who happens to be intimidated by older people, and without thinking about it she approaches only shoppers under about 35 years of age. If the age of the respondent isn't on the questionnaire, management may never know the results represent only younger customers whose opinions may be different from those of older people. In this way the survey results are biased toward part of the population.[3]

Here's another example: Suppose a survey counts foot traffic past a location to see if it's an appropriate site for a retail store. The nature of the traffic is likely to be different on weekends and weekdays and at different times of day. Hence the survey should be defined to observe during all of those periods. If observations are made, say, only on weekday mornings, the results will be biased. Notice that this day of the week and time of day concern is also relevant in our supermarket example.

Conducting the Research

The two basic approaches to gathering data are observation and interviewing. Observation involves watching people or recording the results of what

---

[3] The classic example of a research bias occurred in the 1948 presidential election when pollsters using telephone surveys concluded that the republican candidate Tom Dewey would beat democrat Harry Truman in a landslide. However in those days lower income families frequently didn't have phones. Hence telephone surveys were automatically biased toward more affluent voters who tended to be republicans, and the survey results were totally wrong.

they do. For example, we can count the number of shoppers passing a location and the number entering a store to get an idea of the percentage of walk-by traffic that comes in. Then we can look at the number of sales of particular items to determine what percentage of shoppers buy them. This can lead to an estimate of sales at a location based on traffic.

Interviewing involves stopping people and asking them questions. This can be done in a place of business, upon people's exit from a place of business, in people's homes by phone or in person, or by mail.

Interviewing comes with a built-in biasing problem. Since not everyone will consent to be interviewed, the question of whether those who do consent fairly represent the population always exists. For example, if only satisfied customers consent to be interviewed, survey results will be favorably biased.

A great deal of valuable information can be gathered at surprisingly little cost through the kind of surveys we've described. Using high-school or college students to gather information is quite cost-effective. Be careful, however, to hire only serious, motivated young people, and to monitor what they're doing.

Analyzing the Data

The analysis and interpretation of survey data depend on the nature of the information sought or the problem being investigated. It's generally a good idea to display data in tabular form and show averages. That generally makes it easier to see what's going on than sifting through a large number of individual responses.

Consider our earlier restaurant illustration in which we asked exiting customers to rate the establishment from 1–10 on several criteria. Suppose the survey showed that the average customer rated the food a 7 but the service a 4. That would rather quickly pinpoint the problem. The next thing to investigate would be whether the problem was with the servers or with a slow kitchen.

Marketing Strategy and Business Planning

A small company's business plan is a vehicle for selling the firm, its strategy, and its prospects for success to investors. Without investors, the best strategy in the world is useless because the business never gets started or withers away from lack of funding.

This makes the presentation of the market and competitive situation in a small firm's business plan an important issue in strategic management. If it isn't done in a way that captures investors' attention and convinces them that the business is a good one, everything else is lost.

In the last chapter we made the point that small businesses don't generally create separate strategic and operating plans. Rather each produces a single all-purpose business plan that presents both strategic and tactical ideas at the same time. This makes it worth spending a little time on the presentation technique.

The General Approach to a Marketing Presentation

A good plan begins with a description of the product or service being offered and ties that to a detailed analysis of the market and the company's approach to it. These arguments are made using the tools of strategic analysis we've presented thus far.

This product-market analysis leads to a long-term revenue forecast for at least the next three but probably five years. Such a forecast should provide estimates of unit sales by product and type as well as of total revenue dollars.

The market analysis also leads to a detailed sales forecast for the next year. This should be conceptually distinguished from the longer-term, strategic revenue forecast. The sales plan focuses on exactly what the firm intends to sell to which customers in the short run. It also includes information on pricing and who in the salesforce is going to make it happen. Pricing assumptions lead to an estimate of gross profitability while the question of who will do the selling leads into plans for managing and compensating the sales force.

The Mix of Product

When a firm sells more than one product or several versions of the same thing, it's important to support revenue and sales projections with unit forecasts and pricing assumptions based on the product mix assumed in the plan. Frequently small firms forecast total revenue/sales dollars based on a standard product ignoring the mix issue. This relieves marketing of much of its planning responsibility and makes the finished plan less useful for control later on.

Here's an example to illustrate why mix is important: Assume a company sells products X and Y at different prices which yield significantly different levels of profitability as follows:

	X		Y	
	$	%	$	%
Price	$10	100%	$5	100%
Cost	6	60%	4	80%
Margin	$4	40%	$1	20%

Notice that the gross profit margin on a unit of X is 40 percent while on a Y it's only 20 percent. Imagine that the firm's plan is to make total sales in X and Y of $1,000,000 and to earn a combined gross profit of $350,000 or 35 percent. It's important to understand that such a profit projection dictates how many units of X and Y have to be sold to achieve the plan. (Approximately 75,000 units of X and 50,000 of Y.)

Achieving the goals of the plan doesn't just mean making sales totaling $1,000,000, because if all Ys are sold, the bottom line will be missed even though the sales goal is made. (Gross margin would be $200,000.)

Stating sales goals in terms of total revenue alone can build a negative bias into the plan. Low-margin products tend to be easier to sell, so salespeople are likely to do most of their business at the bottom of the product line which makes the revenue plan but not the profit plan.

To prevent this, sales goals should be specified by product, and sales departments should be required to achieve targets in each line, not just in overall revenue. Individual sales effort is managed through the commission plan by putting low commission rates on low-margin products and higher rates on more profitable lines.

Motivating the Sales Force – Commission Plans

Motivating employees in support of strategy is important in effective implementation. We discussed the administration of incentive compensation (bonuses) for management in chapter 8, but deferred consideration of sales personnel until now. Since sales and marketing represent the "leading edge" of most firms' strategic efforts, managing the salesforce is a strategically crucial task. The goal is to get salespeople to sell the products that are strategically important to the company, and to motivate the best performers to put out as much effort as is humanly possible.

Since all sales are not of equal strategic value, a major goal of the commission plan is to motivate the salesforce to sell in the preferred areas. Sales of one product may be preferred to another because of higher profit margins, over-stocked inventories or the need to promote something new.

Sales are directed into the more desirable lines by putting higher commission rates on those lines. It's a mistake to believe salespeople will sell where management wants them to for any reason other than compensation.

Drawing out Maximum Effort – The Backward Bending Supply Curve of Labor

Commissions are part of the payment made for sales labor. In effect they're the price of labor offered (supplied) by the salesperson. A higher commission rate essentially means a higher price in the labor market. It's generally management's goal to draw as much effort as possible out of salespeople, especially the good ones.

A concept from economics helps us to understand how managing commissions can get the best out of a salesforce. The idea is called the backward bending supply curve of labor. It reflects a basic characteristic of human nature.

The supply curve for most goods looks like figure 10.2a. A higher price means a larger quantity supplied, so the curve slopes upward to the right more or less without limit. The supply of labor services, however, behaves differently. Its shape is illustrated in figure 10.2b.

As the price of labor increases, the amount suppliers (workers) offer increases initially, but then decreases as the wage gets higher. In other words, the curve bends backwards meaning people offer less labor as the price they're paid for it goes up. In the case of salespeople, paying higher commission rates eventually makes them work less. Put still another way, the curve tells us that if people who control their own schedules are paid too much, they'll quit early. That's exactly what management doesn't want them to do.

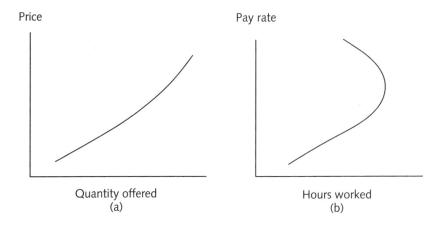

Figure 10.2   The Backward Bending Supply Curve of Labor

This phenomenon exists because unlike other goods, the amount of labor a person can offer is limited. First, it's impossible to work more than about 15 hours per day for any length of time. Second, working implies a tradeoff with leisure. The concept comes down to the fact that if people are highly paid, there comes a time when they have all the money they need and they choose to take more time off.

Managing the Backward Bending Curve

The backward bending phenomenon can be addressed in two ways. One approach is keeping the salesforce hungry by constructing the commission plan so that people are always below the point where the curve bends backward. The problem, of course, is that this may drive the best people away.

The second approach uses accelerators, which are higher rates for additional sales over specified levels, i.e., as the bend is approached, the rate of pay gets higher. This pushes the turning point higher. Accelerators can get larger as performance gets better. For example, if the normal commission rate is 4 percent, an accelerated plan might pay 6 percent for sales between 100 percent and 150 percent of a pre-established quota and 8 percent for sales over 150 percent of that target.

Timing

Commission plans are also designed to keep sales coming in regularly by giving salespeople bonuses for making each quarter's target within the quarter, but not if it's caught up afterward. An annual bonus has a similar effect at year end and keeps people who are behind motivated.

chapter 11

Financing Strategies

The term *financing* refers to raising money to do or acquire something. We finance a car or a house when we borrow money (usually from a bank) to acquire those assets. We can finance a college education with savings, or loans, or scholarships or a combination of those things. Financing a business means basically the same thing, acquiring money to start or run it. There are, however, a few variations that make business financing more complex than personal financing.

In business, we need a distinction based on time. A company can be thought of as spending "long-term" and "short-term" money. Short-term funds are used to support day-to-day activities like buying inventory and paying wages, rents and other recurring expenses. Long-term funds are spent to acquire lasting assets like buildings and equipment, and on activities that go on for some time, like big projects and new ventures. One such long-term use of funds is setting up and starting the business itself.

Strategic financing generally refers to this last idea, raising money to start or expand a business. It should be obvious that strategic financing is crucial to success, because without startup money, there's no business to run, regardless of the quality of management's other strategic thinking.

In other words, since entrepreneurs don't generally have startup money laying around in the bank, and since not many companies have enough free cash available to fund major expansions, financing is a strategy critical activity for most small businesses. This is so even though raising money seems to have little to do with the activities we've been calling strategy up until now. In fact, management has to have a strategic approach to raising money just as it has a strategic approach to its employees, its organization and its markets.

Financing often represents a difficult hurdle for small firms at least partially because managers are unfamiliar with the workings of the financial world. Therefore, before going further, we'll spend a little time on some basics concerning the forms financing can take and a few of the more important rules of the game.

Basic Principles

Financing comes from investors. These are people or organizations who are willing to advance money to firms in the hope of earning a return on their funds. Inherent in the idea is that investors are willing to take some risk with their money to secure higher returns. An important distinction between investors is the amount of risk they're willing to expose themselves to and the amount of expected return they'll demand for bearing that risk.

This is an important idea. Any investor can secure a modest return with virtually no risk by putting his or her money in a bank or buying US Treasury securities. It is the quest for higher returns that motivates people to invest in riskier opportunities like the stock market or small businesses. Indeed, small businesses are generally considered very high-risk investment vehicles, so investors demand either very high expected returns or some of the offsetting safety features we'll describe later.

Investment in businesses comes in two basic forms, debt and equity. That is, the firm raising the money (the firm being financed) either borrows from an investor or sells shares of its stock. The sale of stock conveys a part-ownership in the company to the investor who is then said to have an equity interest in the firm. With respect to equity, it's important to understand that investors who own minor portions of a firm's stock don't generally have an important say in how the firm is run.

The money borrowed (debt) or paid for the stock (equity) is called the proceeds of the financing transaction. It is the money raised, and is employed by the company for the long-term activities we described initially.

Borrowed funds must, of course, be repaid with interest which is the source of the investor's return. Equity funds, however, are generally not repaid, and the investor's return comes from dividends and/or appreciation in the stock's value.

Financing by Borrowing – Debt

Debt financing means borrowing money. An individual or an organization such as a bank lends a business money with the expectation of being repaid with interest. The two major forms of business debt are loans and bonds.

Bonds are a device through which a number of people lend to a company in one transaction. For example, imagine that a small business needs to borrow $100,000 but can't find a single source willing to lend that much. But suppose ten people can be found who are each willing to lend $10,000. Rather than make up ten separate loan agreements, the firm can issue ten $10,000 bonds under a single contract and "sell" one to each investor. Each person who "buys" a bond lends the company $10,000. The terminology is a little strange. We talk about buying and selling bonds even though the underlying transaction is a loan. Bonds are very popular with large companies, but are rarely practical for small firms.

Business loans, on the other hand, are similar to personal loans in that a single borrower faces a single lender in the transactions. Loans are the major vehicle for small business debt financing, so we'll consider them in some detail.

Term Loans

Loans are classified according to term, the time until they're completely repaid. Short-term debt must generally be repaid within a year, while long-term debt is generally outstanding for more than five years. Sometimes people refer to intermediate-term loans, meaning debt that lasts up to about five years.

As a general rule lenders demand that the term of debt match the use of the money. Hence a long-term loan is required to buy equipment that's expected to last 30 years, while short-term borrowing might fund a temporary cash shortages that arises from slow collection of receivables.

Lenders generally anticipate that long-term borrowing will be repaid out of profits. Short-term repayment is expected to come as soon as the need is over, e.g. as soon as the receivables are collected.

Short-term loans are considered safer than long-term debt. That's because if a borrower is in good financial condition today, a short-term loan doesn't give it very much time to get into trouble, but its condition can deteriorate quite a bit in several years. That generally makes long-term strategic borrowing more difficult to obtain than short-term financing.

Loan Payments

Virtually all loans require the regular payment of interest on the unpaid balance of the principal, usually monthly. Most also require that the principal be repaid or "amortized" regularly over the loan's term. (In contrast, bonds typically require only semiannual interest payments until "maturity" and a lump sum repayment of principal at maturity.) The total payment called for on the debt is known as debt service.

This is an important and dangerous feature of financing with debt. Debt service must be made regularly regardless of whether the borrowing business is currently making money. This requirement increases the borrowing firm's risk of failure, because missed payments default a loan and enable the lender to put the borrower into bankruptcy.

Covenants

Covenants are clauses in loan agreements which restrict the operation of the borrowing businesses while the loans are outstanding. Lenders demand them to insure the loan's repayment and thus their own safety.

A covenant might preclude the company from paying dividends during the life of the loan. Another might prevent the entrepreneur from drawing or borrowing money from the business, or might limit the compensation paid to officers. Covenants are designed to ensure that the company's cash is used to service the loan before it can be used in more discretionary ways.

Covenants can also be designed to limit routine operations in the interest of the lender's security. For example, it's common to require that certain levels of profitability and cash liquidity be maintained. It's also not unusual to prevent management from taking on risky ventures that might drain cash away from repayment while the loan is outstanding.

When a covenant is broken the loan is in default. Then an "acceleration clause" usually makes the entire principle due and payable immediately. This allows the lender to sue for the entire loan amount and can easily bankrupt the borrower.

Loans to Small Businesses Require Collateral

Lenders consider many if not most small businesses too risky for loans. They therefore require that marketable assets called collateral back loan obligations before they'll advance debt money. If a company defaults on a loan, the collateral asset becomes the property of the lender, and the proceeds from its sale are used to pay off the loan. Collateral assets can be owned by the borrowing business or the owner personally. It isn't unusual for entrepreneurs to collateralize business loans with their homes.

"Purchase money" loans that are used to buy equipment or real estate are usually collateralized with the assets purchased. Short-term loans to cover inventory and receivables are often partially collateralized by the inventory and receivables.

The collateral value a bank will allow on an asset is usually a fraction of its cost because lenders don't expect to be able to sell defaulted property at full value. Hence to buy an asset with a loan collateralized by that asset a firm generally has to put in some of its own cash. This is a familiar concept. Residential mortgages and car loans are collateralized by the houses and cars bought, and usually require a cash down-payment.

A loan collateralized by an asset is said to be secured by the asset and is called a secured loan. A loan without collateral is said to be unsecured. Lenders tend to make unsecured loans only to businesses they know and that have long histories of stable operation.

Debt Financing and Control

Control in the context of financing involves whether financing sources can exert any influence over the way in which business owners run their companies.

In that regard debt financing generally implies a relatively small loss of control under normal circumstances. The main source of debt-related control problems stems from restrictive covenants that limit management's autonomy. However if covenants are negotiated carefully they don't generally present significant difficulties.

Equity Financing

The term *equity* means an ownership interest. In the context of business investment an equity investor is generally someone who buys stock in the company. Of course, the business has to be organized as a corporation to raise equity financing that way.

Stockholders are part owners of the company, so there's generally a control issue involved in this kind of financing. Holders of a relatively few shares have virtually no control over the firm's management while people with substantial portions can wield considerable influence. Anyone who owns more than 50 percent, of course, controls the company.

We're all familiar with buying stock in large companies. In those transactions there's generally not an issue of control. We just call our broker and buy, say, 100 shares of General Motors at the current market price. We then expect to receive dividends while we hold the shares and hope some day to sell them at a higher price than we paid.

Financing a small business with equity is a rather different proposition. First, there's no market price on which to value the firm or a share of its stock. Second, dividends are unlikely to be paid to shareholders for a long time. The value of stock is therefore just dependent on the appreciation in the value of the company that people expect. That's extremely arbitrary because it depends on subjective assumptions about the firm's future performance. An example will illustrate the problem.

EXAMPLE 11-1

Harry Washington has an idea for a new kind of company in the insurance industry. He has twenty years of experience in insurance and knowledgeable people think his idea has a good chance of being very successful. He's lined up customers that will give his firm an initial business level of about $2m per year. Estimates of his success vary widely. Nearly everyone thinks Harry's business will grow at least 10 percent a year indefinitely. Some people think a 50 or 60 percent growth rate is not at all unlikely. And some, including Harry, think the growth will be explosive and he'll be grossing over $200m in five years.

Harry needs $500,000 to get started. He has $200,000 of his own savings that he'll put into the business. The firm is incorporated with 1,000 shares of stock outstanding, all of which currently belong to Harry. He wants to sell some of this stock (equity financing) to raise the other $300,000. If the company is really successful Harry will have to raise at least another $1m to support its rapid growth over the next few years.

Harry is negotiating with a venture capital firm that represents a group of wealthy investors. It's in the business of making equity investments in very promising new firms.

Problem: How much stock, i.e., what portion of the company, should Harry be willing to give up for the $300,000 in startup capital? Conversely, how much stock should the venture capitalists demand for putting their money at risk? It's important to notice that because the company is new, its earnings are speculative, and since no one regularly buys or sells the stock, it has no established market value. Hence the value of shares, and consequently the company, is a negotiable issue between Harry and his investors.

Analysis: It should be obvious that there's no easy answer to this question. Harry is supplying some money and several intangibles including the idea, the expertise, and the energy. But the venture firm is supplying 60 percent of the money without which Harry can't get started. They'd probably like to get 60 percent of the stock putting little or no monetary value on Harry's intangible contribution. Harry would probably like to give them 10–20 percent putting a big value on his non-monetary efforts. He also needs to save some share of the company for future financing.

The result is going to depend on how much each party thinks the company is eventually going to be worth. The more the venture firm thinks of Harry's idea, the less of a share they'll be willing to accept for their $300,000.

Notice also that there's a control issue here. Although Harry's not likely to give up more than 50 percent initially, he could be maneuvered into having to do so when more financing is needed later on. This can create major problems even if the investors own less than 50 percent. Equity investors usually have little interest in day-to-day operations under relatively normal conditions, but can become very difficult in bad times if they feel their investments are in jeopardy.

We'll have a little more to say about how all this works later on.

Strategic Financial Thinking

Now that we've covered some basic material, we can turn our attention to strategic concerns related to raising money. Strategic thinking in financing involves two distinct steps. First we have to determine exactly how much financing the business will need over the period we're planning. In a strategic context, that's generally several years. Then, having decided how much needs to be raised, we can consider where to get the money and how to approach the sources we select.

It's important to realize that any time a small business seeks outside financing, its case has to be presented in a formal business plan. This is because the source generally insists on knowing the details of how it will get its investment back. This is especially true for long term "strategic" money. We described business planning briefly in chapter 9. In the remainder of this chapter we'll assume that a business plan/financing proposal has been prepared and is available for presentation to the financing source.

The amount of financing required is a product of the business planning process, specifically the financial projections. In what follows, we'll assume that those projections have been made in some detail, and that we have an estimate of how much money we'll need to launch or expand our business.

The issue then becomes whether to go after debt or equity financing, and how to prepare a business plan and supporting proposal that will appeal to whichever source we choose.

Success will turn on how well we prepare our case for presentation to the two different kinds of investor. In that regard, it's fundamentally important to understand how the different investor types think, and what they look for in a funding proposal. The variation is significant enough that a proposal which will succeed with an equity investor, typically a venture capitalist, is almost certain to fail with a debt investor like a bank. Conversely a proposal that will succeed with a bank is more than likely to fail with a venture capitalist.

We'll first consider the venture capital market for equity financing.

Strategy for Venture Capital Financing

Venture capital is the most talked about field of financing but actually provides only a fraction of the money raised by business. As we'll understand shortly, this is because most businesses don't meet the requirements of venture capitalists.

To understand venture capitalists we need to focus on the extremely high forecast returns they demand before they'll invest. Their requirements are high because their business is extremely risky in that the vast majority of new firms fail, including many they back. Hence, to offset the failures venture firms have to make a lot on their successes. As a result, to qualify for consideration a proposal generally has to promise a return in the neighborhood of 50 percent compounded annually for a period of five or six years.

The strategy for success is to make sure our plan meets that requirement. Doing that takes a few calculations based on the way a successful venture capital deal works. The venture firm first invests in a startup for stock (equity). Then the startup operates and grows rapidly for about five years after which it's either sold to a large corporation or taken public.[1] In either case the venture capital firm gets its appreciated investment back and can go on to something else.

EXAMPLE 11-2

Tom Crestful has a data communications product for the burgeoning internet service industry. The product's sales prospects look very good, but he needs about $4m to launch a business to make and market his device. Candidly, he doesn't know how sales will pan out. Reasonable arguments can be made for a wide range of sales and profit forecasts. What figures should he put into a business plan to attract the interest of a venture capitalist in his company?

Let's look for a solution. Assume the following: Tom wants $4m. He's willing to give the investor 40 percent of his business. Successful firms in similar businesses earn profits of about 8 percent of revenues. The starting point for valuing companies is generally about ten times earnings. Then make the following calculations:

The investor's interest must grow at 50 percent per year for five years yielding a value of $30.4m:

$$\$4m \times (1.5)^5 = \$30.4m$$

This amount represents 40 percent of the company's value, so the whole firm will be worth $76m:

$$\$30.4m / .4 = \$76m$$

If firms are valued at about ten times earnings, Tom's fifth year earnings

---

[1] Going public is the procedure by which a corporation's stock is made available for sale to the general public. Being publicly traded establishes a price for the stock and thereby a value for the firm. If the firm has done well, the venture capitalist can sell its stock on the open market at a much higher price than it originally paid.

will have to be around $7.6m. And, if earnings are to be 8 percent of revenues, fifth year revenues will be about $95m:

$$\$7.6m / 0.08 = \$95m.$$

We'll use a round $100m.

Hence to raise $4m from a venture capitalist, Tom should prepare a business plan that projects a revenue stream that grows to $100m in five years and shows a profit of about $8m at that time. To put this in perspective, a business of that size might well employ 1,000 people and have assets in the $80–$100m range. It will also need a good deal of additional financing over the five-year period.

A good rule of thumb might be that the fifth year revenue forecast should be about 25 times the investment.

It may not be advisable to submit a plan with financial projections that exceed those in the example by very much. A more aggressive forecast might be viewed as unrealistically optimistic.

It's clearly not worthwhile to submit a plan with projections like these in a slow growth industry.

It should be obvious that showing financial projections that meet venture capital growth requirements alone won't guarantee funding. The plan also has to establish a credible market and convince the investor that the product can reach it. Indeed, the bulk of the entrepreneur's plan and proposal are devoted to establishing these things. We're just focusing on finances here.

The proposal also needs to convince the investor of the competence of the management team. This is done with a summary of each person's background and education including a listing of accomplishments in similar endeavors. The best experience possible is having participated in the successful launch of a venture before.

Venture capital firms tend to develop expertise in specific areas such as high tech, health care, or energy. It's usually futile to submit a proposal to specialized investors that's outside their field of interest.

Who Qualifies for Venture Capital Financing?

Although venture capital receives a great deal of press, very few business propositions qualify for that kind of funding because of the rapid growth requirements we talked about earlier. Such performance is generally associated with some new market where a previously unknown demand literally explodes. Examples include integrated circuits, cellular phones, personal computers and pharmaceuticals.

Contrast any of those with a more traditional business like restaurants. To grow, most restaurants have to take business away from similar establishments. That doesn't usually happen at extraordinarily high rates.

Supergrowth opportunities are most common in high technology industries, but occasionally turn up elsewhere. Federal Express is a good example.

Venture Capital Firms

Venture capital companies, often called "funds," are usually limited partnerships. A limited partnership is a form of business organization that allows the limited partners to invest money without liability beyond their investments. The organization is run by a general partner who typically doesn't put in a great deal of money, but manages the fund choosing the ventures in which it invests. For this he or she receives a percentage of the earnings. The limited partners are usually other investment companies and wealthy individuals.

Entrepreneurs usually approach venture capitalists by sending them unsolicited business plans. Unfortunately, venture firms get a large number of such proposals, so the chances of success are slim. It helps to have a personal contact or introduction to the venture community, but that's hard to establish for an average person. All this makes venture capital financing very difficult for typical businesses.

Sources of Venture Information

Locating and approaching venture sources is a subject unto itself. There are several publications that may help entrepreneurs who feel their ideas may qualify for venture financing. *Who's Who In Venture Capital* is published by Wiley-Interscience and the *Venture Capital Journal* is published by Venture Economics. *Venture* and *Entrepreneur* magazines can also lead to sources.

Strategy for Lenders – Usually Banks

A bank's orientation is dramatically different from that of an equity investor. To appreciate why we'll go through a little story that illustrates the difference between equity (stocks) and debt investments.

Suppose an entrepreneur approaches two different investors. He proposes a stock sale (equity) to the first and a loan (debt) to the second. To his surprise, both ask the same two questions. The first question and his answer to each prospect are as follows:

Question #1 "What happens to my investment if your company fails?"
Answers:
  Loan (debt) investor: "You lose your money."
  Stock (equity) investor: "You lose your money."

The answer is the same in both cases, a disaster for the investor. Neither is very happy about that, but they proceed with the second question:

Question #2 "What happens to my investment if your company does spectacularly well?"
Answer:
Loan (debt) investor: "You get your investment back plus interest."
Stock (equity) investor: "You get rich!"

The point should be clear. The downside is the same for both investment methods – total loss. But the upside is vastly different. The equity investor shares in the business's success, while the debt investor receives only a modest return.

Appealing to Lenders

It's the lack of upside potential, a chance of doing really well, that differentiates the lender's focus from the stockholder's. Because lenders' returns are modest, they won't want to risk anything more than a modest loss. This means a banker will generally demand collateral before extending a loan to a new business. It also follows that a proposal for debt financing has to focus on the business's stability and the cash flows that will service the debt.

A banker isn't likely to buy into a plan that interests a venture capitalist. She'll consider a 50 percent growth rate far too risky. She's also likely to focus on the fact that a business growing that fast will need more cash in the future rather than generating enough to pay off a loan.

Bankers need assurances that their depositors' money will be safe. Safety requires history, security, or both. History means banks like to lend to businesses with long records of stable operation. Security means they like collateralized loans.

Don't Depend on Borrowed Money to get Started

All this adds up to the fact that one generally can't expect to start a business with borrowed money unless the loan is fully collateralized. For many middle-class entrepreneurs that means putting up the equity in their homes.

This is a very important idea and a basic financing fact that should be understood at the outset by anyone interested in starting a business. Let's restate it in somewhat different words. Most of the money behind small business start-ups comes from the entrepreneurs themselves and from family and friends. We're not saying that financing is impossible, but as a rule much of the money has to come from the entrepreneur's savings or the sale of other assets. That is, it's not realistic for entrepreneurs to assume they can start businesses without money of their own.

Non-Financial Requirements

After the different cash flow requirements are recognized, a plan for a bank depends upon the same key points as a venture plan: A proven market with a credible plan for reaching it, and the competence and experience of management.

More Detailed Guidelines to Working with Banks

Since most small business funding comes from banks, we'll spend a little time on dealing with them. In spite of the conservatism we've been talking about up until now, it's important to recognize two things about banks and small business loans. First, banks want to make loans. It's the business they're in, and in most areas it's a competitive business. If we check the rosters of local Rotary, Kiwanis, and Lions clubs, we'll find bankers on all of them. That's because banks want to be involved in the business community, and want to make loans to local businesses. Second, and perhaps more important, about 75 percent of loans to small businesses are made by small and medium-sized banks. That means the chance of securing debt financing is better with a bank that's small enough to value an entrepreneur's business. In other words, the banking relationship is a two-way street. Small business needs banks, but banks need small businesses too.

Approaching a Bank for a Loan

The goal in approaching a bank should be to get an opportunity to make a complete, thorough presentation to an interested loan officer. It isn't a good idea to try to do that by walking in and pulling out a proposal on the first visit. It's better to go in the first time to identify the right person, meet him or her briefly and set up a second meeting. It's important to be sure they allow enough time for the entire presentation on the second visit.

Information Requirements

Banks have loan application forms which have to be filled out regardless of the fact that much of the information is in the applicant's business plan. Typical information requirements are summarized as follows:

Company/Business
A description and history of the business.
General plans for its future.
The exact amount and purpose of the loan.

Proposed repayment terms showing the source of the cash.
The ratio of debt to equity in the business.
Details of existing or planned leasing agreements.
Proposed collateral.
Insurance coverage on the business and its owners.
Detail of assets by type: inventory, equipment, real estate etc.
Financial statements going back at least three years.
Federal tax returns for at least the past three years.
Projected financial statements for the next three years.
Summary of the assumptions behind the financial projections.
A worst-case contingency plan.

Personal on Owner
Professional qualifications – work history and education.
Professional references.
Credit history and references.
Personal financial statements stressing net worth.
Copies of personal income tax returns for three years.

The Entrepreneur's Equity Investment

Banks prefer to lend to businesses in which the entrepreneur has a good deal of his or her own money invested. That equity is important for two reasons. First, investors feel that people simply try harder and are more careful when their own money is at stake. Therefore there's an extra margin of safety available when a good deal of the owner's money is on the line. Second, if the business starts to fail, equity is lost before debt money, so equity cushions the bank's investment against operating losses.

Always Borrow Enough to do the Job

It's important to borrow enough money to accomplish the loans' purpose. It's not good for a banking relationship to get a loan for some reason and then have to go back later for more money for the same reason. The calculation of the amount requested should be documented carefully. Then if the loan officer suggests borrowing significantly less, it may be a good idea to consider another source.

Don't Be Easily Discouraged

Applicants shouldn't be too discouraged by refusals. They're often for reasons that don't have much to do with the applicant. For example, a particular bank may already have a number of loans in a business area and not want any more. There are also times when money is tight, and there isn't much available for anyone. On the other hand, six or eight refusals should prompt anyone to reconsider their idea.

The Ongoing Banking Relationship

It's important for small businesses to continue to pay a good deal of attention to their banking relationship after a loan is obtained. There's a tendency to forget about it the way most people put a mortgage out of their minds after they buy a home. Business loans are somewhat different because business conditions are so volatile. Further, there's often a lot a bank can do to help a small business through tough times.

For example, suppose a company is making its loan payments, but is experiencing increasing operating difficulties, and foresees the possibility of a cash shortage later on that could cause it to miss one or more payments. When their businesses aren't doing as well as they'd hoped, people tend to be reluctant to share the bad news, especially with their investors because the experience is likely to be confrontational. But investors including banks, don't like surprises, especially bad ones. It's very important to keep the bank informed about what's going on. The worst thing a borrower can do for the relationship is to default without warning. Most of the time a bank that's kept informed will be willing to work with a business to get it through temporary rough spots.

Small Business Administration Loans

The Small Business Administration (SBA) is a government agency whose mission is to assist small businesses. It runs a number of programs providing counseling and advice and offers some financial assistance related to loans. Unfortunately, the nature of the SBA loan program is frequently misunderstood. The SBA doesn't generally lend money itself, rather it guarantees loans made by banks. The guarantee lowers the bank's risk which lets it charge a little less interest, and permits some businesses to borrow that otherwise wouldn't qualify.

To get an SBA loan, a business must have been turned down by all available conventional channels. Information on SBA loans is available through local Small Business Development Centers which are listed in the phone book.

The Five C's of Credit

The five C's of credit is a checklist banks and other lenders go through in evaluating loan applicants. It makes a lot of sense to keep it in mind and to posture oneself to do as well as possible when evaluated against it.

- **Character:** The probability that a person will attempt to pay off the debt and how serious is their intention.
- **Capacity:** A judgement of the borrower's ability to pay.
- **Capital:** The general financial condition of the borrower as reflected in its financial statements.
- **Collateral:** The assets offered as security.
- **Conditions:** General economic conditions and circumstances peculiar to the borrower's industry or geographic area. The best of businesses can fail in the worst of times.

Corporate Financing of Divisions

Divisions of larger companies face financing requirements similar in principle to those faced by smaller firms operating on their own. In the large company environment, the funding source is corporate headquarters, and the decision makers are the parent company's top executives. In general there's a competition between divisions for limited amounts of strategic financing available from the top. This is in fact similar to the competition among independent companies for financing from lenders and venture capitalists.

If division managers want to maintain their positions in charge and secure financing for their projects, they have to cast plans and proposals in terms that meet the strategic objectives of top corporate management.

The Effect of the Stock Market

Top corporate executives tend to focus on two business measures: Sustained growth and short-term profitability. It isn't difficult to understand why. Those are the criteria upon which Wall Street rewards stocks with high prices. Since stock price maximization is the first and foremost goal of CEOs and board chairmen, these yardsticks filter back to the business unit level as the underlying criteria for the evaluation of performance.

The overriding valuation formula in the stock market is rather simple. It's based on the price earnings ratio and earnings per share. The price of a company's stock, P, is given by:

$$P = EPS \times P/E.$$

In this formula, EPS is earnings per share, bottom line profit (earnings) divided by the number of shares of stock outstanding.

P/E, the price earnings ratio, is a number pinned on a company by the stock market that determines how much the market will pay for each dollar of earnings. It's simply the stock's price divided by the company's most recent EPS. Lately the average P/E is about 15 or 16, but more glamorous issues command ratios of 30 or more. Countless studies of stock market performance have shown that although P/Es depend on a number of things, their primary determinant is expected growth.

In other words, the strategic hot buttons for corporate funding flow from this equation. More profit means a higher EPS while more growth means a higher P/E, both of which mean a higher stock price.

This emphasis on sustained growth and short-term profit leads to the general rule that division funding proposals that in one way or another purport to enhance growth and/or profitability have the best chance of success. Further, the more credible and immediate the connection between the funding proposal and growth and profit, the better are its chances of success.

Private Sources of Money

Private financing sources called "angles" are occasionally available. They're typically wealthy individuals who might be interested in an unusual investment. Finding them just about always depends on a personal contact. Accountants, lawyers, and bankers sometimes know clients who are possibilities. This kind of financing is hard to find.

Make Use of the Way People Read Plans and Proposals

The people who evaluate funding proposals can't read all they receive carefully, because they get too many. They tend to scan through the pile quickly eliminating most after a brief reading. Those that show promise are put aside and examined more carefully later. It's important to write a plan or proposal so that it has a maximum chance of getting into this read-later category.

The quick scan tends to focus on three things: the executive summary describing the nature of the business; the financial projections which should detail how the funding will be used; and the background of the entrepreneur and the management team.

Keep in mind that the executive summary in a business plan has a very unique function. Generally executive summaries are designed to enable busy people to avoid reading the summarized document. In a business plan or funding proposal the intent is exactly the opposite. We want to interest the reader enough to get him or her to read the whole thing. Do that by putting the best pieces of information you've got about each major area in the summary, and downplaying problems and weak points. Write briefly about the important strategic issues that underlie the plan. Also summarize how the requested money will be used and how it will be paid back or how big an equity investor's return will be. Finally, summarize management's credentials if they're impressive and relevant.

Write the executive summary emphasizing "Three Ms," the Market, the Money and the Management and be sure it's easy to find the key points in the marketing, financial, and management sections, i.e., highlight revenue growth or loan payoff in the financial projections and key experience in the management section.

chapter 12

Break-Even Analysis

Introduction

Break-even is a well-known technique of financial analysis. It allows us to take apart a firm's cost and pricing structure to determine how much volume will be necessary to just survive. As the name implies, the break-even calculation shows just how much a business has to sell given its cost and pricing to create a wash at the bottom line. That is, no profit and no loss. A simple extension of the calculation shows how much more business will be necessary to achieve any desired level of profit or return on investment.

Break-even is an important element of strategic thinking because it forces us to develop an understanding of the cost/price structure of the business which can then be laid up against the reality of the long-term marketplace. The basic calculation is quite simple and straightforward. What is more subtle and strategically important is that break-even gives us an insight into the sensitivity of the business to pricing and cost and their interaction with market demand.

Gross strategic errors are very common in small business. We've all seen retail stores and restaurants that seem to go out of business overnight and product ideas that never get off the ground. Much of the pain and loss associated with those kinds of failures can be avoided with a combination of break-even analysis and strategic thinking. Big companies make that kind of error too, but a lot less frequently. The reason is that their analyses tend to be more competent along these lines.

Break-even planning does at least two things. It forces entrepreneurs, who often don't understand finances well, to come to a better understanding of the fiscal workings of their businesses. Going through the process makes them aware of just how important their next sale is and how many sales they need to stay in business. Additionally, since break-even shows the minimum sales level a business can live with, it can reveal whether or not a proposal is viable.

Fixed and Variable Costs

Break-even analysis begins with the separation of a business's costs and expenses into fixed and variable categories. The terms refer to whether the cost item changes in the short run with the level of production.

A variable cost increases or decreases in direct proportion with the level of a firm's output. The costs of material and labor used in a product are good examples. Fixed costs, on the other hand, are items that don't change with volume. The rent on buildings is an example. Fixed costs are often called overheads. Unfortunately, all costs don't fit neatly into one of the two categories. An example will illustrate these ideas.

EXAMPLE 12-1

Suppose Samantha Spade stays up late one night watching television and sees a classic Humphrey Bogart movie in which he played a mythical private detective also named Sam Spade who became famous in the 1940s by dashing around San Francisco in a trenchcoat. Intrigued by nostalgia and the coincidental name, Samantha, who we'll call Sam from now on, decides to start a business in which she makes classic, Bogey-style trenchcoats for both men and women under a "Sam Spade" label. She plans to sell the coats to clothing stores in her area.

Sam begins by renting some space and hiring a few employees to sew the material into trenchcoats. To keep the illustration simple, imagine the workers are part-timers who only get paid for the hours they work. Sam also buys some sewing machines and a delivery truck.

Suppose in the first month Sam makes and sells 100 trenchcoats, but in the second month she only does 50. The fixed/variable cost distinction hinges on which costs are the same in the first and second months and which are different.

The rent on Sam's work space clearly won't change from month one to month two, so that's a fixed cost. But the cost of materials and labor will be half as much in the second month, so those costs are variable. Other fixed costs might include the depreciation on the truck and the sewing machines and things like the phone bill. Other variable costs might be inbound freight on the material and gas to run the delivery truck. If Sam hires a full-time employee like a salesperson, an office worker, or a production supervisor, that person's wage will also be a fixed cost because he or she is paid the same amount each month regardless of the level of production.

Many costs aren't entirely fixed or variable. That is, they don't fit neatly into either category. Consider the delivery truck. Depreciation and insurance are clearly fixed costs, but gas and oil may be variable if fewer deliveries are made in slow months. However, if the truck makes an equal number of deliveries but each is smaller in slow months, gas and oil will be the same as in busy months, and should be thought of as a fixed cost.

Heat and light in the workshop can reflect the same kind of fixed/variable ambiguity. If the shop employs fewer people in slow months but is open all day every day, heat and light will be the same as in busy months, and can be thought of as fixed. But if in slow periods, Sam only opens half as many days as usual, heat and light will be less than in busy periods, and should be considered variable costs.

In spite of problems like these, break-even analysis requires that all costs be separated into either the fixed or variable categories. Sometimes a single cost element is arbitrarily separated into fixed and variable components for break-even purposes. For example, we might decide that heat and light are 60 percent fixed and 40 percent variable, and split the total accordingly. Although that's a somewhat arbitrary judgment, it probably reflects a more realistic assessment of the business's cost structure than just considering the entire item a fixed cost.

In what follows we'll assume that all costs and expenses are classified as either fixed or variable.

Break-Even Diagrams

The quickest and easiest way to understand break-even analysis is through a graphic representation (figure 12.1). Start with plots of fixed and variable cost versus the firm's sales volume. Plotting cost along the vertical axis and sales along the horizontal axis results in the following:

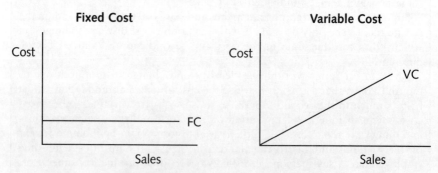

Figure 12.1 Fixed and Variable Costs

Fixed cost is constant as sales increase, while variable cost increases proportionately with sales along a straight upsloping line.

The two diagrams – fixed cost and variable cost – are combined by

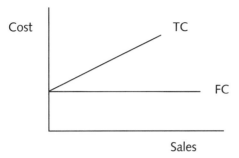

Figure 12.2   Total Cost

plotting variable cost on top of fixed cost. The resulting line represents total cost (figure 12.2), the sum of fixed and variable elements.

Figure 12.2 reflects the business's cost structure, the relationship between fixed and variable cost as volume changes. Next, revenue is introduced as an upsloping line through the origin. When the horizontal axis is sales dollars (rather than units), revenue appears as a 45° line. The traditional break-even diagram is shown in figure 12.3.

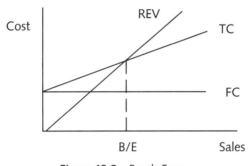

Figure 12.3   Break-Even

Break-even is the point at which revenue equals total cost. On figure 12.3 it's the point at which the Total Cost line and the Revenue line intersect. The break-even sales volume is directly below that point on the horizontal axis.

Break-Even Calculations

The graphic approach is easy to understand, but is difficult to apply to a real situation. In practice it's better to figure out the break-even volume arithmetically.

The Concept of Contribution

Whenever a sale is made, some variable cost is incurred. Generally the selling price is substantially above variable cost. The amount by which the selling price exceeds variable cost is called the contribution made by the sale.

EXAMPLE 12-1 – CONTINUED

Suppose Sam Spade's trenchcoat factory can make a coat for $70 in labor and material, and that these are her only variable costs. Assume also that she can sell the trenchcoat to a retail store for $100. Then the contribution on that sale is $30. The term contribution means that the sale contributes $30 toward Sam's profit and fixed cost (overhead).[1]

Contribution is often expressed as a percentage of sales. In Sam Spade's case the contribution of $30 is 30 percent of the $100 sale. Expressed as a percentage, the figure is called the contribution margin. If a business sells a number of products at different prices and contribution margins, an average value can be used for the percentage contribution margin in break-even computations.

The Break-Even Calculation

The break-even calculation is really quite simple. It just asks how many sales have to be made each month to contribute enough money to cover all of the firm's fixed costs.

EXAMPLE 12-1 – CONTINUED

Assume Sam Spade's fixed costs are $1,800 per month. If each unit sold contributes $30, she has to sell 600 units ($1,800/$30) to break even. Since each unit sells for $100, break-even sales in dollar terms are $6,000 ($100 × 60).

---

[1] Sam's wholesale price to the retailer of $100 implies the coats would probably sell to customers for somewhere between $150 and $200.

But there's an easier way to get to the same result. Just take the total fixed cost and divide it by the contribution margin expressed in decimal form:

$$\$1,800 / 0.30 = \$6,000.$$

This calculation essentially says: how many dollars that contribute 30 cents each does it take to make $1,800?

Extending Break-Even to Include Profit and Return on Investment (ROI)

It's a simple matter to extend the break-even technique to calculate the level of sales required to achieve a given level of profitability or Return on Investment (ROI). We just treat a profit requirement as an additional fixed cost and go through the calculation exactly as before.

EXAMPLE 12-1 – CONTINUED AGAIN

Suppose Sam Spade invested a total of $25,000 on her delivery truck, her sewing machines, and anything else she needed to set up her trenchcoat business. Further suppose she wants to earn at least a 12 percent return on those invested funds (ROI). What level of sales is required to achieve that goal?

First we'll assume that Sam is in the 33 percent tax bracket including federal and state taxes. ROI goals are usually stated in after-tax terms, so we have to figure out what pre-tax return will result in a 12 percent after tax return. Since a 33 percent tax rate implies that the taxpayer gets to keep 67 percent of each dollar of income, we're asking what return times 0.67 equals 12 percent. We get this by simply dividing 12 percent by 0.67.

$$12\% / 0.67 = 18\%$$

This says that Sam must have a pre-tax profit that is 18 percent of her investment of $25,000.

$$\$25,000 \times 0.18 = \$4,500.$$

However, that is an annual requirement. The additional monthly profit required is one twelfth of that or $375.

Sam's fixed costs are $1,800 per month. Adding the required profit gives $2,175. Her contribution margin is still 30 percent, so the volume required to make the goal is:

$$\$2,175 / 0.3 = \$7,250.$$

In other words, to make her target return, Sam must sell at least $7,250 a month or $87,000 per year. Since each trenchcoat sells for $100, she'll have to make and sell about 870 per year to consider herself a success.

Using Break-Even Strategically – A Retail Location

Entrepreneurs frequently make dramatic mistakes in selecting retail locations. The problem is that people find it very difficult to tell whether or not the traffic at a site will support a particular kind of business. Break-even analysis can help to answer the question.

In retailing, fixed costs typically include rent,[2] utilities, property taxes, depreciation, and the salaries of salespeople and management (including a reasonable salary for the entrepreneur himself if he intends to work there). A retailer's variable costs generally include the wholesale cost of goods and a small amount of inbound freight. If salespeople are paid commissions, those are also variable costs.

Retail pricing is commonly based on a markup over wholesale (variable) cost. A 100 percent markup means price is two times cost; or conversely, that cost is 50 percent of list price. A 50 percent markup means price is one and one half times cost, so cost is two thirds or 67 percent of list price.

A complicating factor is that retailers don't sell everything at list price. In fact, some sell most of their goods at discounts. Hence the effective relationship between price and variable cost is somewhat different from the list relationship.

EXAMPLE 12-2

Harvey Grimes is going to open a clothing store. He plans to price his merchandise at a 150 percent markup. That is, he'll set his list price at 2.5

---

[2] Retail rents can be a little tricky with respect to fixed and variable analysis. Most retail sites are let on percentage leases which charge a base rent plus a percentage of the tenant's revenue over some annual minimum. For example, a landlord might charge $1,000 per month plus 5 percent of annual revenues over $300,000. Hence rent always has a fixed component of $1,000 per month, but when sales exceed $300,000 we have to add 5 percent to variable costs. We'll ignore this complication for the sake of keeping our example simple.

times his wholesale cost. At that markup, a sale at list price has a cost of (1/ 2.5 =) 40 percent of revenue. Harry recognizes, however, that freight and discounting will increase his cost as a percentage of sales somewhat. On the average, he thinks cost will be about 45 percent of sales, which works out to an effective markup of 122 percent (1/.45 = 2.22).

That is, for every dollar of sales, Harvey will pay the wholesaler 45 cents, and keep a 55 cent contribution to profit and overhead. Equivalently, his variable cost is 45 percent of sales and his contribution margin is 55 percent.

Harry has estimated his store's total overhead, or fixed cost, at $5,000 a month in a location that he likes a lot. He's concerned, however, about the traffic past the spot. He knows that most of his business will come from shoppers walking by, but doesn't have anything but a vague feel for how heavy the traffic has to be to reasonably ensure a viable business. Sites with more traffic tend to be more expensive.

What analysis will help Harry with his location decision?

Solution: We'll begin by finding Harry's break-even volume. If 55 cents of every sales dollar is a contribution to overhead, how many of those dollars are needed to just cover the $5,000? In other words, how many "55 cent dollars" are there in $5,000? To get the answer simply divide $5,000 by .55:

$$\$5000 \,/\, .55 = \$9,090.91.$$

The store has to sell $9,090.91 to just break-even. This won't give Harry any profit or a return on his investment but he won't be losing any money either. We'll round the number to $9,100 for convenience.

Required Traffic Count from Break-Even Volume

Now let's work backwards to traffic count. Suppose that it's known that the average sale in a store of this kind is $30. That means that in order to break even, the business must make at least ($9,100 / $30 =) 303 sales transactions during the month. Let's suppose experience tells Harry that roughly one walk-in customer out of four buys something. That means he has to have (303 × 4 =) 1,212 walk-ins a month. Next suppose Harry observes other stores and notices that about one person in twenty walking by comes in. That implies he needs somewhere in the neighborhood of (1,212 × 20 =) 24,240 walk-bys a month. If the store is open seven days a week, that means the location must provide at least (24,240 / 30 =) 808 walk-bys in an average day to survive. To make a profit will take more.

How does Harry tell if the location he has in mind will provide that kind of traffic? Obviously, by having someone stand outside and count for a few days.

Admittedly the analysis is rough, but suppose Harry's count shows only 400 people walking by a day. That would imply his business doesn't have much of a chance at that location, and that he should look elsewhere.

Sensitivity Analysis

It's important to notice how break-even gives us insights into the workings of a business and its sensitivity to changes in our assumptions about the way it will operate. For example, someone might challenge Harry's analysis by saying that the assumption of a 55 percent contribution margin is too high. She might claim that 55 percent doesn't adequately reflect discounting, so an average contribution margin of 40 percent or 50 percent is more realistic. It's easy to work through the numbers and see what the traffic implication of the lower margin assumption is.

If Harry had constructed his argument in less precise terms by saying, for example, that traffic was "good" or "high," there would be no way to effectively refute the objection.

chapter 13

Strategies for Service Businesses

Introduction

Operating businesses which primarily provide services can involve managing a number of difficult, essentially administrative issues that don't come up in product-oriented operations. Pricing is a good example. In the last chapter we discussed a retail situation in which the rationale behind price was just a markup on wholesale cost. Pricing a service is a far more complicated issue. For example, consider that the services of an automobile mechanic cost most of us $50 or $60 an hour, but the mechanic gets only about $15. Does that mean the garage owner is marking up cost by $300%? If so, isn't that excessive, a ripoff? By retailing standards it seems so, but we'll see shortly that it probably isn't unfair.

Administrative issues like this may seem less than strategic. Pricing is a good example, is it generally a strategic matter? Certainly a retail price reduction as in a sales promotion is not a strategic move. It's usually nothing more than a short-run tactical response to market conditions. It's important, however, to distinguish this kind of short-term pricing action from the more fundamental issue of the level of a business's prices. That gets at whether or not a firm can survive at a competitive price in the market. That's a strategic issue in that it goes to the heart of the business's operation and how well the entrepreneur understands its nature.

It's very common for service businesses to doom themselves to failure at the outset by under-pricing what they have to offer or by over-pricing to the point of not being competitive. This usually happens because the entrepreneurs haven't properly considered what the price of an hour of service has to cover. This very fundamental pricing question is certainly a strategic issue.

Actually, a number of "administrative" issues in small business can be considered strategic in the sense that they're capable of sinking the business. The overwhelming majority of small business failures aren't due to the owners' not knowing how to do whatever they're in business to provide (e.g., a restaurateur not knowing how to cook). Most are due to an inability to carry out some seemingly administrative function like pricing or financing or managing inventory. Whether this makes these things strategic or not is less important than understanding that they're critical factors in running the business.

In this chapter we'll concentrate on learning how to price a service offering. That's a sticky problem that gets a lot of people in trouble whether you call it strategy or tactics.

Defining a Service Business

In a service business, the customer buys personal services from the seller. That's pretty obvious. The problem is that in most service businesses there's a good deal of product sold too. Auto repair is a good example. When you get your car fixed you pay for parts, but the shop is primarily in business to sell labor. Contrast that with a restaurant. There you're buying a product, the food, even though preparation and table service are a large part of what you're paying for. Clearly the distinction is a matter of degree, since most services provide some product and many products are delivered with some labor. In this chapter, we're concerned with businesses in which the emphasis is on the labor side. These include:

Maintenance and Repair
Consulting
Health Care
Janitorial and Cleaning
Some construction businesses
    Plumbing
    Electrician
Professional business services
    Lawyer
    Accountant

Pricing a Service

Incorrect pricing is a common cause of failure in service-oriented businesses because most entrepreneurs aren't familiar with the calculations needed to price services correctly. Because of their complexity, it's important to document pricing calculation in some detail.

Service rates seem high to most people. An auto mechanic's labor is charged at $40 to $60 an hour, while repair time on a large computer is generally over $100 an hour. Contract computer programers bill at more than $150 an hour. This seems a little outrageous considering that the repair person probably makes only from $25,000 to $35,000 per year, which is between $12 and $17 an hour, and programers rarely make over $60,000, which is about $30 an hour.

To understand all this we'll go through a pricing calculation for a typical service. Our example will concern a maintenance/repair service on a technically complex piece of equipment that's done at the customer's site.

Billable Hours

Pricing begins with an estimate of billable hours, the total number of hours in a year that an average service person will spend working on equipment.

Billable hours starts with the total number of working hours available in a year not counting overtime. That's usually 2080 hours, 40 hours a week, times 52 weeks. That figure is then reduced by several factors about which we'll make the following assumptions.

We'll assume employees get two weeks of vacation each year, for 80 hours, and five sick days for 40 hours. Ten paid holidays account for another 80 hours. Then we'll recognize that service workers do some paperwork, and allow three hours in each of the remaining 47 weeks for that, another 141 hours.

Technical service people generally need periodic training to stay current. Two weeks per year is a fair estimate of the time spent training at the manufacturer's factory. That takes out 80 more hours.

Next we reduce the remaining hours by an efficiency factor that allows for breaks, going to the rest room and anything else that isn't strictly work. Fifteen percent is a reasonable efficiency factor.

Finally, since we're assuming the service is performed at customer sites, we'll assume the technician travels about one hour for every three spent working on equipment. That reduces the time available by one fourth. We'll assume there isn't any dead time spent sitting around waiting for calls.

Summarizing, we have the following:

Total Annually Available Hours			2,080
Less:	Vacation	80	
	Sick	40	
	Holidays	80	
	Paperwork	141	
	Training	80	421
Net Available Hours			1,659
	Efficiency		× 85
Net Working Hours			1,410
	Travel factor		× 75
Annual Billable Hours			1,058

Cost of Service

Next we have to consider cost assuming it has to be covered entirely by the price of the billable hours we've just calculated. For simplicity, we'll assume that service is our only business, i.e., any parts sold are at prices that just cover their own cost. We'll also assume that ten technicians work out of a single office staffed by one manager, one inventory control person and one clerical/dispatch person.

Assume the technicians earn $30,000 a year, the manager makes $50,000 and the inventory and clerical people make $18,000 each. All wages are accompanied by a benefits burden of 30 percent. Total annual payroll expense is then:

Ten technicians @ $30,000	$300,000
Two office workers	60,000
Manager	50,000
	$410,000
Benefits @ 20%	123,000
Total	$533,000

Also make assumptions about office expenses as follows:

Rent	$30,000	per year
Utilities	7,000	"
Dispatch phone	12,000	"
Supplies	5,000	"
Depreciation	2,000	"
	$56,000	per year

Next assume the cost of technical training is about $2,500 per person week including travel and lodging. For ten technicians at two weeks a year that's $50,000.

Then consider travel expenses. Assume each technician drives about 25,000 miles a year in a truck that costs $20,000. Assume the trucks are depreciated over four years on a straight line basis. Further assume that operating a truck costs about $.20 a mile for gas, oil, tires, repairs, and insurance. That's $5,000 per year. In addition, each truck depreciates by another $5,000 per year, so the total expense is $10,000 per year for each of ten trucks. Total vehicle cost is then $100,000.

Summarizing costs we have:

Salaries and wages	$533,000
Office	56,000
Training	50,000
Vehicles	100,000
Total Cost	$739,000

Calculating the Rate per Hour

Each technician has 1,058 billable hours, so the ten-person organization in total can bill 10,580 hours. Therefore, the cost per hour of providing service is:

$$\$739,000 / 10,580 \text{ hours} = \$69.85 \text{ per hour}$$

If the firm's financial goal is a pre-tax profit of 20 percent, gross that figure up by dividing by 75 percent (1–25 percent)

$$\$69.85 / .75 = \$93.13$$

This figure is the rate at which customers will be billed. Notice that the service technician's wage is only $14.42 per hour ($30,000 / 2080 hours), but the business isn't making an excessive profit.

Modifying the Rate for Different Businesses

These calculations can be modified to reflect different businesses. If the customer comes to the service provider there's no travel or vehicle cost. If employees drive their own cars, the firm just pays a mileage rate. In some businesses, the company doesn't have to pay for travel. For example the owner of a maid service just tells his or her employees where to show up. If employees are part-timers the company may not have to provide benefits, vacations, or holidays.

Some businesses, however, have additional cost and time elements. If expensive equipment is needed there's more depreciation than just the trucks in our example. In consulting, a good deal of non-billable time has to be set aside for marketing and business development. Advertising expense has to be added in a majority of small businesses.

Another important addition may be a factor for dead time spent waiting for calls. This can be especially important in a startup where the firm initially doesn't have enough business to keep its workers fully busy. The billing rate we've just calculated won't cover cost and profit if the technicians aren't working all the time. Unfortunately, in that situation raising the rate too much can make it uncompetitive compared to established firms who are able to fully utilize their workers.

Comparing the Calculated Rate with Competitors

The calculated rate always has to be compared with whatever the competition is charging. If rivals are charging a lot less the business may not be viable, especially if competitors are more efficient. Other reasons include the following: A competitor may be pricing service at a loss to attract other business. A rival may be slowly going out of business, but can disrupt the market until it's gone. The market may be over-populated with sellers resulting in intense price competition. Think twice about entering such a business.

Other Factors to Consider

The following issues may also have to be considered depending on the business.

Service on Site or at a Service Center

In some cases it makes sense for customers to come to a service center while in others the provider travels to the customer. The difference generally hinges on the moveability of whatever is being serviced. Automobiles and people (health) are serviced at central locations. Houses are serviced where they stand. The distinction has a lot to do with how the servicing organization is set up and the magnitude of its costs. Remember when doctors made house calls?

Your Market Area

A basic strategic issue in service is the size of the business's market area. For most firms that's dictated by the distance a car can drive in a reasonable time. To plan for the issue, draw a circle on a map of that radius, and decide whether there are enough customers within it to support the business. Further consider how many technicians are likely to be required to service the area.

Health-care services are related to the population within the circle and to the average age of people in that population. Equipment-related services depend on how much equipment is in the area and how often it fails or needs to be maintained. Adequate strategic thinking obviously demands that there be enough need within the service area to support the business.

Time and Materials vs. Contract

With a service contract the provider supplies maintenance and fixes anything that goes wrong with equipment over some period for a set fee. Extended warranties on consumer products are essentially service contracts. Similarly, an HMO is a service contract for health care. In service contracts the customer pays a modest amount whether service is needed or not, and the provider supplies as much service as she needs. The arrangement is very much like an insurance policy. It transfers the financial risk of equipment failure from the customer to the provider.

Service without a contract is generally available as needed. In industrial settings it's often called a time and materials arrangement, because that's what the customer pays for. Providers like service contracts better than time and materials arrangements because the contracts stabilize income. They also provide for periodic maintenance which is often ignored when customers aren't on a program.

Getting There Quickly

The time it takes to get to the broken equipment is more important in some businesses than in others. Response time is obviously important in things like emergency health-care services, but it can also be critical in areas like computer repair. When a business computer breaks down, in some cases the whole company can stop. Then the time it takes for the repair person to arrive is a serious matter.

The rapid response problem for service providers is that guaranteeing a quick arrival requires maintaining extra staff. That implies people are idle some of the time which costs money. The classic example is a fire station. In order to have fire fighters available all the time, they have to spend a lot of time sitting around the fire house. The commercial approach is a separate contract for customers who need fast service and are willing to pay extra for it.

chapter 14

Location Analysis

People in commercial real estate often say "The three most important factors in business success are location, location, and location." The strategic question, of course is whether this conventional wisdom is true for a particular business.

While location is critical to some businesses, it's less important to others. A good location generally means one that's easy to access and that has high traffic. However, the strategic analysis involves the fact that better locations cost more money, so a business owner has to balance a location's quality against its cost to arrive at a cost-effective decision.

In many small businesses, especially retail firms, location can be the single most important strategic decision made by an entrepreneur. Hence this short chapter is devoted to the art of selecting a location.

A Science or an Art?

There's a tendency to talk about location analysis as if it was an exact science. People speak as if there was some secret formula that once applied guarantees selection of the perfect spot for a business. There's actually no such formula. Location analysis is a matter of sifting and organizing a lot of information and then making an informed decision. In the end it's a personal judgement. Experience helps, of course, and commercial real estate professionals tend to have insights developed over the years that beginners lack. In what follows we'll point out a number of things that should be considered and weighed carefully in the decision.

The Dimensions of Location

The location of a small business has two separate dimensions. The first is a consideration of community. It gets at the question of whether the people and businesses in a community have a demand for the product or service our business offers. For example, you wouldn't want to put a sophisticated designer clothing store in a low-income, rural, or blue-collar community.

The second issue involves selecting a location within the chosen community. Most businesses strive to select locations that maximize their attractiveness to customers within limits dictated by cost. That selection is related to the nature of the product or service being offered.

Not all businesses are location-sensitive. It isn't too important, for example, for service providers that go to their customers. A plumber is a good example. People don't care where his office is because they don't go there. They just need to know there's a plumber in the area who will come when they call. The same is true for a great many service businesses. Employment agencies, maid services, etc. don't depend on a specific location within a town. They do, however, have to be sensitive to the community's overall demand for their product or service.

Choosing a Community

A successful choice of community involves evaluating population, demographics, and competition. The first step is determining if enough potential customers are located in an area the business can reasonably expect to service.

First, decide how far people will drive to get the kind of thing the business sells. For fast food that might be a mile or two, for household goods and decorations it might be ten or fifteen miles. This is the business's market radius.

Next, look at potential sites and draw circles around them of that radius on a map. Then examine the population within each circle for potential customers.

This involves developing a customer profile for the business. A profile is a listing of the important characteristics of a buying unit, usually a household. These include age, family size, income, etc. A typical profile might look something like this:

Age	35–50
Family size	3–5
Income	$50–$100,000
Education	College graduate
Children's age	5–15

Next get some idea as to whether the people in an area match the profile. Demographic information for census tracts is available in larger public libraries. The town hall or county seat may have some information as well. A good sense can also be gotten by just driving around on a sunny Sunday afternoon.

However, be careful of subtle traps. Not everything shows up in the profiles. For example, there are important market differences between a university town and one supported by an auto assembly plant even though ages, family sizes and incomes might be similar. A fast-food restaurant might do well in either, but what about an art gallery, a bicycle shop or a health-food store? These would probably do better in the college town. On the other hand, an auto parts store, a motorcycle shop or a body-builder's gym would probably do better in the blue-collar environment.

Competition also has to be considered. It's important to find out how many similar businesses are already there. A town may be able to support several fast-food restaurants, but two health-food stores may kill each other.

Profiles, competition, and demographics are important to the community decision but so is walking around with your eyes open.

Choosing a Site Within a Community

The second location question involves choosing a site within a community. A major preliminary issue here is the importance of location to the customer. If customers don't come to the business often or ever, its exact location probably isn't important. Service businesses usually fit that description. They use advertising to reach customers and communicate on the telephone, then the service is brought to the customer's home or place of business. Conversely, location is critically important to most retail businesses.

Retail location revolves around walk-by and/or drive-by traffic. Traffic is the reason for the success of many stores in modern shopping malls. The mall draws customer traffic based on its large anchor stores as well as the number of smaller shops. Small stores that would fail in most outside locations can do well in malls because of the walk-by traffic. People don't go to the mall intending to visit the small store, but they stop in as they walk past.

To be effective a location has to be both visible and accessible. If a business is visible because it's located on a road with high automobile traffic, but it's difficult for people to get off the road and into the store, the traffic won't do much good. The speed of drive-by traffic is also important. Being visible from cars doing 65 mph isn't nearly as good as being visible from cars doing 20 mph.

Two issues are important in evaluating traffic, quantity and quality. Quantity is a simple matter of numbers, i.e., how many people go by in a day. That can be measured by standing in front of a location and counting for a few days. It's important to count on different days of the week. Weekdays are likely to be different from weekends. Hiring a high school or college student is a good way to get counting done if the person is reliable.

Quality is a more difficult issue related to whether passers by are potential customers at the time they're passing or at all. Here's a real-life example.

EXAMPLE 14-1

Bill Watkins opened a store carrying decorating accessories in a suburban strip center. He located between three established businesses: an upscale restaurant, a lady's health studio, and a large supermarket. He thought success was very likely because of the traffic going in and out of those businesses. He reasoned that women do most home-decorating, that they would be going in and out of the spa and the supermarket regularly, and would stop into his store.

Bill got a real shock when he found that women going to the spa tended to change into exercise clothes at home, drive to the spa, park, and run almost head-down from their cars to the studio. They returned the same way. They weren't about to go shopping in their leotards!

Supermarket shoppers behaved similarly. A woman on her way to the grocery store is a woman with a mission! Once she's parked in the supermarket's lot, she tends to go directly into the store and then directly home. There's no time to shop for decorations while the ice cream's melting.

The point is that traffic made up of people who aren't potential customers is low-quality and doesn't count. Walk-in customers for an art gallery need to come from people who are leisurely cruising around if they're not out shopping for decorating items. That's why there are so many art galleries in resort communities. Assessing the quality of traffic is a tough judgmental call.

Bankers and Realtors

Entrepreneurs in search of sites should consult a banker and a commercial realtor in the community.

Bank loan officers have insights into the kinds of businesses that work in different locations developed from experience in lending to small firms, some of which do well and some of which don't. Bankers tend to catalogue the reasons for success and failure which include location.

Realtors show what's currently available in a community, and may be knowledgeable about what kind of business is likely to work where if they're experienced in the commercial market. However, it's important to keep in mind that realtors earn their livings on commissions. They want to sell or lease the property that makes them the most money. That's generally their own listing.

For example, suppose an entrepreneur contacts a real estate agent to find a site for her business. Also suppose two viable sites are listed, one by that agent and another by someone else. The agent can sell either property, but gets twice the commission for moving her own listing. Any agent is likely to push her own listing harder, but it wouldn't be unusual for one to neglect showing the other agent's listing entirely. Agents also commonly offer "soft advice" to get business. They'll rarely lie outright about a property's merits, but may give the impression of great expertise when saying it would be a good site for a business.

In any event, be sure to use a commercial realtor rather than someone in residential sales. A realtor that sells houses is likely to know little or nothing about business property, but may take the assignment anyway to earn the commission.

chapter 15

Diversification

Entrepreneurs already running businesses sometimes become interested in expanding either into other operations of the same type or altogether different enterprises. When one business gets involved in another, the process is called diversification. The firm is diversifying its interests by participating in more than one enterprise. The concept is similar to an investor diversifying a stock portfolio. The idea gets an enormous amount of attention in the large company context, where most of the activity occurs in a field known as mergers and acquisitions. When one company merges with or acquires another, it is diversifying its interests. Diversification also occurs when a firm, large or small, starts a new venture from scratch.

A branch of strategy called Corporate Strategy deals with multiple business units operating under one ownership. Corporate strategy is divided into two sub-areas which treat (1) the diversification process and (2) managing the diversified enterprise thereafter.

Diversification has turned out to be a risky proposition. The track record isn't good in either large or small companies. Most large firm mergers don't work out well frequently resulting in poor performance and lost value. Many are taken apart a few years after they're put together. In the small company context taking on new businesses or opening branches often results in over-extended resources and financial distress.

The potential benefit of diversification, of course, is rapid growth and ultimately ownership of a larger and more profitable organization. That's a tempting reward for which many people are willing to take considerable risks.

Defining Small Business Diversification

In a large company, diversification means opening or acquiring a new business in another field. (Acquiring a competitor is loosely considered diversification too.) On the other hand, expanding a business isn't diversification. For example, an East Coast firm isn't diversifying if it builds a plant on the West Coast.

In small business our definition needs to be a little different. Clearly if a successful restaurateur opens a car dealership, that's diversification. But what if he or she opens another restaurant, is that diversification or expansion? The distinction is somewhat arbitrary, but we'll choose to call it diversification. Our reason is that for a small firm such a move contains a large part of the risk associated with the more traditional definition that also requires moving into another field.

How Diversification is Accomplished

There are two ways to get into another field: Either by starting an operation in a targeted industry or acquiring a firm already in it. The same is true for a small business diversification that's an expansion in one line of business. A new branch can be opened, or a competitor can be acquired.

Acquiring Another Company

Acquisition has two big advantages. First, it's fast. An acquired firm continues in business, so the acquirer is a player in the targeted industry immediately. When starting from scratch, it takes years before an entrant is strong enough to be noticed.

Second, acquisition can hurdle obstacles. This idea refers to the fact that participating in most industries requires certain skills and assets, access to technology, relationships with customers and suppliers, and connections with people in key positions. These requirements are called *barriers to entry* in that a firm without them can't get into the business. A start-up may not be able to get over all the barriers. However, acquiring a firm that's already in the industry neatly circumvents most of them.

The major disadvantage of acquisition, on the other hand, is cost. Operating companies are generally sold for a great deal more than the cost of their assets. So acquiring a going concern in a field generally costs more than starting a new operation from scratch.

Start-up

Alternatively, a diversifying company can start a new venture in a targeted industry. That's generally slow and subject to the barriers to entry problem discussed in the last section. That makes success a bigger risk too, because no one knows for sure whether the diversifier will have the things it takes to succeed in the new business.

Start-up usually works best when the new business is in the same industry as the core business or in something very similar. Then the diversifying company is likely to have the resources it needs. For example, successful restaurants rarely acquire other restaurants, they start copies of what worked for them elsewhere.

The big advantage of starting from scratch is that it's usually a good deal cheaper than acquiring someone else.

In summary, starting from scratch is cheaper, but probably takes a lot longer and has a higher chance of failure than acquiring an existing company.

When and Why Firms Diversify

Before getting into the reasons that should be behind a well thought-out diversification, we'll review the pros and cons of not diversifying in order to have a point of comparison.

Advantages and Disadvantages of a Single Line of Business

Doing just one thing in one place has a straightforward appeal. The management team can put all of its resources and attention into that one thing and become very good at it. The firm builds competences in the skills and abilities that are important to the business, develops connections with customers and suppliers, and establishes a long-term reputation for commitment and attention to detail. All this enhances the probability of sustained success.

The disadvantage is equally straightforward. All of the business's proverbial eggs are in one basket. If anything goes wrong with that one line of endeavor, whether it's management's fault or not, everything can be lost. Imagine, for example, an independent drug store which has been successful in a neighborhood for many years. Then suppose a large chain opens a store nearby. That generally signals the end of the road for the independent. The owners may be in trouble if that's their only business and source of income.

Conditions in the Core Business

We'll refer to an existing business, the one we're diversifying away from, as the core business. This is an important idea. We'll see that the core business plays an important role in diversified organizations.

It is crucially important to consider the condition of the core business before getting into diversification issues. That's because we generally depend on the core to be a platform which supports the new enterprise for some time.

That support comes in a number of ways. The core may provide cash to purchase or start up another enterprise or to fund early operations while the new business isn't pulling its own weight. Depending on the nature of the two operations, the core may also provide technical knowledge and support, entrance into distribution channels, contacts among suppliers, and a reputation in the customer base. Generally the core also has to support the entrepreneurs and their families until the new operations start making money.

It's also important to keep in mind that the core is usually a lot less risky than a new operation. Hence it's a source of stability for the combined enterprise.

Problems in the Core

All this is important because people frequently consider diversification as a way to escape a core business that isn't doing well. That's not a good reason to diversify unless the plan is to exit the core business very soon.

As a general rule, if the core is having trouble, but is a viable business in a reasonably attractive industry, it's better and safer for the owners to put their energy and resources into improving the core than into trying to find something new.

Prosperity in the Core

There are also times when the core business is doing well, but it's still not a good idea to diversify. If the core contains significant growth and profit opportunities, energy is generally better expended to exploit them than in attacking something new. This usually occurs if the core business is in a rapidly growing industry or if it's in a weak market position relative to its rivals.

The Right Conditions

Diversification is generally a very good idea if the core business is in a strong position in a stable, slow-growth market. That generally means it's making a good profit and is generating cash. Cash is available because slow growth implies it doesn't have to reinvest its earnings to provide assets to support its own expansion. Such a business more or less runs itself, freeing its owners to deal with diversification and also provides cash to work with.

Good Reasons for Diversification

There are basically only three valid reasons to diversify a small business: safety, synergy, and a bargain.

Safety The safety rationale is related to the idea of having all of one's eggs in one basket that we discussed earlier as a disadvantage of single line of business firms. If something goes wrong with that line of business, the enterprise is out of luck, so it's better to spread activities around.

There's also a stability dimension to the argument. Many businesses are cyclical and go through good and bad periods. Having more than one kind of operation tends to flatten out the peaks and troughs in earnings.[1]

Synergy The synergy argument says that under certain conditions two or more companies operating under one ownership may perform better collectively than the sum of their performances separately owned. In essence, synergy says that under certain conditions two plus two can equal five.

The most significant reason for synergies is that some activities and costs can be shared. For example, suppose the salesforces of two similar but different companies call on the same customers. If the firms combine, one salesperson can sell both products on a single call, and the firm needs a much smaller sales group than the sum of the two before combining.

Quantity discounts are another good synergistic effect. If two firms buy from the same supplier, they can place larger orders and negotiate better deals.

The synergy argument means one company can acquire another at a fair price that reflects its full value standing alone and still get a bargain. The bargain comes from the fact that both the acquired and acquiring companies can experience improvements as a result of working together.

A Bargain It's axiomatic that a diversification can pay off if an acquisition is made at a bargain price. That means that for some reason a firm is offered well below its true value. That happens but not often. When it does, an acquirer still needs to be careful because a bargain won't make a venture work if the acquiring entrepreneur has no interest in or knowledge of the business.

A Bad Reason for Diversification – Ego and Empire

A lot of diversification activity can't be justified by safety or synergy or a bargain. People simply seem to want to run larger organizations even if it doesn't seem likely they'll make any more money doing so. It often seems pretty likely they'll make less. Nevertheless people get into ill-advised expansions and diversifications all the time. It happens in big as well as small companies. Commentators speculate that there's an ego phenomenon but that can't be proven.

Basically, entrepreneurs and CEOs are too willing to believe outrageously favorable assumptions about the costs and benefits of moves that may contribute to their empires. That leads to paying too much to get into something new.

---

[1] The safety/stability argument can't be applied as convincingly to large companies. They tend to be owned by stockholders who are just investors. If a stockholder is unhappy with a firm's safety or stability, he can diversify by selling some of its stock and buying another company's. Hence there's no financial reason for management to diversify for the benefit of shareholders.

Obviously, we can't caution against this kind of behavior too strongly. Diversification is always risky, and should be evaluated carefully and with a very critical eye.

Types of Diversification

Strategically, diversifications are classified as either related or unrelated.[2] The difference is conceptually very simple. In a related diversification, there's some meaningful connection between the diversifying company and the new firm (which may be acquired or started) or its business. In unrelated diversification there's no connection whatsoever. Unrelated diversification is also called conglomerate diversification, but that term is usually used in the context of large firms.

Related Diversification and Strategic Fit

The advantage of related diversification is based on the concept of strategic fit. To say that two firms enjoy a strategic fit means that when combined under one ownership there's a basis somewhere in their operations for a synergistic benefit. Synergies usually involve some kind of cost saving. Here's an example:

EXAMPLE 15-1

Toledo Inc. is a moderate-sized firm that makes lawn mowers. Its factory runs in the fall and winter so the product is available for sale in the spring and summer when the factory is essentially idle. Across town the Apex Corporation makes snowblowers. Its factory produces in the spring and summer so the product can be sold in the fall and winter when its factory does contract sheet-metal work because it doesn't have enough of its own work to keep busy.

The skills and technology necessary to make lawn mowers and snowblowers are very similar. Both require fabricating sheet-metal parts with small gasoline engines to deliver power to a rotating working unit controlled by a walk-behind operator.

Toledo and Apex have a strategic fit opportunity. If the firms combine they can operate out of a single factory that runs year round producing lawnmowers in the winter and snowblowers in the summer. The combined company can

---

[2] Thompson and Strickland, *Strategic Management*, pp. 218–30.

then close one factory completely and save the associated overhead expenses. Further, the unused factory can be sold to reduce the assets on the combined firm's books.

These actions mean the combined company will be able to do the same things the two separate firms could do, but with fewer expenses and assets. This will make the combined operation more profitable and give it a higher return on invested capital than the financial results of the separate firms added together could have achieved. This is the 2 + 2 = 5 idea of synergy.

Notice that the term strategic fit appears appropriate because of the nature of the benefit. Eliminating a factory is a long-term move dealing with permanent resources. It's the kind of thing we've been calling strategic all along.

Can you think of any other strategic fit benefits that might be available in a merger of Toledo and Apex?[3]

Sometimes the advantage of strategic fit isn't a cost saving but a free or low cost benefit.

EXAMPLE 15-2

Charlie Hogan lives in rural Vermont and has made his own maple syrup since boyhood. Everyone who's tried it agrees it's better than anything else available. Five years ago Charlie formed Vermont Maple Inc to manfacture and market his syrup. He struggled for years but never could get his product accepted into the grocery distribution system anywhere but in a few local stores that he visited personally.

A year ago Charlie was approached by Wilson's Inc., a nationally-known manufacture of frozen waffles. They bought Charlie out, keeping him on to run production for which he'll get a salary and a share of the syrup product's profits. Putting Wilson's name on Vermont Maple gave it immediate access to major supermarket chains and national brand recognition among consumers. Sales have been great ever since even though Wilson doesn't advertise the syrup separately.

The synergy here was combining Charlie's quality product with Wilson's access to distribution, advertising clout, and name recognition.

---

[3] Marketing – The two firms probably sell to the same retailers who in turn sell lawn mowers in the summer and snowblowers in the winter. A salesforce that sells winter and summer and is smaller than the sum of the two may be possible. Is there any potential benefit in advertising and promotion?

Purchasing – Higher volumes of engines and sheet-metal may mean larger quantity discounts than either company could get alone.

Engineering –The same engineers can probably work on both products.

Administration – The two companies' accountant and personnel departments can probably be combined into one that's smaller than the sum of the two when independent.

Kinds of Strategic Fit

Strategic fit opportunities are generally described as marketing fits or operating fits. Marketing fits occur whenever the benefit has something to do with the connection between the company and the customer. That can be in sales, marketing, advertising, or promotion. Example 15-2 illustrates a marketing fit.

Operating fits occur anywhere else like manufacturing, engineering, or administration. Example 15-1 illustrates an operating fit. Things like delivery or after-sale service can be defined in either category.

Some writers also talk about a management fit. This theory says a synergy is available if the two combining firms face the same kinds of management problems, and executives get very good at handling them. However, it's hard to think of examples in which such a situation wouldn't also imply marketing or operating fits.

Finally, there's a concept called financial fit. It's somewhat different than the others in that it doesn't deal with synergies in the same sense. Firms fit together financially if their cash flows balance. For example, a new venture into another business is likely to require cash contributions for some time before it's able to sustain itself. If the core business generates the cash the new business needs, we say the two fit financially. But if the core doesn't generate the required cash, they don't.

Unrelated Diversification

Unrelated or conglomerate diversification is a straightforward idea. It simply means the two business units involved have nothing in common. For example, suppose an electronics manufacturing company opens a restaurant. There's no basis for strategic fit, and there's unlikely to be any synergy available.

The only advantage lies in the argument that having the two firms under one corporate umbrella tends to smooth out the ups and downs associated with cyclical business conditions in one or both of the industries.

In small business, this is a reasonable argument. In the big company context, as we've already described, it doesn't make as much sense.

Justifying the Cost of Getting into the New Business

Diversification just about always has a cost. Starting a new venture usually means buying all kinds of equipment and other assets, and generally requires funding operating losses for the first year or two. Acquiring another firm means paying the acquisition price to the current owners.

The decision that always has to be made is whether the future benefit of owning the new business justifies the present cost of getting into it.

The Financial Decision – Capital Budgeting

Diversification decisions should be based mainly on a financial analysis of the proposed new business. The process is known as Capital Budgeting, and uses a technique which recognizes the Time Value of Money.*

The analysis involves making a projection of the future cash flows that will come from the new business, and comparing the present value[4] of those future flows with the current cost of making the acquisition or start-up. If the future inflows exceed the current outflow required for entry into the business, all on a present value basis, the idea is financially justified.

EXAMPLE 15-3

Zack Sanders runs a successful hardware store and is thinking about opening another one in a neighboring town. He has estimated the initial cost of opening the new store will be about $350,000. He's done a detailed market analysis, projected the new unit's sales, considered all of its costs and expenses and come to the conclusion that it will generate cash after-tax profits of about $60,000 per year.

The relevant return on investment (interest rate) for the idea is 15 percent.

---

* For a thorough explanation of both time value concepts and capital budgeting see William R. Lasher, *Practical Financial Management*, 2nd edn (South-Western College Publishers, 2000).

[4] The present value (PV) of a future sum is the amount that must be deposited at interest today to have that sum at the future time. For example, if $100 is promised in one year and the interest rate is 5 percent, the present value of the promise is $95.24, because

$$\$95.24 + \$95.24 \times .05 = \$95.24 + \$4.76 = \$100.00$$

Notice that

$$PV = \$100.00 / 1.05 = \$95.24$$

If the promise is two years away, we just extend the calculation as follows:

$$PV = \$100.00 / (1.05)^2 = \$90.70$$

An important related result derived with a little math is the present value of an indefinitely long stream of equal payments. The formula is simply

$$PV = PMT / k.$$

where PV is the present value of the stream, PMT is the periodic payment amount, and k is the interest rate in decimal form.

For example the present value of $1,000 per year expected to be earned indefinitely is

$$PV = \$1,000 / .05 = \$20,000.$$

That's much higher than bank deposit rates, because there's considerable risk associated with investing in business ventures.

Assuming Zack's estimate of his yearly income is correct (the forecasting process is complex with a lot of places to make errors), his capital budgeting analysis proceeds as follows.

The present value of his future income is

$$PV = \$60,000 / .15 = \$400,000.$$

Subtract from that the \$350,000 outlay currently needed to get started to arrive at the Net Present Value (NPV) of the project.

$$NPV = \$400,000 - \$350,000 = \$50,000.$$

Since this is a positive number, it indicates that on a present value basis the project's inflows exceed its outflows. That implies it's financially acceptable if all the underlying assumptions are reasonable (see note 4).

Overriding Strategic Considerations

Sometimes it seems that other considerations contradict and override the results of financial analysis. Here's an example.

EXAMPLE 15-4

The Dinsdale family owns one of four competing gas stations in the town of Ardmore. The competitors are all about the same size, and offer auto-repair services along with gas. None are doing exceptionally well or poorly.

A discount gas chain whose stores don't offer repair services operates in a nearby city. It hasn't made any moves toward Ardmore as yet, but the four local owners have been concerned about it for several years. When the discounter opens a location, it degrades the business of the traditional stations nearby by taking some of their gasoline sales.

Harriet Dinsdale has been thinking about diversifying into another business for some time. She's looked into several retail opportunities and an air-conditioning service business. She's done some financial analysis and concluded that the air-conditioning business looks best. In fact it looks more lucrative than the core gas/service station business. So she's decided to invest \$220,000 to get started.

Last week Harriet's son Sam came in with some interesting news. One of the other gas stations is for sale due to the owner's retirement. It's available for \$205,000. The Dinsdales are interested in buying, but a financial analysis shows it doesn't look as profitable as the air-conditioning business for roughly the same investment. Besides, they're tired of the gas business, and would like to try something new in addition to running the station. They don't have enough money or time to do both.

Which opportunity should they choose, the new air conditioning business or another copy of the old gas station?

Solution: Although the financial results seem to indicate that starting the air-conditioning business is the better option, buying the competing gas station is probably the smarter thing to do. The critical reasoning has more to do with what's likely to happen if they don't buy the station than what they'll make out of it if they do.

Someone is eventually going to buy the station. If that's someone new, things will probably continue as before with four competitors in the local market. But if one of the other owners buys it, there will be just three competitors left, one of which is twice the size of the other two. The larger firm may then be in a position to dominate the market making things difficult for the others. It could conceivably even drive the others out of business. Given that possibility, the Dinsdales would probably rather be dominant than dominated.

Worse yet, the discount chain might see the station being sold as an opportunity to enter the Ardmore market. If the chain buys into the area, much of Dinsdale's gas business is history.

The right decision in this case is to protect the core business. That's more important than diversifying into something new which should be considered only when the core is secure.

The Conflict with Financial Analysis. Notice that our advice seems to conflict with the Dinsdale's financial analysis which said the air-conditioning business was the better choice. It really doesn't.

The analysis was made assuming the core gas station business would continue as before under either decision. That's the usual situation in diversification decisions, and all we have to do is explore the proposed new business to come to a conclusion.

This case isn't like that. If the Dinsdales choose the air-conditioning option and let the gas station go to someone else, the core business may get a lot worse. That degradation should be subtracted from positive results of the air-conditioning projection. When that's done the air-conditioning option will look worse financially than the gas station alternative.

Summarizing the Financial Issues

Any diversification worth doing will be in an attractive line of business (industry) with good long-term profit potential and will not cost so much that the benefits are given away at the outset. That means we must be careful never to pay too much for a business. We have to be willing to walk away from the negotiating table if the finances don't work!

This is a major problem. People get caught up in chasing after a particular deal, and wind up overpaying. Once that's done the acquisition can never recover to make financial sense.

A classic example of paying too much happened not long ago in the big company world. It's worth mentioning as an illustration of what not to do. In November of 1994, Quaker Oats Co. negotiated a deal to pay $1.7 billion for Snapple Beverage Corp. Snapple had grown phenomenally during its short life, having been a leader in the "new age" drink market. But by the time of the acquisition its growth was already slowing due to the entrance of other competitors, some of whom were market leaders. A number of things went wrong from the start and Quaker sold the business in March of 1997 for $300 million. That's a loss of $1.4 billion in about two and one half years.[5] One can't help but wonder at the analysis that led Quaker to make the decision to pay that much for Snapple.

---

[5] Source, *The Wall Street Journal* March 28, 1997.

part V
Restructuring Strategies

chapter 16

Cost Reduction and Downsizing: Planning to get Leaner or Smaller

Introduction to Part V

The chapters in Part V are intended to shed light on the issues of cost reduction and restructuring. Before tackling this section in earnest it is worthwhile setting out precisely what we intend to do.

Strategic changes very frequently come about when companies are in trouble. This is especially true in small business where people tend not to think about strategy too much until they find themselves losing money. Then there's a frantic scramble to rethink their approach to the market. Most of the time that rethinking is accompanied by an even more frantic scramble to cut costs and return to profitability as quickly as possible.

This means that strategic analysis is more often than not played out against a backdrop of layoff, cost reduction, and restructuring or, to use a more recent term, downsizing. But such adjustments in cost can themselves be strategic events. Minor layoffs generally aren't strategic, but deeper cuts in cost and the traumatic idea of downsizing or restructuring into something smaller have very long-term consequences and are fundamentally strategic exercises.

Unfortunately, the general cost-reducing phenomenon is poorly understood by managements. What seems especially difficult for people to get their arms around is what happens when cost reducing moves from being a tactical cleaning-out of deadwood into being a strategic exercise with long-term, potentially negative implications. Upper management tends to impose cost-reduction targets on lower management without paying much attention to issues of function or how the reductions are to be accomplished. Then they're surprised when the intended financial results are circumvented or accompanied by unintended functional failure.

The chapters in this part are intended to shed some light on these issues. Chapter 16 is a bit of a romp through economic theory which we'll use to try to gain some insight into why major long-term cost reduction, lately called downsizing, is as difficult and problematic as it is. Then in chapter 17 we'll take a closer look at technique on how to get cost out of an organization. At the same time we'll appreciate some of the unexpected results that can occur. We'll end that chapter with an illustrative case in an appendix as well.

Reducing Spending

Businesses reduce spending levels when they're in financial trouble. The degree of reduction depends on the depth of the crisis and can vary from minor adjustment to major reorganization. Minor adjustments are referred to as trimming the fat, reductions in force (RIFs), layoffs and cutbacks. Major changes tend to be called retrenchments, restructuring, and downsizing. As we progress from one end of this spectrum to the other, we need to understand the financial and operational implications of our actions. A retrenchment is not a big layoff. It's something very different. In order to make either happen effectively, management must understand the economic and organizational phenomena that occur and realize that its goals may be constrained by those phenomena. Reductions without insight result in mortally wounded businesses which fail in the long run or are crippled for years.

It will be our goal to first understand in fundamental economic terms what differentiates a large reduction from a small one and then to explore some of the details involved in the implementation of each. We will also look at certain features of the planning and reporting process which can make management of expense reductions difficult. Finally we'll talk a little about focus and the ways in which people behave that impact how they handle reductions.

Downsizing

A long economic expansion came to an end at the close of the 1980s, and many companies found themselves overextended and in trouble. The solution was often to retrench or "downsize." That is, to shrink by plan. At the corporate level this usually means divesting certain business units that aren't contributing. At the single business level, downsizing means reorganizing to survive profitably at a much lower revenue level. Essentially, it's growth in reverse.

To those who haven't been through it, such shrinking may seem little more difficult than growing in the first place. It isn't uncommon to hear words to the effect of: "We were profitable at $50m five years ago, why can't we do it again?" (Last year's sales were $120m.) In other words, we just go back to what we were five years ago and everything will be okay –

right? Wrong! The fact is that growing backward is much harder than growing forward because of the infrastructure and responsibilities we develop on the way up.

Growing backwards can be particularly difficult if senior managers don't have much experience at it. Senior people generally come out of successful businesses or divisions. Their experience is mostly in managing growth. Sure, everyone's been through a minor downturn or two, but sustained, bone-crushing contraction is not in the experience of many top managers.

That's a problem because people tend to approach crises with techniques that worked for them in the past. Unfortunately, the moves that worked on the way up are usually dead wrong on the way down. But they're all the top people know. Hence it's not surprising that senior managers often seem to attack cost reduction and downsizing ineptly. They've got the wrong set of tools in their experience bag.

Before going any further, let's spend a little time analyzing the kind of conditions that bring companies into tough times.

The Economics of a Crunch

Companies can be thrown into crisis for any number of strategic or tactical reasons. Competition can get ahead of them, distribution can go awry, R&D efforts can fail, and costs can get out of control. Most frequently, however, the underlying problem manifests itself in a falling off of sales. The company becomes unable to sell as much product as it did at accustomed prices. This can happen suddenly or slowly, but is generally recognized with something of a bang. Costs frequently get out of control in the period leading up to the bang, and that tends to make matters worse.

Let's look at the economics of the conditions which can lead to a crunch severe enough to require substantial cost reduction or downsizing by an individual firm. In order to do that we'll need a little basic theory. So we'll look at simplified versions of several ideas in economics: supply and demand for an industry, supply and demand for a firm, and the concept of a firm's cost function.

Supply and Demand Analysis for an Industry

An industry demand curve is a graph relating price and quantity in the market for a product (see figure 16.7). It reflects the desires and abilities of buyers at a particular point in time. The vertical axis represents price while the horizontal axis indicates the quantity purchased in the current period.

Theory says that buyers are perfectly happy to operate anywhere along the demand curve. Further, it says that virtually all demand curves worth

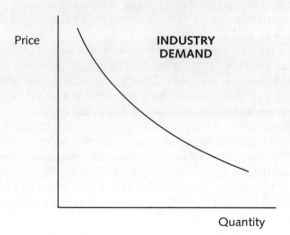

Figure 16.1 Industry Demand

worrying about slope downward to the right. That simply means that people will buy more if the price is low and less if it is high.

We're enjoying a stable market when the demand curve's position relative to the axes remains unchanged from period to period. That is, people's tastes, preferences, and ability to buy remain constant as do the options provided them by industries producing substitute products.

An industry supply curve relates prices with quantities supplied by producers. In general, the curve is upsloping, indicating that suppliers are willing to produce and sell more product at higher prices than at lower prices. This is an intuitively appealing idea even though the reasoning behind it is quite involved. Again, the theory says that suppliers are happy to operate anywhere along the curve. Further, a stable market implies that the supply curve stays in the same place from period to period relative to the axes. This says that the number and ability of suppliers remains more or less constant.

Drawing both curves on the same axis shows that there's only one point at which both buyers and sellers are happy, the intersection of the two curves. The market tends to operate at that point and we say that it is in equilibrium. The market in equilibrium is said to clear at price P* and quantity Q* (figure 16.2).

Supply and Demand for a Single Firm

So far we've been talking about industry supply and demand curves. The individual firm faces something quite different.

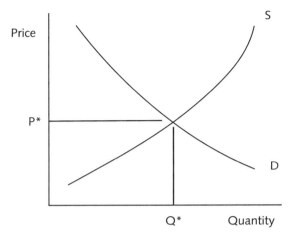

Figure 16.2   Industry Supply and Demand

The Demand Curve Facing a Single Firm

Economic theory is best developed for companies operating at the two extremes of the competitive spectrum. At the one end, we have perfect competition in which each firm's product is a commodity indistinguishable from that of competitors, and no competitor has a significant advantage over any other. Therefore, the individual firm simply accepts the industry price. This means that demand to the individual firm appears as a horizontal line at the market clearing price which is determined by industry supply and demand conditions (P* in figure 16.2).

In other words, a company facing many competitors with an undifferentiated product can sell all it wants at the market price or below, but nothing above that price. Pricing above market will simply drive customers to the competition, while lowering price will attract them in droves.

At the other extreme, the firm has little or no competition. That case can be described as a near monopoly situation. The key distinguishing feature of this case is that the individual firm faces a demand curve much like an industry's. That is, it slopes significantly downward to the right. This means the firm chooses the position along the demand curve at which it operates. It does this in accordance with its own supply curve which is related to its costs of production.

Neither of these situations is particularly representative of the vast majority of companies operating today. Most companies enjoy some product differentiation and customer loyalty, so their products are not entirely commodities. However, the differentiation and loyalties are not enough to overcome significant price differentials versus the competition.

What this means operationally is that most firms face demand curves which are shallowly downsloping to the right, and whose overall level is set by the intersection of industry supply and demand. The concept is illustrated in figure 16.3 where the left panel (a) represents an individual firm and the right (b) is the industry in which it operates.

The Individual Firm's Supply Curve

The amount of production offered by an individual firm at any given price is its supply curve. It is generally upsloping to the right like the industry curve, but it has a peculiar shape on the lower left end.

There is a price below which the firm loses money on each additional unit it sells. This is the point at which price equals the firm's variable cost of production. Let's call that price p#, the lower-case letter indicating that we're talking about an individual firm. Such a price is illustrated in figure 16.3(a).

Prices below p# are unattractive in the short run. In other words our firm, at its current size, would rather not play the game below p#, so it offers no production there. Its supply curve doesn't exist in that price range so graphically the curve goes straight to the vertical axis at that level.

We should understand that prices slightly above p# may not cover overhead (fixed costs), so the firm can't survive in that range very long. The individual supply and demand picture for a typical firm is illustrated in figure 16.3. Lower-case letters (except for P*) are used to distinguish the firm from the industry picture:

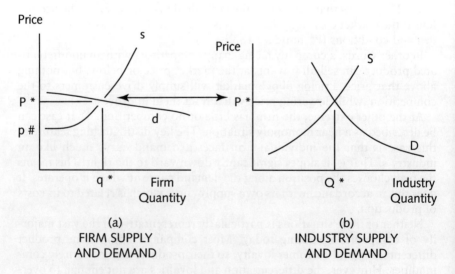

(a)
FIRM SUPPLY
AND DEMAND

(b)
INDUSTRY SUPPLY
AND DEMAND

Figure 16.3 Supply and Demand For a Single Firm

The industry supply curve is simply the sum of the supply curves of all the participating firms. Notice that it does not become horizontal at p#. This is because the cutoff price, p#, may be different for different companies depending on how cost-effectively they each produce.

It's important to understand that the curve d in (a) moves up and down as conditions change in the industry and the market price, P*, moves up and down in (b). It is our goal to understand what happens to the individual firm as these changes occur.

Cost Curves for a Firm – The Essence of Downsizing

The Cost Curve Concept

Firms produce based on a cost function that relates average unit cost with production volume in a time period. In the short run, the company is (by definition of the short run) constrained to operate with the physical plant, systems, and organization that currently exist. We therefore talk about a short-run cost function or short-run average cost curve, usually abbreviated SAC. The typical shape of the SAC is shown in figure 16.4.

The SAC's shape is important because it has major strategic implications. At low production levels average cost decreases quickly with increasing volume as overhead is spread over a larger number of units. Hence the curve

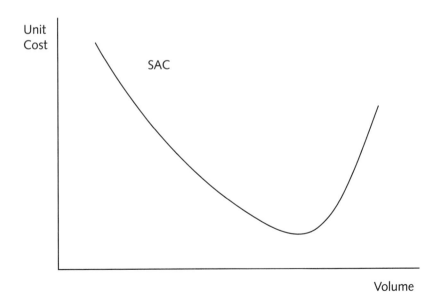

Figure 16.4   The Short-Run Average Cost Curve (SAC)

slopes downward as volume increases. The decline continues until output approaches the plant's capacity. As that happens, additional costs are incurred such as overtime and shift premiums. These tend to push unit cost up with increasing speed. Well beyond the design capacity of the plant, one must rent space and machinery, pay labor premiums, and often pay increased material and transportation costs. As a result, the SAC rises rapidly.

Cost Curves for Bigger and Smaller Plants

If a production level substantially beyond the upturn of the SAC is required, a bigger plant must be built. In general, the bigger the plant, the lower the unit cost at design capacity. It is informative to draw the SAC for a bigger and a smaller plant on the same axes. This is done in figure 16.5 where SAC' represents the larger plant.

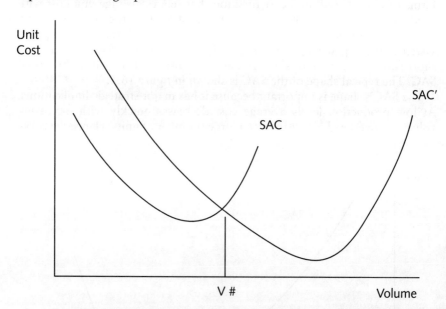

Figure 16.5 Short-Run Average Cost Curves for Two Plants

Notice that the lowest unit cost of production is achieved at the bottom of SAC', the larger plant. However, if production is going to be less than V#, the point at which the two curves cross, the firm is better off in the smaller plant.

This is a crucial point. If the volume available to an individual firm falls below some level, it can find itself trapped in a plant that is too large. There isn't enough volume to spread the overhead over, and costs become uncompetitively high.

The Meaning of Plant Size

It's important to understand what is meant by plant size in this context. It isn't just the physical size of the factory. The concept implied here encompasses the entire company. The "plant" also includes the computer system and the organizational structure of the firm as well as its operating methods and procedures. In other words, it encompasses the very nature of the way the company does business. In a larger company there are more specialists, analysts, and expediters. Both physical and informational process are usually more automated. In general there's more fixed overhead, but it is spread over a much larger volume, so cost per unit can be lower than in a smaller firm. The idea relates to complexity, capacity, and capability as well as to physical size.

For example, while a larger "plant" may have service representatives stationed around the country for quick response to customer needs, a smaller plant might dispatch service from a central location. A larger plant stocks enough inventory to fill 99 percent of orders immediately. A smaller plant has to backorder 15 percent of the time. A larger plant has an online order entry and billing system so that the status of orders can be queried and established instantly, while a smaller plant has a batch system and can only give updates weekly. Variable costs can be different too. The larger plant orders in quantities that yield volume discounts relative to its smaller cousin. The large plant does in-house training which develops more skilled labor. The smaller plant has to hire who it can from the outside.

When companies grow, they move to the right along a particular SAC curve. When they pass the bottom of the curve, they (in essence) build a new plant which has a cost curve like SAC' with a lower bottom.

In reality, companies "build" their new plants a little at a time. Each increment is accomplished by upgrading a particular resource area within the company. Each of these upgrades represents a new, slightly larger plant. For example, adding a new computer system is a movement to a new plant size. That element of capacity, the computer and its associated systems, is larger. In terms of figure 16.5, the firm has effectively stepped up to an SAC' from an SAC.

It's critically important to understand the process involved here. In the real world a new, substantially larger plant doesn't have to come about all at once, but it does involve moving in discrete jumps. A new computer system might be added in one year, a high-volume production machine in the next, and so on. Capacity growth is not a continuous process, but a series of discrete steps. Of course, building a new and larger factory is a large, discrete increment in plant size.

The organization can be enlarged almost continuously, but most of the systems and facilities come in lumps: a new computer, a new order entry system, a new building. Each lump is designed to handle a higher volume than the thing it replaced. And each lump requires an investment in money and time.

Shrinking – Growth in Reverse: Cost Reduction vs. Downsizing

When companies shrink they have to reverse the process by moving left along the current SAC curve. If the movement left is far enough (past V# in figure 16.5), and if it is expected to last, it becomes appropriate to downsize, that is to shift back to the smaller plant. In the figure it means jumping from SAC' back to SAC.

Downsizing isn't the same as reducing cost. Cost reduction means running the existing organization and facility (plant) as economically and efficiently as possible. It means getting the SAC for a given sized capability as low as possible.

Downsizing means admitting the company is in the wrong place along the volume axis by a substantial amount – too far to the right. It means that the firm has to move left so far that it must fundamentally change what it is by becoming smaller. That is, it must shift from a larger to a smaller plant, from an SAC' to an SAC. Generally, the shift has to be several steps to the left, not just one.

Moving from one SAC to another means changing the company's infrastructure. It generally means getting rid of one system or piece of equipment or building and acquiring another. When the company is growing, it means getting rid of a smaller one and adding a bigger one. People expect this to cost money. When the company is shrinking, it means getting rid of a big resource and picking up a smaller one. That costs money too. Unfortunately, the trade-in value of the old, larger resource rarely approaches the acquisition value of the new, smaller one. It's like trading an old station wagon in on a new compact car, you still have to come out of pocket with some money. In other words, a substantial cost reduction generally requires a capital expenditure. The cost isn't always just hardware. If, for example, the computer is being downsized, the new machine may need new software, and the way the company does things may have to be redesigned.

The basic mistake that managements make in coping with sustained hard times is failing to understand the difference between cost reduction and downsizing and mixing up what it takes to accomplish each.

People assume that a large transition to the left can be made continuously rather than in major jumps, and that it can be accomplished without incremental expense. They try to cost-reduce too far. The result is that they gut the organization into something that can't perform without damaging itself and its reputation, sometimes to the point of failure. The error stems from what people want rather than what is real. In hard times companies are desperately short of money. The idea of spending money to save money is hard to accept if you don't have any.

We'll discuss this more later. Now let's see what makes companies need to move to the left in the figure and discuss when downsizing is the right thing to do and when it isn't.

Why it's Harder to Shrink than Grow: Organizational Hysteresis

The term *hysteresis* is borrowed from physics, and applies to electromagnets. It refers to the phenomenon that occurs when current is increased and then decreased on a magnetic core. As the current is increased the core's magnetism increases. When the current is decreased, magnetism decreases, but not along the same path. Rather, magnetism takes a higher path on the way down than on the way up. There is a residual magnetism that stays with the core on the way down. Graphically it looks like figure 16.6:

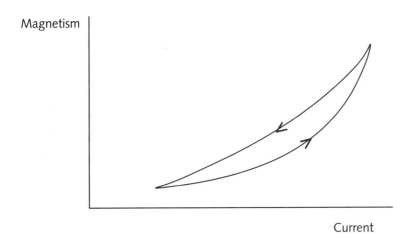

Figure 16.6   Magnetic Hysteresis

The lower path occurs on the way up, and the higher on the way down. The core seems to hang onto some of the magnetism or be reluctant to give it up.

Something similar happens when organizations grow and then shrink. Costs tend to be higher on the way down at a given size than they were on the way up. If we measure size by revenue dollars, then a graphical portrayal looks like figure 16.7.

This happens for several reasons. First, cost structures tend to have a

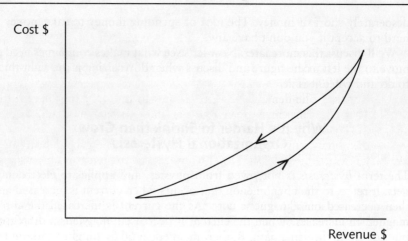

Figure 16.7 Organizational Hysteresis

number of features that are difficult to get rid of. The most pervasive is the requirement to support old products. A ten year-old product still has to be maintained, serviced and spared, but the service revenue may not justify the overhead. Nevertheless, the firm's business reputation depends on supporting old products for some time.

Distribution channels can be under-utilized. Suppose for example, we opened a West Coast sales office based on $10m per year in sales, that amount being just enough to cover the overhead. Today, sales are $6m but we have a number of customers out there who need our support, and we're not willing to give up on the idea of selling there either.

Ten years ago we hired someone to do a particular job. Today, he's still doing the same job, but he's had ten years of raises in the meantime. During good times those raises may have greatly exceeded the inflation rate so we're paying a higher real amount to get the job done.

In addition to this kind of thing prices tend to be lower on the way down, because the product is older, competition is stronger, or demand is lower. Lower prices mean that direct cost is a higher percentage of revenue than on the way up.

Changes in the Market

Let's return our attention to the industry picture. The market in equilibrium is represented by figure 16.2. We have an upsloping supply curve, a downsloping demand curve, and a market clearing price and quantity, P^* and Q^*. Suppliers are on their supply curves, buyers are on their demand curves, and the market clearing price, P^*, is substantially above each individual firm's variable cost, p#, to ensure a reasonable profit. Everyone is happy.

All this is great until the market changes. Market changes are represented by a shifting of either the industry demand or the industry supply curve (or both). An increase in demand, for example, says that people will buy more at any given price. The demand curve translates to the right (not necessarily parallel to itself). This can happen if buyers suddenly have more money or if their tastes change so that they want the product more.

An increase in supply can occur if new competitors enter the industry or if a leading competitor decides to lower its prices, say to increase market share. Collectively, more is offered at any given price, so the supply curve shifts to the right.

Supply and demand can also decrease, by shifting to the left. A decrease in demand occurs when people buy less during a recession or when a substitute product from another industry becomes cheaper or in some way more attractive.

We can also think of the up and down shifts in the curves. For example, a decrease in supply occurs if input prices increase and firms must charge more at any quantity level. Such a shift up of supply is equivalent to a leftward shift.

A Crunch for the Individual Firm

Individual firms get into trouble when changes occur that lower the market clearing price, P*. Things really get tough when P* drops into the range of a company's shutdown price, p#, in figure 16.3. If the market price just equals p#, a sale brings enough money to cover variable costs, but there's nothing left for overhead or profit. If the market price goes below p#, the company will generally stop production immediately, because money is lost on every unit sold. If it is somewhat above, the firm may produce for a while, but its days are numbered if it doesn't do something drastic.

Two general types of market change move P* down. These are a decrease in demand and an increase in supply. The movements of the industry supply and demand curves are illustrated in figures 16.8 and 16.9 respectively.

Demand can fall off for a number of reasons. These include a general reduction in business activity, a failing of popularity of the product due to tastes or obsolescence, or an increase in the attractiveness of substitute products from other industries. Any of these lead to a leftward shift of the demand curve as illustrated in figure 16.8. The original demand curve, labeled D, shifts left to a new position, D'. The result is a lowering of the point of intersection with the supply curve and a drop in market price from P* to P'.

An increase in supply, shown in figure 16.9, can come about through the entrance of new competitors or by an increased aggressiveness on the part of existing firms. In either case, the result is a movement to the right of the supply curve causing a lowering of the point of intersection with the demand curve. In figure 16.9, the original supply curve, labeled S, shifts to a new position, S′, which causes a drop in market price from P* to P′.

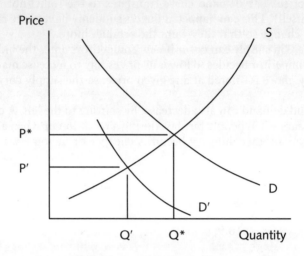

Figure 16.8 Decrease in Demand

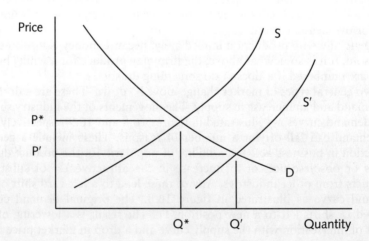

Figure 16.9 Increase in Supply

It is important to notice that while market price drops in both cases, the quantity sold in the industry moves in opposite directions. An increase in supply expands industry volume while a decrease in demand contracts it. This can be seen by observing the position of the new industry quantity, Q', relative to the old one, Q^*, in each diagram.

A firm entering troubled times usually observes a decrease in its ability to sell at accustomed prices, but it is often not immediately obvious which of the two phenomena described above is going on. Sometimes a combination seems to occur as existing firms attempt to maintain volume by aggressively cutting price in the face of a decrease in demand.

From a strategic perspective, it is critically important to understand which phenomenon is going on in the market. The appropriate reaction will be different depending on the firm's goals and the direction in which the size of the industry is moving from a quantity sold perspective. Let's look at each case separately.

The Response to an Increase in Supply

If the price available to the firm has fallen as a result of an increase in supply as illustrated in figure 16.9, a downsizing exercise is usually not appropriate. In that case although price has fallen, there is actually more being sold in the industry. The real question is how hard the firm wants to fight to maintain its share of what's being sold.

Supply usually increases for one of two reasons. New firms enter the industry, or an existing firm becomes more aggressive in pricing. The aggressive pricing is usually a result of either a willingness to sacrifice profits for market share or of a newfound cost advantage that's being passed on to the customer.

In either case prices drop. Referring to figure 16.3, we see that a lowering of industry price will drive the firm's demand curve down. This in turn will push operations down the individual supply curve to lower volumes. If this happens to a significant degree, the firm can find itself at a volume level from which a smaller plant size looks attractive (see figure 16.5).

The problem is that backing up to a higher SAC in response to an increase in competition makes one less competitive in the long run. On SAC the firm's lowest achievable price is higher than it was before on SAC'. Remember that industry volume is up in this case. The competitor who captures that volume will be able to build a very large plant whose costs are lower than anyone else's. Unless a company is planning to retreat out of the business entirely, downsizing is probably not the right thing to do.

A firm in this situation has five options:

1   Push the current SAC as low as possible through cost reduction in an effort to maintain competitiveness and hold volume levels at least as

high as they were before without losing capacity and functionality.
2 Build a larger, more modern plant to get cost down and compete aggressively for the increased volume.
3 Attempt to shift to non-price competition and become a niche player.
4 Exit the industry taking resources elsewhere.
5 Go through a downsizing to achieve reasonable profitability at the lower volume level hoping that prices and volumes are not squeezed further later.

An important dimension of the decision among these alternatives is the expected duration of the pressure.

Aggressive behavior on the part of a strong competitor, new or established, is sometimes designed to get marginal firms out of the industry or to pump the aggressor's market share to some specific level. In the meantime, the aggressor himself may be losing money. Such conditions are often not expected to last. The aggressor may either achieve his goals or eventually tire of the cost of the fight. In either case he can be expected to resume normal pricing in the future.

In such a temporary situation, downsizing by smaller players is probably not a good idea. Downsizing generally costs a substantial amount of money, and entails a reduction in capacity which has to be built back up if the demand facing the firm eventually expands. If the supply shift is temporary, that money is wasted in the long run.

If the pressure is expected to be temporary, the best option is usually number one. That is, skinny down as much as possible without destroying capacity, and hang on by the fingernails. Of course the danger is that the pressure persists longer than expected, and firms run out of resources.

Option two involves building a bigger plant to compete head-on with the forces pushing the supply curve to the right. This is essentially what the American automobile industry did in the 1970s and 1980s in response to the pressure from imports from Japan. Japanese factories were newer and more automated, and their people worked for less. In order to stay competitive, a number of US plants had to be modernized and labor had to give up some of their previously won benefits.

Option three, finding a niche, involves looking for a quiet corner in which the largest, most aggressive firms won't notice you. Clearly, this only works under special circumstances.

Option four, exiting the industry, is always a possibility, but can be very costly. Nevertheless, it's better to do this in a planned, systematic way than to be driven out bankrupt.

The fifth option involves going through a downsizing in order to hang on longer. It's a dangerous proposition since the downsized company is inherently at a cost disadvantage due to its small size. It can easily be squeezed out at a later date.

The Response to a Decrease in Demand

A falling off of demand for a product is represented economically as a shift to the left of the industry demand curve. The condition is illustrated in figure 16.8, and can be due to any number of causes. Buyers' tastes may have changed so that they no longer choose to spend as much money on the product. A substitute product produced by another industry group may have become in some way more attractive, i.e., better or cheaper. Or, buyers may not be spending as much on anything as is the case in a recessionary period.

As shown in figure 16.8, a decrease in demand causes a drop in price and a simultaneous drop in industry volume. The volume effect is opposite that in an increase in supply. When demand falls, there is less volume to be shared among participating players. That means that either everyone must sell a little less, or that some firms must sell a lot less while others maintain their volume. In severe cases, everyone may have to sell substantially less. Of course, marginal firms sometimes leave the industry.

Another phenomenon occurs frequently. In order to maintain market share and volume, some firms will aggressively lower prices in the face of a decrease in demand. If leading firms do this, the effect on smaller players seems like a combination of an increase in supply and a decrease in demand. The effective market price drops away like a stone forcing the individual's sales level down dramatically.

Clearly, when a firm is forced to sell a substantially reduced volume, it will have to move to the left along its SAC or move to a lower cost curve. Once again, the expected duration of the downturn is a key issue.

The firm in this situation has two reasonable options:

1   Cost-reduce and hang on until demand picks up.
2   Downsize at a cost in order to achieve short-term profitability.

The first option is best if the downturn isn't expected to last forever, and the current price is high enough for survival.

The second option involves a current outlay for the downsizing followed by another to rebuild capacity if and when demand returns. This option is appropriate if the duration of the downturn is expected to be very long. It may also be best if there is a fundamental change in the nature of the industry such that the firm is unlikely to ever return to its original volume levels.

The Issue of Can vs. Must – Who Are We?

Who we are makes a big difference in these decisions as well as the depth of the hole we're in. When a small firm is under pressure intense enough to drive price into the neighborhood of cost, the issue may be downsize or fail. The same is true if an entire large company is under pressure. In other words a firm in really deep trouble may not have the luxury of anything but Draconian cost cutting regardless of the fact that the actions are crippling in the long run.

But that's not always the case. Sometimes the current problematic condition means low profits but not negative cash flows. Or there may be funds available from other operations, as when one division of a large company is in trouble but others aren't. Then the short-run vs. long-run issue discussed here becomes very relevant.

American companies are very subject to making the downsizing decision based on short-run considerations. Management can downsize and show the expenses of a move to a smaller SAC as a one-time restructuring expense. This minimizes the impact on stock price and pumps earnings quickly. But in the longer run, it's a really big mistake.

chapter 17

Cost Reduction and Downsizing: Practical Applications

In this chapter we'll get into some detail regarding cost reduction. Keep in mind cost cutting is tactical when it deals with eliminating inefficiency and excess but strategic when it impacts the functional capability of departments and reshapes the company in terms of size and configuration. Also keep in mind that cost cutting and downsizing are related to strategic thinking because they so often come along at the same time. That is, we're often prompted to consider general strategic changes by the same external events that wipe out profitability and force us into a cost-cutting mode.

Cost Reductions in General

When we approach reducing an organization's size, we need to think in terms of three distinct and separate levels of action. It is the failure to recognize the distinction between these levels that leads to most implementation problems in shrinking organizations. The three levels of action are as follows:

1 A reduction without significant modification of functional responsibilities within the organization.
2 A reduction in which the responsibilities of the sub-units within the organization are reduced or redistributed.
3 A move in which the basic structure and capability of the business is modified, i.e., a downsizing.

The first action is a "tightening up" or "leaning down" of the organization. It involves a review of what people are doing, identifying waste and inefficiency and moving to eliminate them. Such a program is appropriate in response to mild business downturns or situations in which it doesn't look like the organization is going to achieve its plan. They're also appropriate from time to time to keep the organization lean and "fit."

The second level is called for in response to more serious and usually sustained downturns. It is critically important to have a good feel for the line that is crossed when we move from the first type of action into the second. It is in this second area that cost reductions can begin to do more harm than good if they aren't handled correctly.

The third level is what we have already been discussing, reshaping and redefining the business into something smaller and more viable in a changed environment. Here again serious problems arise if we try to treat a third-stage problem with second-stage tools.

Reducing cost revolves around managing our most flexible resource – overhead labor. Companies sometimes purchase a few services that can be readily eliminated, but these don't generally amount to a great deal. Cost reduction in the short run deals with getting rid of people and modifying the way the people we have spend money. As we move into deeper levels of cut, we have to start addressing fixed costs. These are harder to get out of the organization because we have to modify the way we do things and the tools that we have to accomplish our tasks. We had also better pay a great deal of attention to which tasks we really want to get done.

The First Layer of Reduction

Most organizations can cut 10–20 percent from "normal" levels of staffing without loss of function and without major reorganization. This is accomplished with a combination of attention to efficiency, weeding out deadwood, and foregoing "nice to do" things. There are a number of areas that typically can stand improvement. Here are a few:

- The organization often contains people who are marginally effective, having been promoted during organizational "weak moments." Take a hard look at people whose credentials aren't consistent with jobs:

  Manager of professionals without a degree
  Programing manager who has never programmed
  Ex-bookkeeper running an accounting department
  Technician in charge of an engineering area

- Question functions in which managers have only one or two people under them.
- Look at people with generally flaky reputations.
- Challenge organizations in which job titles, functions, or headcount within functions are substantially different from other parallel parts of the company, e.g., sales/service region with five support engineers while others have only one. A sales department with a financial analyst that no one else has. The only manufacturing department with an expediter, etc.

- Take a hard look at job titles like coordinator, expeditor, analyst, administrator, consultant, advisor, etc.
- Review the need for people and organizations with vaguely defined "make things better" missions, e.g., manager of "profit improvement programs."
- Review people who were hired to do something that never materializes or turns out to be a lot less significant than planned, but who are still there doing something else.
- Look hard at span of control. Managers with four or fewer direct reports may be consolidated, or should be working managers.
- Always look hard at the number of secretaries and administrative assistants.
- Look at overtime records. Organizations that never put in any O/T are probably overstaffed. Constant O/T isn't cost-effective either if the work is being accomplished at premium rates. O/T should be used in an orderly manner for peaks.
- Look at the pattern of charges between departments, especially manufacturing, engineering, and field support. Is excess labor being charged around the company because there isn't enough work in the home department?
- Look at headcount and spending levels in prior periods. Have there been increases? If so, are the increases justified in terms of workload?
- Look for excess equipment. Does everyone need a state-of-the-art PC?

The Manpower Analysis

Once we've gone through the organization looking for obvious problems we must employ our most powerful tool, the manpower analysis.

Subordinate managers virtually always resist reducing their staff. Even in the face of disastrous business conditions people will seriously argue that they can't do their job with any less people. Senior managers generally cope with this attitude by imposing a relatively arbitrary level of cut on the subordinate either in terms of dollars or headcount. There follows a give-and-take argument after which both managers agree on a somewhat reduced cut level.

The process generates a "more than we need" phenomenon on both sides. The subordinate demands more resources than he really needs or resists a cut that he knows he can live with because he's afraid of being cut further. The senior asks for a deeper cut than is really necessary because he expects to be argued down.

A different behavior occurs when the senior manager takes an intimidating posture with respect to his subordinate. In effect he says, "Resist my cut efforts, and I'll fire you!" In that case subordinate managers have been known to give in to unrealistically deep cuts imposed by someone who doesn't understand their department's inner workings. They and the organization get in trouble later when they can't do the job.

The real problem here is that people argue their way through the cost-reduction exercise in vague and imprecise terms. A statement like, "I just can't do the job with 10 people, I need 12" isn't backed up with anything more detailed or concrete than the gut feel of the manager. His boss's response and eventual decision isn't any more firmly grounded.

An enormous step can be made in the direction of rationality if senior managers require that subordinate managers justify their headcounts on a workload/productivity basis at least in rough terms. Some measure of work needs to be defined for every type of effort within a department along with the amount of production that can be expected from an average worker.

For example, in Accounts payable work depends primarily on the number of invoices that have to be processed and secondarily on the complexity or number of lines on each invoice. It is not difficult to determine how many invoices a day a good worker can process. It is also possible to estimate how many invoices a month any level of business implies. Putting these two numbers together takes a good deal of the guesswork out of how many payable clerks the company needs. A little leeway remains with respect to scheduling, overtime and intensity of effort, but not much. Forcing a staffing level lower than that implied by such calculations simply means that bills won't get paid correctly. That can lead to unhappy vendors who stop sending product.

Worse, it can lead to paying unverified invoices which generally means overpaying or paying for product you haven't gotten. This is our first example of a cutback that costs more money than it saves because of impaired function in the cut department.

Productivity measures can be stated in terms of dollars or some physical unit or process. Here are some examples:

Revenue per Salesperson.
Calls per Salesperson.
Sales support per $ of revenue.
Procurement dollars per purchasing agent.
Daily transactions per accounting clerk.
Equipment installations per field engineer.
Lines of code per programming day.
Employees per personnel representative.

Managers can be challenged to reduce costs by improving productivity as measured by these indicators, but it rarely makes sense to expect more than a 10 or 15 percent improvement from ordinary levels.

This is a really important point. Doing more with less or the same work with fewer resources can only be taken so far. Overhead departments that are cut too far stop functioning effectively, and it's easy for that ineffectiveness to cost more than the cuts save. The insidious problem is that those kinds of costs don't show up in the income statement for some time.

Getting "Lean and Mean"

The key to finding the elusive "lean and mean" position is getting each subordinate manager to identify with doing a good job with the fewest resources. Most managers don't think in those terms. They think in terms of:

1 Do the best job, but let someone else worry about the resources, or
2 do the best job within budget, where I try to wrangle the highest budget possible out of the boss.

The problem here is that people are usually rewarded for doing a good job (within budget) but are never singled out and praised for doing an okay job with a lot fewer resources.

Think about that. Our prizes always go to the biggest, the fastest, the most accurate, and so on, with little regard for cost though it's generally assumed that we're within budget. Does anyone get an award for reducing quality a little while saving a lot? Not often if at all. Yet when we're in a crunch, that's just what we want to do.

We have to instill an attitude, or culture in which spending is as important as doing. The best way to do that is to measure production in each department and reward increased effectiveness. That is, getting more transactions per person per day, not just more transactions.

The best way to find the lean and mean place in a subordinate department is to motivate the manager to find it for you. If we don't do that we're always playing head games with our managers. Ideally a subordinate manager will come to his senior and say, "Look, I can reduce by three people if you can accept a delay in peak time processing of an extra day. Can I do that?" The way most of us do it, you cut him by three people and wait to see what happens.

Subsequent Layers and the Issue of Function

So far we've been talking about taking the slack out of the organization while remaining at the current plant size. Suppose we locate the elusive lean, mean position but find that the company is still performing below par. If we decide to cut headcount further, we must proceed with caution. At this point and beyond it's easy to do more harm than good, especially in the long run.

Reducing headcount below the most tightly stretched but fully staffed level means giving up function. This is probably the most misunderstood or ignored facet in the way senior managers approach downturns. Budget directives usually involve imposing lower spending levels on subordinate managers and nothing more. The implicit direction is to continue doing all of the things they did before. It is also implicit that a "manager" should be able to run his department without being told "how" to do it, so all he is given is the new budget constraint in terms of dollars and/or headcount.

This is fundamentally unsound thinking. Beyond some point it becomes impossible to execute all of the functions of a fully staffed organization even in a ragged manner. The key to successful expense reduction beyond that point lies in the consideration of which functions management is willing to give up.

Senior management must analyze operations and decide what it's willing to do without. If management doesn't do that, the organization will make the decision for them. When the organization implicitly makes the choice through action, what is given up will usually not be what senior managers would have chosen had they thought about it.

The organization will maintain visible activities on which it receives feedback on a day-to-day basis, but will forgo less obvious functions that may be more important in the long run. This makes a layoff seem successful in the short run, but builds insidious problems that can sink the firm in the longer term.

EXAMPLE 17-1 – AN MIS DEPARTMENT

The Management Information System or MIS department, which runs the company's computers and controls the way information is stored and disseminated, is a frequent cost-reduction target. Most companies charge user departments for computer services in one way or another. When a crunch comes everyone says his or her charges are too high. The obvious question is how can they be reduced?

The usual approach is to demand that the MIS director reduce her expenses by say 20 percent – generally without reducing service. The result is that service goes to hell and in a short time costs go back up due to hiring outside help.

This is the wrong approach. The right approach is to simultaneously ask:

How can we live with fewer services?
How can we provide those services at the lowest cost?

Let's think through a sensible approach to the problem.

First consider the MIS cost structure. MIS expenses are generally separable into three areas, equipment, operations and programming. Here's a rough breakout:

Hardware (rental or depreciation)
Software (rental or depreciation)
Maintenance (contract or time and material)

Operations
  Personnel
  Supplies

Programming
  Systems
  Applications
    Maintenance
    Enhancement
    Development

Now let's consider what cost reductions are possible under three scenarios: (1) Essentially no change in day-to-day services provided to user departments; (2) somewhat reduced routine service but no major structural change in the department or its capability; and (3) fundamental changes in structure and capability, i.e., downsizing the department.

At this point it's worth noting that MIS is a classic example of the problems inherent in reducing overhead cost. The rest of the organization depends on its services but generally feels they cost too much. Costs are generally allocated to users based on how much of the resource they use. That's generally based on something like the number of report pages they receive, or the number of interactive workstations they've got. MIS costs are capital intensive and more related to capacity than to current usage.

Scenario 1: Essentially no change in services

Examine the MIS cost structure. If services are to be essentially maintained and the organization is already in a lean condition, all we can really cut out is programming in the development and enhancement areas. We can give up as much development of new programs as we like without impacting today's services. We can also give up enhancement of existing systems, but users are generally clamoring for changes to programs and consider that virtually day-to-day service. Maintenance can't be touched or systems don't run.

In most organizations development programming isn't more than 10 or 15 percent of the total budget.

Scenario 2: Reduced services

Suppose we want to go further, still in the cost-reduction mode. Small improvements can be made by reducing the frequency with which some reports are run and eliminating some reports altogether. (Eliminating a particular report or run, not the system, software or data base from which the report is generated.)

Most user departments are willing to do this but expect big savings in their charges. The problem is that if MIS charges are based at least in part on reports used, those charges carry the overhead of the hardware and software. If only one department reduces its reports by 20 percent, it will have a big reduction in charges. (Less than 20 percent, however, because of the respreading of overhead.) But other departments will see an increase in their charges due to the reallocation of overhead over fewer reports.

The big problem comes if all departments reduce their reports by 20 percent each expecting to see a big reduction in their charges. Everyone is shocked and upset when their charges are virtually unchanged. The problem is that the only real saving is the incremental cost of paper since all the overhead is still there. It's been allocated on fewer reports, but since everyone reduced their requirements by the same 20 percent the relative proportion of overhead going to each user department is unchanged. Hence their charges are only minimally reduced. This generally creates a lot of animosity between user departments and MIS.

The next step is to give up data requirements. If we track less data we can sometimes save on storage and data base management costs.

But so far the available cost reductions are minimal because capacity is still intact:

We still have the same computer so rental (depreciation) and service charges are still the same.

We still have all the same software so rental, maintenance, and enhancements are still the same.

The next thing we can give up is entire systems. Most companies have a number of systems, some of which are absolutely required and some of which are in varying degrees nice to have. We have to have financial systems for the general ledger, receivables and payables, and most firms need their inventory control systems, but we may be able to do without sales tracking, commissions, on-line order inquiry etc. We may also be able to downgrade the sophistication of some systems, e.g., by going from on-line to batch processing. Eliminating a system enables us to save considerably in MIS in software, data, and programming. Moving away from on-line saves in software, data communications, and hardware (terminals). However, the efficiency lost in other departments may offset the savings.

This is where things really start to get tense. We're still in the cost-reduction mode. We now have to start getting serious about giving up function to save money.

Reexamine the cost structure of MIS. How are we going to get any more money out if the department has to keep doing the same things with the same equipment? It can't be done. But managements try all the time. The result is that the company's information system fails. If the firm remains in business, people rush around trying to do quick fixes and wind up spending more money than they would have in the first place.

Scenario 3: Downsizing the department

The next step is downsizing, meaning we have to step down to a smaller system. This isn't easy and takes a great deal of senior management attention. The smaller system will generally handle less volume and do fewer things.

The transition involves several steps:

1 Decide what the requirements of the new system will be, i.e., what function reductions is the firm willing to live with?
2 Identify the smaller system that will retain as much of the current system as possible, e.g., software, peripherals, etc.
3 Estimate the ongoing cost reduction between the new system and the old. Be sure to include additional costs in other departments where the smaller system means more manual work.
4 Estimate the cost of conversion:
    a) Disposal of old hardware and software (consider asset write-off, lease breaking, sale proceeds, etc.) Be sure to include tax effects.
    b) Acquisition of new hardware and software.
    c) Implementation: Redesign, reprogramming, installation, changeover costs in all departments.

Before starting, do a present value analysis (capital budgeting) to see if it's worth doing. The advantage needs to be substantial and involve a large reduction in headcount as well as other cost.

A Simple, General Approach to Analyzing a Department in a Cost-Reduction/Layoff Situation

The general approach to functional analysis in a layoff situation is to simply lay out who does what in a department on a chart. That is, we match job titles with tasks to rationalize the number of people we have in each job category. A chart like figure 17.1 works best:

	Job A	Job B	Job C . . . . Job N
Task 1			
Task 2			
.			
.			
Task M			

Figure 17.1 Personnel Analysis

In each cell put the number of hours of effort expected to be dedicated to each task by employees in each type of job in order to get the functions accomplished that management has decided are necessary. Then sum the columns to get the number of manhours of effort in each job title needed. Compare that with the number of people actually on board in each job category.

Estimating the Improvement Available Through Layoff Action

Most managers have a hard time understanding how much bottom-line improvement is available through cost-reduction actions. This is especially true with respect to first-level actions in which the intention is to more or less maintain function. That's usually a straightforward layoff.

In other words, it isn't uncommon to see managers propose layoff solutions to budgetary problems that require more drastic restructuring. They grossly over-estimate the effectiveness of layoff actions in improving profitability. For example, suppose a company or division finds itself with a budgetary problem that's estimated at $1m. Some managers will propose solving the problem with a layoff even if the amount is as much as 50 percent of the total payroll. It's rarely feasible to cut personnel that deeply and stay in business.

When we have to get cost out of an organization and consider a layoff, it's imperative that we understand the magnitude of what can be done.

EXAMPLE 17-2

Assume a manufacturing concern's sales have fallen off by 20 percent and that the income statement has deteriorated as shown below. A deterioration in cash flow has also occurred which resulted in increased borrowing and the increase in interest expense shown.

	Normal		Current	
	$	%	$	%
Revenue	100	100	80	100
Cost	50	50	44	55
Gross Margin	50	50	36	45
Expense	30	30	30	38
Interest	4	4	6	7
PBT	16	16	0	0
Tax	5	5	0	0
PAT	11	11	0	0

Assume that normally manufacturing cost is made up of material, labor, and overhead as follows:

M	60%
L	15%
O	25%

Where overhead is 40 percent labor and 60 percent other costs like rent, utilities, and depreciation most of which are fixed in the short run.

Analyze the Changes in Cost

The direct labor (DL) and direct material (DM) content of product don't change when the revenue drops, so the detail of cost changes is as follows:

	Normal	Current
M	$30.0	$24.0
L	7.5	6.0
O	12.5	14.0
	$50.0	$44.0

It's important to follow the numbers here. DM and DL fall by 20 percent with sales and production to $24 and $6 respectively. However, the $12.5 in manufacturing overhead is still being spent. Moreover, the $1.5 of DL that isn't required to build the reduced volume spills into manufacturing overhead. There's nowhere else for this labor to go until we lay people off. These dollars may show up like this or as unfavorable labor or overhead variances, the end result is the same. An element of confusion can be added if such a variance winds up being capitalized into inventory.

People Costs Overall

The people cost in manufacturing overhead is

$$40\% \text{ of } 25\% = 10\% \text{ of cost.}$$

That's about 5 percent of normal revenue since manufacturing cost is normally 50 percent of revenue.

We'll assume other expense areas like marketing and finance are about 60 percent people cost, that's a typical amount. Then people cost in expense is

$$60\% \text{ of } 30\% = 18\% \text{ of normal revenue.}$$

So total people cost as a percentage of revenue under normal conditions are

DL	7.5%
Mfg Ovhd	5.0%
Expense	18.0%
	30.5%

30.5%   also $30.5 in this example

Now, what range of performance improvement is feasible through layoff?

Assume that our DL standards are okay so we can get rid of the unused DL that has so far slopped into manufacturing overhead. This is 20 percent of DL because we've had a 20 percent revenue decrease. This is 1.5 percent of normal revenue or $1.5.

Outside of DL, we have overhead and expense. In these areas the limit of non-functional reduction is about 20 percent if we're starting from normal times, the limit with functional reduction but without downsizing may be another 15 percent. In total that's 35 percent of the people cost outside of DL.

$$35\% \text{ of } 23\% = 8.1\% \text{ of normal revenue}$$

Adding back the DL, we get 9.6 percent or $9.6 as our maximum pretax improvement. The company just can't do any better than that without a major plant size shift in at least some areas. But the profit shortfall is $16 before tax, so the layoff isn't enough. This result is very important. Companies can't always get where they want to go through even the most drastic layoffs.

Let's continue by looking at what an adjusted income statement looks like. First, here's what can be achieved in cost:

	Normal	Current	Adjustment	Doable
M	$30.0	$24.0	$ -	$24.0
L	7.5	6.0	-	6.0
O	12.5	14.0	3.3*	10.7
	$50.0	$44.0	$3.3	$40.7

```
* $1.5 + $1.8 = $3.3
    35% of $5 = $1.8
```

Then in total the income statement becomes:

	Normal		Current		Layoff	Doable	
	$	%	$	%	Adjustment	$	%
Revenue	100	100	80	100		80.0	100
Cost	50	50	44	55	3.3	40.7	51
Gross Margin	50	50	36	45		39.3	49
Expense	30	30	30	38	6.3*	23.7	30**
Interest	4	4	6	7		6.0	7
PBT	16	16	0	0		9.6	12
Tax	5	5	0	0		3.0	4
PAT	11	11	0	0		6.6	8

*35% of $18 = $6.3
**Notice that we've roughly maintained our cost and expense ratios to revenue by taking a percentage cut out of people that's almost twice the percentage drop in revenue.

The best we can do is get back to a running rate of a little better than half of normal profitability. And so far we haven't accounted for the costs of the layoff.

Post-Layoff Spending

It's a fairly common occurrence for managers to increase certain discretionary spending after a layoff in an effort to maintain their department's function when responsibilities have been left intact but have become unattainable because of the reduction in people.

This can happen when the cost reduction is delineated in terms of headcount and/or people expenses, but managers still have discretion in other spending. Some common tricks are as follows:

Rehire same or other people as "consultants."
Extensive overtime (O/T) (at premium rates).
Subcontract work out.
Purchase material with labor content already in it.

It's important to understand why this happens. The organization is in the cost-reduction mode, but has tried to treat a level-two problem with a level-one approach. By ignoring function, management has implicitly said: "Do everything you were doing before. Further, you're graded on accomplishing function, not on reducing costs." Subordinate managers react by circumventing the intent of the cost reduction to get what they perceive as their jobs done.

A related practice is to let key work back up to crisis proportions without telling anyone until the last minute. When the crisis hits, upper management must authorize completion of the work quickly in order to make a company commitment, usually at premium rates.

Here's an example. Suppose a system must be shipped to a customer by a certain date. Certain testing must be done prior to shipment. Testing isn't done, and the day before the committed shipment the VP Manufacturing tells the General Manager that we won't make the ship date unless he authorizes the labor necessary to get the job done in the last day. This generally involves a big premium. Usually enough confusion exists between marketing, manufacturing, engineering, and field service that no one actually gets blamed for the event.

It's important that management prevent things like these from happening. The best way is to analyze function to be consistent with a fully-stretched workload for the remaining staff.

Timing and Cost Effects of Expense Reductions

When we plan force reductions we have to consider two timing issues: (1) the time until implementation and (2) time equivalence of severance and other administrative costs.

The time from when we start to think about a layoff until we do it is generally at least two months.

We also have to estimate the total severance cost in terms of months of salary. This can range from two weeks to over a year depending on the longevity of the employee group. A reasonable average might be a month. Things to think about include:

severance pay;
accrued vacation (accrued or unaccrued on books);
outplacement;
consultants or specialists hired to help;
agreements in which terminated executives are kept on the payroll for a while; and
clerical services provided for those looking for new jobs.

Can We Make a Plan We're Missing Through a Layoff?

Large companies run on plans to a much greater extent than small firms. In larger firms, division management is usually graded on achieving the division's annual plan. When financial results during the year start to look as if the plan will be missed, people often think that recovery is just a matter of having the guts to go through a substantial layoff. Generally, however, once we're far enough into a year to be sure we're missing the plan by a significant amount, catching up through cost reduction is very difficult.

EXAMPLE 17-3

Suppose the income statements in Example 17-2 represent the annual plan and the annualized running rate at the end of the first quarter for a troubled company.

	Plan		1st Qtr Annualized	
	$	%	$	%
Revenue	100	100	80	100
Cost	50	50	44	55
Gross Margin	50	50	36	45
Expense	30	30	30	38
Interest	4	4	6	7
PBT	16	16	0	0
Tax	5	5	0	0
PAT	11	11	0	0

If we start thinking about layoff action at the end of the first quarter, we can expect it to be implemented and to have its financial effects behind us by the beginning of the third quarter. How close will this bring us to making the plan?

Notice that we're projecting being behind by $11 after tax at year end, or equivalently $16 pretax. To make that up we need to achieve an annualized pretax profit rate of $32 in the second half.

Now recall that the maximum annualized improvement available through layoff – with drastic functional cuts but without downsizing – was $9.6 pretax. Assume we can get additional non-people expense reductions of half again that much, or about $4.8 (this is a generous assumption). Thus our total available improvement is about $14.4 or less than half of what we need.

Downsizing won't help because in order to get the spending rate lower through downsizing we'd have to spend a chunk of money on getting rid of old equipment and procedures and putting in new ones. Further, it takes a longer time to plan and execute a downsizing, and we might well not want to compromise our long-term abilities.

In other words, the plan was shot in the first quarter. This kind of revelation can come as a devastating shock to executives who haven't been through it before.

Preparing for Cost Reductions in Risky Times?

If times are such that there is a substantial probability of a downturn during the plan year, there are a few things that can be done to avoid being caught like this:

1 Have reduction in force (RIF) action plans prepared in advance. Think through the people we'll let go, the services we'll provide for them and the functions we'll give up at various levels of cut. Have these plans ready to go.
2 Do your agonizing in advance.
3 Select "Trigger Points" on some key indicator – usually profit or sales shortfall – at which we can implement and still recover.
4 Have the courage to pull the trigger when the point is hit. Most people wait to see another month or two of results before they're convinced the miss is real, but by then it's too late.

Morale Effects

Reductions in force can understandably have a devastating effect on morale. The negative feelings are worst when people are holding their breath waiting for the axe to fall. The rumor is out that a layoff is coming and no one knows for sure whether their job is safe. This is tough on employees, but from a company perspective the problem is that productivity goes down the drain in such periods.

The worst situation comes about when a firm makes a series of layoffs. That usually happens because market conditions continue to deteriorate after the initial action and more reductions are necessary later on. We're all familiar with major companies that go through a series of layoffs over a period of years as their fortunes tumble. After a while the remaining employees lose all loyalty and become minimally effective.

An exacerbating phenomena has to do with severance. The first group to go generally gets very generous packages, because the future doesn't look too dismal yet, and management feels it can afford to be kind. Successive RIFs, however, get poorer treatment as the company's long-term prospects look progressively worse. After a few rounds, the remaining employees recognize that they'll get little more than a shove out the door when their time comes, and become even more bitter and resentful.

Surprisingly, however, the morale effect of a layoff isn't too bad on the remaining workforce if people don't expect another. The laidoff employees are gone, out of sight and out of mind so to speak, and soon forgotten, and everyone tends to move ahead without too much recrimination.

All this means that it's generally much better to do one big layoff than two or three small ones. Cut hard and deep the first time and hope that's all that's needed. Tentative moves hoping to minimize the suffering as likely as not make it worse.

People-Related Expenses

There are a number of expenses that tend to rise and fall with headcount/payroll. Some depart with the fired employees, but others have to be overtly cut. Here are a few:

1 Fringe benefits depart with the people. We generally simply add a percentage to salary and wage computations to cover this when we talk about people costs. The largest benefits are payroll taxes and health insurance and pension contributions. The total is often as high as 30 percent of payroll.

2 Training and education. As a general rule during hard times company paid training and education should be limited to that immediately required by the job, or that required to keep from losing key people. Some specific cautions apply:

   In-house training – must reduce the training department.
   Outside trainers – be sure we don't send more of the remaining employees to as many classes as we used to before.

Tuition Reimbursement – goes with people, but be sure it's job-related.

3 Personnel Department. Fewer employees should mean fewer administrators. In addition we might want to give up some of the benefit programs that seem like good ideas in better times, e.g., counseling, health club, cafeteria subsidy, newspaper, etc.

4 Phone costs should go down. Remove extensions. Train people not to talk casually on long distance. Is the telecommunications package the most cost-effective?

5 Equipment – PCs, typewriters, desks, etc. – should become available. Be sure someone else doesn't buy a new PC when there are surplus ones around. If you don't plan to reuse, sell some off.

6 Dues and subscriptions. Should go down when people leave, but subscriptions have to be cancelled.

7 Supplies generally go down with fewer users.

8 Travel and entertainment. Fewer travelers generally spend fewer dollars but it's necessary to make sure that the remaining employees don't make more trips. Travel and entertainment (T&E) is a real sink for money. Institute rules that eliminate unessential travel. All trips should require two levels of management approval (boss and boss's boss.) Challenge the number of people to go. Is everyone a necessary participant? Look hard at getting discount air fare. Share cars. Limit meal expenses. Make one long trip instead of two short ones. Stay in mid-range or economy hotels.

In virtually every area, it's necessary to put in controls to make sure the remaining employees don't spend the money that those who have left would have.

Layoffs in Sales

Some people argue that a layoff of sales people is like cutting your own throat. In hard times you need to expend more effort to sell product to keep the company going. Sometimes that's true and sometimes it isn't. It's important to be careful, because sales departments can suck up expenses faster than anyone.

We always need to sell product. But if we generate a great deal of expense to sell additional deeply discounted product, it isn't always worth it. In fact, we can be worse off.

There are typically three kinds of activity in the generic sales area – marketing, sales, and sales support. We'll consider each separately.

Marketing

A little goes a long way. During good times departments tend to build up to do a great deal of research, tracking, and analysis. The first dollars spent here can have a tremendous impact, but the increments get small real fast. The problem with analyzing marketing effort is that you can never absolutely prove the worth of anything. What would we have sold if we didn't do this – you can't tell. But beware of insidious increases. During good times Marketing/Sales presentations get very fancy. It's not uncommon to see presentations prepared by outside graphic art firms at a very hefty cost. When tough times come, these costs are buried in our way of doing business, and have to be rooted out. Marketing groups tend to be very quick to use consultants and outside help. Another popular practice is subscribing to industry research publications. These can be helpful, but the information is often available in the library.

Sales Support

This consists of administrative and technical work to support/assist the salespeople in the field. The idea is to free up the salespeople to do more selling. However, if they don't actually do more calling and prospecting, there's no point to having support. Salespeople often develop an "it's not my job" attitude toward paperwork after they've had support assistance for a while.

Sales

Certainly a key resource, but also an easy place to waste a lot of money. An unproductive salesperson can spend as much as a good one. We have to constantly monitor performance to be sure people are pulling their weight. One generally should not attempt to train neophytes in bad times. It's usually better to hire experience and make compensation highly incentive-based. Pay a good person a lot, but be sure a non-producer starves. In tough times having a bunch of amateurs beating the bushes won't sell much more product!

The strategy of redirecting resources into Marketing or Sales can be very dangerous since it's easy to spend money with no benefit in these areas. It must be undertaken very carefully. During hard times there's a temptation to try to pump up revenues. We sometimes do this by hiring more salespeople. Usually we admit that the new people will be less effective than the old hands. Sometimes, however, at the same time we're adding salespeople, we're reducing price, either at list or through a higher average discount. As a result, additional low margin sales coupled with higher expenses don't do anything for the bottom line.

A Few Words About Expenses in General

It's often hard for management to find excessive or wasteful spending. Extravagance is usually buried in accounts filled with legitimate, necessary expenses. So if a reviewing executive doesn't know exactly what he's looking for he isn't likely to find it.

Subordinate managers won't often lie outright to their bosses, but they rarely volunteer information on freehanded spending either. For example, suppose a branch manager who can authorize purchases up to $5,000 bought a new table for her conference room costing $4,800 when the average such table used in the company costs $1,500. She just likes nice furniture. If the boss asks, "Did you buy a $4,800 table?" She'll say, "Yes." But if she's asked if she made any extravagant purchases she'll probably say, "No."

Here are a few things to do and look for.

Strategies to Catch Excess Spending

1 It's a good idea for a senior executive or his representative to spend a day in Accounts Payable every once in a while. Go through every check paid by the company for a week, excluding payroll and inventory. You'll be amazed.

2 Have the accounting department calculate the cost of meals per person present, and report anything over $30 to management. You may be amazed at how many $50 bottles of wine are purchased.

3 Always require that the senior person present at a meal pay, and require approval by his boss.

4 Review the level of hotel people are staying in.

5 Question whether everyone who goes on trips has to go. Always require two levels of approval for travel. The traveler's boss and his boss.

6 Review air fares. Most business travelers simply pay full fare. Is anyone trying to coordinate discounts?

7 Field offices can be particularly bad. Look for coffee services, janitorial services, rented plants, temporary help.

8 Are employment and advertising agencies being used? Such agencies do some things you can't do well yourself, but there's a tendency to also let them do things your own people can do for practically nothing. Are they cost-effective?

9 Appoint a central authority for personal computers, and don't let anyone buy any hardware or software without that person's approval. People often buy the latest model when the company has several older ones laying around that will do the job adequately.

10 Review all payments to individuals and one- or two-person companies.

11 Maintain an approved vendor list and review it frequently. Especially for non-inventory purchases.

12 Close open accounts at stores, restaurants and supply houses. Require that everything come through purchasing. Forbid Accounts Payable to issue checks without a PO from Purchasing.

13 Look hard at company cars. Do the people who have them really travel that much on business?

14 Review your health plan. Is it the most cost-effective for your employees? Do the employees contribute?

15 Review all of the employee programs that were started in good times: health club, subsidized cafeteria, employee newspaper.

16 Look at tuition reimbursement programs. The education should be job-related. A secretary in an MBA program because he or she may someday be a manager isn't reasonable.

17 Review the sales incentive (commission) plan. A good salesperson should make a lot while a poor one starves. BUT if the good seller gets too much for easy sales (usually to repeat customers), he won't be motivated to bring in new business.

Case Study: The Barton Corporation

Barton Corp. is an electronics company in which production is fundamentally an assembly operation. Barton buys components from a number of vendors and holds them in inventory. It then creates its product by assembling different combinations of components into various configurations. Configured product is shipped directly to customers from the factory. The assembly process is conceptually simple but physically detailed and tedious. It often takes several weeks depending on the complexity of a particular configuration.

Barton's salesforce advises customers of the product configuration that will best suit their needs. Once a sale is made, the salesman phones the order in to a Materials Management Department at the home office. This group is responsible for getting the order assembled and off to the customer.

The Materials Management Department

The Materials Management Department performs a pivotal role at Barton. Many employees feel that it represents the operating heart of the company. The department is managed by a longtime employee, Joe Moretti. Joe started in the department as an inventory clerk 15 years ago and has worked his way up to his current position. He has done nearly every job in the department and is intimately familiar with the entire operation. He prides himself on running a tight, efficient group. Joe had two years of college before starting to work at Barton, and is currently going to night school to finish his Bachelor's degree in Business Administration. He has had relatively little exposure to top management concerns such as market position, profitability or cash flow, but does have a general understanding of these ideas. Joe's department has a low turnover and he has worked with most of his employees for over eight years. He considers each of them a good friend, especially his subordinate supervisors.

The Materials Management Department consists of 20 people organized into several sub-departments. Each sub-department is run by a working supervisor. The sub-departments are:

Purchasing	Inventory Control
Receiving	Shipping
Inspection	Administration

Overall, Materials Management does the following functions:

1   Orders for components are placed with vendors by a purchasing group. Orders are based on sales forecasts which are received from the Sales Department on a regular basis. Sales forecasts the configurations it plans to sell as well as the most likely dates the customers will request delivery. Materials Management explodes the forecasted orders into components and time phases its ordering to account for delays in delivery, production, shipping etc. (An MRP exercise.)

2   A receiving group receives the goods and checks the quantity received against the PO, noting differences. They fill out a receiving document and send it to Accounts Payable. When a shipment is short against an order, the inventory control group keeps a record of the fact and follows up with the vendor until the rest of the order is received. This follow-up is important because short receipts often mean delays in filling customer orders which can result in irritated customers, conflict with the Sales Department, and cancellations.

3   The inspection group inspects and tests incoming inventory and returns defective parts to vendors. Defective goods are generally not identifiable as defective through simple observation but tend to fail after a limited period of use. Once product is configured and placed in service a failed component becomes difficult to identify. A technician must be sent to the customer's site, and the product must be taken out of service while it is being worked on. Early failures upset customers a great deal and are very bad for Barton's reputation for reliability. The failure is not generally blamed on the incoming inspection group, since there is usually no way to tell if the problem is one they should have caught but didn't.

4   The Inventory Control group tracks inventory in the usual sense, it checks items in and out, maintains records and physically handles the material. In addition the group monitors inventory and suggests disposal of aging

goods at reduced prices. Goods that get too old lose all their value, largely through obsolescence. A substantial amount of inventory falls into this category, since purchases are based on sales forecasts that are inherently inaccurate. Forecasts are especially weak with respect to product mix rather than dollar value. That is, the Sales Department usually has a pretty good handle on how much it can sell in a given month, but has a hard time predicting the precise configurations that will be ordered. This means that peripheral components are often in over or under supply.

5   When Materials Management receives an order, they pull the appropriate inventory to configure it. They then send the components to a manufacturing area to be assembled. They monitor the order through assembly, eventually receiving the completed product back. Finally they package and ship the product to the customer. All this generally goes on under considerable time pressure. It seems that once customers decide that they want Barton's product, they want it yesterday. There is generally an urgency surrounding the order-assemble-ship process. The order comes in through Administration, but most of the monitoring function is done by Inventory Control.

6   Problems frequently arise during assembly regarding the correctness of a configuration or the availability of components. Materials Management acts informally as an expeditor or coordinator in these cases getting the required parts or knowledge to the right place to keep the process moving. Administration and Inventory Control handle this effort.

7   The department is in constant contact with field sales regarding the status of orders. Ship dates often must be revised due to problems at Barton or customer problems. Materials Management functions as a focal point through which information passes between the factory and the field. This function is relatively unofficial, but contributes substantially to the smooth running of the company. Sales calls in to Administration to ask about order status.

8   Old customers order replacement components and in some cases upgrades and enhancements directly from Materials Management. This didn't used to amount to much, but has been steadily increasing over the years. The group pulls and ships these orders coordinating billing and credit with accounting. Orders come in through Administration and are passed to Inventory Control.

The Crisis

June 1 was a bright sunny spring morning and Joe Moretti came to work in unusually good spirits. When he got to his office he found a message stating that Bill Barton, the founder and president of Barton Corp. had called an unexpected meeting of all department managers for 9 a.m. Joe was a little uneasy. This was very unusual, and didn't sound good.

At the meeting Bill came right to the point, the company was in trouble. About a year ago, two of the companies that Barton purchased components from had decided to integrate forward and assemble an end-product similar to Barton's. In addition, a Japanese firm had begun to import another similar product. The result had been a dramatic increase in the competitiveness of the business. Demand for the product was growing, but not nearly as much as supply had increased due to the entrance of the additional competitors. The bottom line had been a substantial decrease in the market price of Barton's product as the competitors fought a market share battle.

Bill explained that it was fundamental to his long-term strategy that Barton hold its unit sales volume at a level at least as high as it had been before the current problem arose. If they shrank back, customers would perceive them as a loser and would migrate away from Barton. Bill felt this was both critical and doable. The current market price of product was high enough to allow a small gross margin on each sale, but nothing like what they had before. He felt they could survive if they could just tighten their belts. Further, he felt that the new competitors might not last long if prices stayed low. The ventures were sidelines for them, and if they didn't make much money they'd probably quit in a year or so.

After all this was explained, Bill said that he was going to make it simple. He believed in cutting back once, but in doing it deeply enough to solve the financial problem in one shot. Therefore he was ordering a 35 percent across the board expense reduction in all departments. There would be no exceptions and no special cases. He knew everyone was running a pretty tight ship already, but it would just have to be done. The alternative was unemployment for them all. He didn't care how managers did it, but he wanted a plan to reduce the running level of expense immediately, and he wanted it by the end of the week. He reiterated that he considered them all responsible professionals capable of running their own departments, so how they got there was up to them.

The staff reaction was reasonably positive. They all were aware of the market problem, and trusted Bill's judgement on how to lead them through it.

The import of Bill's message began to sink in when Joe got back to his office. He had to take over one-third out of his spending level with no decrease in the level of business he had to support.

Joe's current budget appears on the next page.

Joe leaned back in his chair and looked out the window. The fresh spring morning had turned cold and cloudy. He had some tough decisions ahead of him.

MATERIALS MANAGEMENT DEPARTMENT
($000)

	Purch.	Receiv.	Inspc.	Inv C	Ship.	Admin.	Total
Headcount	3	2	2	8	2	3	20
Wages*	110	40	50	170	40	90	500
O/T		5	5	30	10		50
Fringe	33	12	15	51	12	27	150
Equip.						180	180
Phone	15	1	2	10	2	10	40
Travel						10	10
Other					50	50	
Total	158	58	72	261	64	367	980

*Wages are roughly evenly divided among the headcount within each department with the exception of Administration which contains Joe at $50,000, an assistant at $25,000 and a clerk at $15,000.

QUESTIONS

1 How do you think Joe will respond to Barton's demands.
   a) What will his budget look like?
   b) What will his headcount look like? and most importantly,
   c) What will happen to the functions within the department.
2 a) How is this result different from what Bill Barton might have chosen to do if he thought about it?
   b) If he thought about it at some length, do you think Bill might have chosen to reduce Joe's department less?

ANSWERS

1 Joe will probably respond like this. First he'll eliminate as much non-people cost as he can even if some of the budgeted eliminations are unrealistic, e.g., outlawing all overtime is usually popular. Then he'll address the remainder with people. His reduction target is $000

$$\$980 \times 35\% = \$343$$

a) His non-people cuts might be something like this:

O/T	$50
Phone	20
Travel	10
Other	20
Equip	10
	$110

Hence his people reduction has to be planned at

$$\$343 - 110 = \$233.$$

Since fringe benefits are budgeted at 30 percent of wages, he has to reduce the wage line by approximately

$$\$233 / 1.3 = \$179.$$

This works out to just under 36 percent.

b)   Joe's headcount reductions and wage savings are likely to look like this:

	Purch.	Receiv.	Inspc.	Inv C	Ship.	Admin.	Total
Headcount	1	1	1	4	–	1	8
Wages($K)	35	20	25	85		15	180

Part of the rationale will be that shipping and receiving will be combined.

Notice what's happened in Inventory Control. Total effort was $170 + 30 = $200. It's now $85. That's a 58 percent reduction. More than half.

Notice also that shipping and receiving can't possibly be reduced by more than one half person each. Before the reduction it took four hard working guys to physically move the product in and out. We can't conceivably do it with less than three and no overtime. Remember that Bill Barton's goal is to keep shipments up to their previous levels.

Notice that inspection has gone down from $55 to $25, a 55 percent reduction.

Also notice that a clerk has been let go out of Administration for relatively small dollar savings. What was that person doing?

Function

Clearly this group can't do everything they were doing before even though Bill Barton's implicit direction is that they do. It's fairly clear that Barton's mind is on the marketplace and that he expects

Joe and others like him to "manage" their own responsibilities.

The key question is which functions will someone like Joe try to maintain, and which ones will be put off until tomorrow again and again until they never get done?

The first point to note is that the functions they will try to maintain are those that relate to their relationship with the sales department and the marketplace for new product. There's more than one reason for that. First, their outside contact and short-term reward/punishment (strokes) comes from sales. Put another way, sales is their perceived customer who they want to please. Further, Joe and his group understand the strategic importance of sales even in this low margin time. If they forget, Bill Barton is likely to remind them fast.

This says that the most protected function will be receiving sales orders, pulling inventory and shepherding product through the assembly process and back out the door to customers. They'll also try to maintain their role as a provider of order-status information to sales, but are likely to demand that sales cut way down on the number of inquiries. Expediting production will also get done, but probably not very gracefully.

Converting sales forecasts into inventory purchase requirements and purchasing itself will also continue to get done, but with less thought and attention. That will result in more over- and understocks of parts.

The critical insight here is to understand what the department will stop doing or do so poorly that its effect is lost. Barton will have moved into a very short-term world and things that don't have an immediate impact will get lost in the shuffle.

Incoming Inspection will become cursory. This will result in more product failures at customer sites and cause the company to send out more technicians at an enormously greater cost than was saved on not doing the inspections. Further, the firm's reputation for reliable product will begin to slide. Remember that Materials Management is not directly accountable for these failures, so there is little incentive to concentrate on finding the faulty components when the pressure is on.

Follow up and tracking of short receipts will probably come to a halt. This will cause more inventory stockouts and delays in production.

The quality of the safeguarding and control of inventory will decrease. The result of this tends to be binary. Inventory may be lost or stolen or it may not. If it isn't we're lucky and get away with an expense reduction. If there is a loss, it can be very large.

Monitoring inventory for obsolescence will become much less intense and more careless. So will the effort to dispose of inventory before it becomes worthless. This can cost very large dollars.

Finally, servicing old customers will falter. Profit on these sales may be small, but when old customers can't get parts Barton's reputation will deteriorate.

Notice that the jobs that don't get done are the ones that don't have a short-run impact. Why? Because no one says anything to the department about skipping those jobs.

What Will Be The Result?

2a) The department will appear to be doing the job with less resources, because the immediately visible functions will continue to get done. Bill Barton may pat himself on the back and wonder why he didn't do this sooner.

But two other things will also be happening. The company will be

1   Building worthless inventory, and
2   Deteriorating their reputation for quality.

These latter effects are insidious. No one will see the inventory write off on the income statement for six months or more. The slide in reputation may never be identifiable on the income statement as such, but it will eventually be there in lost revenue. It may also result in uncollectable receivables and returns along with the lost customers.

If upper management had the choice, what would they want the group to give up? The least costly give up might be some promptness in order-filling. They could also come to an agreement with sales to reduce the time spent on status inquiries. An online inquiry system might save manpower in the long run but would cost money in the short run.

An important corollary point here is that inventory control clerks are cheap, but obsolete inventory is expensive. It doesn't pay to save a few short-term expense dollars in inventory control at the cost of lost materials.

b) If Bill Barton had taken the time to do some *strategic thinking* it's very likely he'd have cut Joe's budget less. Inventory control is a classic area for short-run/long-run problems. Spending a little money on relatively cheap labor today has the potential to save literally millions later on.

Note: Cheap labor saves big bucks in collections too.

index